Bound to Exile

By the same author

British India

A Survey of the Nature and Effects of Alien Rule

Bound to Exile

The Victorians in India

Michael Edwardes

Take up the White Man's burden
Send forth the best ye breed
Go bind your sons to exile
To serve the captive's need.
Rudyard Kipling
The White Man's Burden

PRAEGER PUBLISHERS
NEW YORK · WASHINGTON

BOOKS THAT MATTER

Published in the United States of America in 1970
by Praeger Publishers, Inc., 111 Fourth Avenue,
New York, N.Y. 10003

Library of Congress Catalog Card Number: 77-100935

Printed in Great Britain

Contents

List of Illustrations   vii

Preface   xi

1   To Her Majesty's Eastern dominions   1

2   This splendid empire   10

3   Bombay ducks   22

4   Benighted province   35

5   City of palaces   46

6   Up the country   60

7   Navel of the world   77

8   Unto the hills   86

9   The wild and lonely places   96

10   At the edge of the abyss   106

11   Up among the pandies   112

12   Bloody assize   124

13   Mirror of indigo   133

14   An imperial assemblage   141

15 The making of a memsahib   146

16 The day's work   162

17 Picnics and adultery   173

18 The last frontier   186

19 The 'damned-nigger party'   193

20 The great queen dies   204

A bouquet of flowers from an Anglo-Indian garden of verse   206

Illustrations: The world of Anglo-India   221

Notes on sources   269

Index   279

List of Illustrations

Except where otherwise stated, all illustrations are from the author's archive

Frontispiece: 'Survey 1840 my tents'. Water-colour by John Brownrigg Bellasis. *India Office Library.*

1   Calcutta from the esplanade. From Charles Ball *History of the Indian Mutiny* (London n.d.).

2   'Our station'. From G. F. Atkinson *Curry and Rice (on forty plates)* 2nd edn. (London 1859).

3   Mulnath House, the mansion of an indigo planter. From Colesworthy Grant *Rural Life in Bengal* (London 1860).

4   A factory-assistant's bungalow in Bengal. From W. M. Reid *The Culture and Manufacture of Indigo* (Calcutta 1887).

5   'The young civilian's toilet'. From William Tayler *Sketches illustrating Manners and Customs of Anglo-Indians* (London 1842). India Office Library.

6   A private dinner party. Anonymous water-colour. India Office Library.

7   The dining hall of Government House, Calcutta. India Office Library.

8   'The last night of his griffinage'. From Captain Bellew *Memoirs of a Griffin; or, a Cadet's first Year in India* (London 1880).

9   'The Indian subaltern's vampire'. From *The Delhi Sketch Book* July 1, 1852.

10 The ice pits at Allahabad. From Fanny Parkes *Wanderings of a Pilgrim in Search of the Picturesque* (London 1850).

11 The bazaar, Simla. From Edward J. Buck *Simla Past and Present* (Calcutta 1904).

12 'Types of Indian servants'. From Joseph Moore Jr. FRGS *The Queen's Empire; or, Ind and her Pearl* (Philadelphia 1886).

13 Anglo-Indian sittingroom. Anonymous water-colour. India Office Library.

14 A cook in Bombay, 1842. From Captain Leopold von Orlich *Travels in India* (London 1845).

vii

15 'Our judge's wife'. From G. F. Atkinson *Curry and Rice (on forty plates)* 2nd edn. (London 1859).

16 Kite-hawks attacking food destined for the table. From William Tayler *Thirty-eight Years in India* (London 1881).

17 'Our cook room'. From G. F. Atkinson *Curry and Rice (on forty plates)* 2nd edn. (London 1859).

18 'Our coffee shop at Rawulpindee', no. 1. India Office Library.

19 'The Indian Pips goes to see the Bobbery Pack throw off'. From *The Delhi Sketch Book* September 1, 1852.

20 'A small boy does the "grand signor" '. From William Tayler *Thirty-eight Years in India* (London 1881).

21 'Our band'. From G. F. Atkinson *Curry and Rice (on forty plates)* 2nd edn. (London 1859).

22 John Lawrence, governor-general of India, with his Council. India Office Library.

23 Lieutenant-General Sir John Bennet Hearsey KCB. From Colonel Hugh Pearse DSO *The Hearseys: Five Generations of an Anglo-Indian Family* (Edinburgh and London 1905).

24 'Business quarter of Madras, with the Mole'. From Joseph Moore Jr. FRGS *The Queen's Empire; or, Ind and her Pearl* (Philadelphia 1886).

25 Merchant Street, Rangoon. From C.S. *Leaves from a Diary in Lower Bengal.* (London 1896).

26 'Madras surf'. From the Rev. W. Urwick *Indian Pictures drawn with Pen and Pencil* (London 1891).

27 'Shipping in the Hooghly, Calcutta'. India Office Library.

28 The Municipal Hall, Bombay. India Office Library.

29 'Some Indian servants'. From C.S. *Leaves from a Diary in Lower Bengal* (London 1896).

30 A civilian in his courtroom. Water-colour by A. F. P. Harcourt. India Office Library.

31 'The planter'. From G. R. Aberigh-Mackay *Twenty-one Days in India* (London 1910).

32 An Indian coffee planter's morning muster. From Robert H. Elliot *The Experiences of a Planter in the Jungles of Mysore* (London 1871).

33 Changing horses on the Grand Trunk Road. From Captain Oliver J. Jones RN *Recollections of a Winter Campaign in India in 1857–58* (London 1859).

34 'Steaming up the Indus near Sewan. Satellite and Sutlej flat'. Water-colour by John Brownrigg Bellasis. India Office Library.

35 'A primitive ferry-boat'. From C.S. *Leaves from a Diary in Lower Bengal*. (London 1896).

36 'Two riders on a camel'. From Captain Leopold von Orlich *Travels in India* (London 1845).

37 'Travelling in a palanquin'. From Captain Leopold von Orlich *Travels in India* (London 1845).

38 'Griffin marching to join'. From Captain Bellew *Memoirs of a Griffin; or, a Cadet's first Year in India* (London 1880).

39 The widow of an Indian slain by a tiger. From C.S. *Leaves from a Diary in Lower Bengal* (London 1896).

40 Cooking tent. From Mrs Robert Moss King *The Diary of a Civilian's Wife in India 1877–1882* (London 1884).

41 'Disarming the 11th Irregular Cavalry at Berhampore'. From Charles Ball *The History of the Indian Mutiny* (London n.d.).

42 '1st Bengal Fusiliers marching down from Dagshai'. From G. F. Atkinson *The Campaign in India 1857–8* (London 1859). India Office Library.

43 'Reinforcements proceeding to Delhi'. From G. F. Atkinson *The Campaign in India 1857–8* (London 1859). India Office Library.

44 John Nicholson. From Captain Lionel J. Trotter *The Life of John Nicholson, Soldier and Administrator*, 3rd edn. (London 1898).

45 Sheet music cover by John Brandard for 'The Delhi Polka', by Charles d'Albert.

46 'The relief of Lucknow by General Havelock'. From Charles Ball *The History of the Indian Mutiny* (London n.d.).

47 'Blowing mutinous sepoys from the guns'. From Charles Ball *The History of the Indian Mutiny* (London n.d.).

48 'Remains of the Presidency [*sic*], Lucknow'. From Joseph Moore Jr. FRGS *The Queen's Empire; or, Ind and her Pearl* (Philadelphia 1886).

49 'Kishnagur dak bungalow'. From Colesworthy Grant *Rural Life in Bengal* (London 1860).

50 'Peter'. From William Tayler *Thirty-eight Years in India* (London 1881).

51 'Our nursery on the march'. From Mrs Robert Moss King *The Diary of a Civilian's Wife in India 1877–1882* (London 1884).

52 'Hyderabad Station, March 1887'. From Colonel Cuthbert Larking *Bandobast and Khabar: Reminiscences of India* (London 1888).

53 Victoria Terminus, Bombay. India Office Library.

54 'Guests at Installation, Gwalior, 1894'. India Office Library.

55 'Mussoorie and the Dhoon, from Landour'. From Charles Ball *The History of the Indian Mutiny* (London n.d.).

56 The club-house, Ootacamund. Water-colour by G. H. Bellasis. India Office Library.

57 Simla. India Office Library.

58 An Indian picnic. India Office Library.

59 'Manners and Customs of Ye Englyshe in India—No. X. The Indian Pips goes to a Pic Nic'. From *The Delhi Sketch Book* July 1, 1852.

60 Exercise in the hills. From a photograph in the possession of the India Office Library.

61 Tiger-hunt camp. India Office Library.

62 'A pig hunt'. From Captain Oliver J. Jones RN *Recollections of a Winter Campaign in India in 1857–58* (London 1859).

63 'The hunters hunted'. From William Howard Russell *The Prince of Wales' Tour: A diary in India* (London 1877).

64 The Delhi durbar, 1877. From J. Talboys Wheeler *The History of the Imperial Assemblage at Delhi held on the 1st January 1877* (London n.d.).

65 Lord Lytton. From J. Talboys Wheeler *The History of the Imperial Assemblage at Delhi held on the 1st January 1877* (London n.d.).

66 Hindu Stewart's monument, South Park Street cemetery, Calcutta.

67 The Victoria Memorial Hall, Calcutta.

Preface

This book is not a political or even a social study of India in Victorian times, but a view of 'Anglo-India', that special country inhabited by the British who lived and worked in India during the long reign of Queen Victoria. It has been assembled, in the main, from their diaries, letters and memoirs, and from the observations of travellers, both British and European. I have also made use of contemporary fiction, because it reveals much that would never have been allowed to intrude into the formality of memoirs—where the authors were usually striking attitudes rather than disclosing realities. The criticisms that emerge from time to time are again almost entirely contemporary. I have tried to keep them completely so, but however sincerely the historian may claim objectivity, such a thing does not exist.

I have also kept the jargon of Anglo-Indian words and phrases to a minimum, explaining those that are used as they appear. But one or two that occur frequently need early definition. In modern times, 'Anglo-Indian' has come to mean a person of mixed blood, a Eurasian, but in the following pages it is used in its Victorian sense—an 'Anglo-Indian' is a Briton in India. 'Civilian' is not simply the opposite of 'military', but, in the sense in which it was used by the British in India, a member of the civil service, and therefore distinct from such other Anglo-Indians as wives, businessmen, planters, and, of course, soldiers.

For those who would like to know the origins of the materials quoted throughout the book, I have added some notes on sources.

What varied opinions we constantly hear
Of our rich Oriental possessions;
What a jumble of notions, distorted and queer,
Form an Englishman's 'Indian impressions'!

First a sun, fierce and glaring, that scorches and bakes;
Palankeens, perspiration, and worry;
Mosquitoes, thugs, cocoanuts, Brahmins, and snakes,
With elephants, tigers, and curry.

Then Juggernat, punkahs, tanks, buffaloes, forts,
With bangles, mosques, nautches, and dhingees;
A mixture of temples, Mahometans, ghats,
With scorpions, Hindoos, and Feringhees.

Then jungles, fakeers, dancing-girls, prickly heat,
Shawls, idols, durbars, brandy-pawny;
Rupees, clever jugglers, dust storms, slipper'd feet,
Rainy season, and mulligatawny.

Hot winds, holy monkeys, tall minarets, rice,
With crocodiles, ryots, or farmers;
Himalayas, fat baboos, with paunches and pice,
So airily clad in pyjamas.

With Rajahs—But stop, I must really desist,
And let each one enjoy his opinions,
While I show in what style Anglo-Indians exist
In Her Majesty's Eastern Dominions.

> G. F. ATKINSON,
> *Curry and Rice (on Forty Plates).* 1859.

1 *To Her Majesty's Eastern dominions*

The news arrived while they were still in Calcutta. The sailor king, William IV, with his blunt language and quarterdeck manners, had died in June 1837 and Britain now had a queen on the throne. But it was only the bare news and everyone waited anxiously for letters fat with the gossip of London.

Nothing had come by the time Lord Auckland, the governor-general of India, with his two sisters, Emily and Fanny Eden, left Calcutta on the last day of October. After travelling up the river Ganges for some two hundred miles on a kind of barge towed by a steamer, they arrived at the town of Rajmahal about four in the afternoon—and went ashore to see the ruins. 'But the real genuine charm and beauty of Rajmahal', wrote Emily that night, 'were a great fat Baboo standing . . . with two bearers behind him carrying the post-office packet'. Fanny's and Emily's letters from England were full of news of that 'charming invention', the young queen. They could 'fancy the degree of enthusiasm she must excite. Even here we felt it'.

The British in India paid tribute to the new monarch in their various ways. In Calcutta, an impressive though not too extravagant ceremony had announced her accession. Elsewhere, descriptions of all the pageants that had been held in London to show the queen to her people were passed around, and everybody agreed that there was reason for enthusiasm.

In London a number of sober gentlemen had conveyed their congratulations to the queen, in a high-sounding petition despatched from their offices in Leadenhall Street. These men were the real rulers of India. Though the queen's ministers decided who should be governor-general, and though the gentlemen in Leadenhall Street were supervised by an instrument of the queen's government called, with great precision, the Board of Control, yet in the strictly legal sense the queen had inherited not so much the Indian colonies as control over the East India Company, which had begun its rather bizarre life during the reign of another queen, 237 years before.

1

For the first twenty-one years of Queen Victoria's reign, those of her subjects who exercised power in India were the servants, first and foremost, of a trading company which traded no longer. Its Directors were the sole source of patronage. No appointment could be made to the civil or military services in India except by them.

Yet even when a young man of about seventeen (the usual age) was fortunate enough to have the ear of a Director of the Company, he still had to pass a fairly stiff examination before going on to the Company's college at Haileybury. 'Each candidate shall be examined in the four gospels of the Greek Testament, and shall not be deemed duly qualified for admission to Haileybury College, unless he be found to possess a competent knowledge thereof; nor unless he be able to render into English some portion of the works of one of the following Greek authors: Homer, Herodotus, Xenophon, Thucydides, Sophocles, and Euripides; nor unless he can render into English some portion of the works of one of the following Latin authors: Livy, Terence, Cicero, Tacitus, Virgil, and Horace; and this part of the examination will include questions in ancient history, geography, and philosophy.

'Each candidate shall also be examined in modern history and geography, and in the elements of mathematical science, including the common rules of arithmetic, vulgar and decimal fractions, and the first four books of Euclid. He shall also be examined in moral philosophy, and in the evidences of the Christian religion as set forth in the works of Paley'.

A formidable array of requirements. But still, 'the art of cramming is, like other modern sciences, carried to such a pitch of refinement (being quite a profession), that most young men of decent education can be crammed into passing without remarkable talent or acquirement'.

Haileybury itself offered an education of no great value to a young man about to go out to India. Much of the teaching, in fact, went clear over the students' heads. Many of the professors were distinguished scholars, of the stature of such men as Malthus, the theorist of population. Not unnaturally, there was considerable emphasis on oriental languages, but too much was unfortunately placed on the study of Sanskrit, 'a language not more useful to an Indian magistrate than a knowledge of the tongue of the ancient Germans would be to a modern commissioner of police, who might now and then discover a slang term to be of orthodox Saxon origin, to the great edification of philologists; yet it may be doubted whether his efficiency would be much increased thereby'.

When a new recruit to the Honourable Company's service arrived in India, however, he was allowed a year to 'master one of the languages principally required in the transaction of public business'. After passing an examination, he would find himself 'pronounced qualified for the public service'. If he failed the examination, and after a further six weeks of cramming failed again, he was 'shipped to England as a hopeless subject and deprived of his appointment in the Company's service'.

Such a fate struck comparatively rarely, for the rewards of service in India—despite all the disadvantages of climate and situation—were very attractive. Salaries were large, and the social position of the 'civilians', as they were called, was excellent. 'The leading civilian is the acknowledged head of the society of whatever place he may be stationed at, while the juniors are regarded, as much from their position as their generally superior attainments, with deference and respect'. Opportunities for sport were 'on a scale of magnificence and affluence unknown to the English sportsman'. In return, the civilian had to live ten years in India before home leave was granted—but what was this, compared with the opportunities that were placed in his way for spreading happiness among the thousands of human beings under his protection? 'Through his instrumentality, the cause of education, and, therefore, of Christian enlightenment, may be advanced—his charities, judiciously dispensed, will save myriads from starvation—and the encouragement he has it in his power to give to the labourer by building bridges, constructing roads, and draining lands, will confer the blessing of employment upon the industriously disposed, while it gives an impulse to the internal commerce of the country, and diffuses health in regions of disease'.

Though some Englishmen subscribed to the belief which was

3

to grow stronger and stronger during Victoria's reign, that the British held India by some kind of moral right, they had acquired it by conquest. As the author of a *Handbook to India* (published in 1844) put it: 'The highest opinion that might be entertained of our character as governors, would, of itself, we apprehend, avail but little in the retention of the country against the schemes of disaffected or designing men, if it were not backed by a well-organised and judiciously distributed physical force'. The British were menaced by all sorts of native ambitions. There were still, in spite of everything so far achieved, 'evil powers within the heart of the empire against whose machinations the greatest amount of political integrity could not successfully contend'. The people were priest-ridden and avaricious, and 'what elements more potent than priestcraft and avarice to excite a populace to rebellion?' All in all, the pragmatic view acknowledged that 'the sword is an indispensable agent in the retention of India; and it is a happy thing for the populace of that empire, that the mercy and humanity which distinguish the administration of the civil government attemper the steel by which the sedition of the disaffected and the incursion of the foreign foe are invariably chastised'.

So the Company had its own armed forces. The army in India numbered around 200,000 men—mainly Indians, though there were some European regiments. The number of British officers did not exceed 5,000. Those young men who chose a military career in the Company's service went to Addiscombe, the Company's military college. Their final examination results decided their fate for them. According to a declining order of merit, they would find themselves in the engineers, the artillery, or the infantry. Entry to the Company's cavalry, however, required no training or examinations at all. Directors of the Company had the right of nomination, and a protegé too stupid for the civil service might easily find himself with a cavalry commission instead. This may perhaps have been the origin of the old story about the cavalry officer who was so stupid that even his fellow officers noticed it!

When his civil or military training was over and a young man was accepted for service in India, he would be appointed, in the case of the civil service, to one of the three 'presidencies' into which British India was divided—Bengal, Madras, or Bombay. All that then remained was for the new civilian to sign his covenant—which bound him, among other matters, not to accept 'presents' from rich natives nor to engage in trade—and for some person approved by the Directors to guarantee 'to pay the sum of £3,000, as liquidated damages, to the Company, for breach of a covenant to be entered into, that the student's nomination hath not been in any way bought, or sold, or exchanged for any thing convertible into a pecuniary benefit'. The military cadet, provided he had reached the age of sixteen on the day of his final examination, received his commission in the branch he was assumed to be best fitted for, and went to the India House in Leadenhall Street to be sworn in. 'He was marched into a room, where some half dozen old gentlemen were sitting at a long table and looking as solemn and dignified as such people can possibly be. There a book was put in his hand, and he was told to repeat a few sentences beginning with "I . . ." and ending with something or other about the East India Company and the articles of war, having done which he received an exhortation from a little man with a cream-coloured face to conduct himself like a gentleman and not kill more natives than he can help'.

At the time of the queen's accession, the customary route to India was, as it had always been, a tedious sea voyage lasting between three and four months by way of the Cape of Good Hope. The price of a cabin was around £100—and, for that, the passenger bought an empty space to be filled at his own expense and according to the standard of comfort he could afford. If he was sensible, he bought cabin furniture which was so designed that it could be converted for use when he arrived in India. But whatever the traveller's taste (and financial resources), the absolute necessities included 'a sofa with mattress, pillow, and a chintz covering for the day-time; a wash-hand stand; a hanging lamp; a looking glass with sliding cover; a chest of drawers in two pieces, the upper part having a ledge around the top for the purpose of holding a small collection of books, or for preventing articles from falling off; a foul-clothes bag and an oilcloth or carpet . . . merely for the sake of appearances'. The personal equipment of a bachelor, for his 120-day journey, began with a basic list of thirty-four different items, ranging from 'ten dozen shirts; a blue camlet jacket; two pairs of merino, camlet or gambroon trowsers' to a 'dressing-case and Russian leather writing-case, suitably filled; three pounds of Windsor soap; six pounds of short wax candles and a bucket and rope (serviceable in drawing up salt water whenever wanted)'.

To lighten the tedium of the journey, 'numerous additions may be made, suitable to the means and inclinations of passengers. Fowling-pieces, rifles, fishing-tackle, colour-boxes, musical instruments, books, scientific instruments, telescopes, cards, chess and backgammon boards . . . and an outline map of the route' were all suggested.

The journey to India, of course, was undertaken not only by bachelors or even unaccompanied married men. There were wives and daughters, too, as well as young ladies destined for the marriage market. As the poet Thomas Hood, put it:

'By Pa and Ma I'm daily told
To marry now's my time,
For though I'm very far from old,
I'm rather in my prime.
They say while we have any sun,
We ought to make our hay—
And India has so hot a one,
I'm going to Bombay!'

Obviously, the ladies' 'necessities' were more extensive than the men's. Apparently essential items included a 'quilling-net and piece-net; hair powder; a good supply of papillote paper; pomatum, smelling-bottle, hartshorn, aromatic vinegar, aperients, and a case of Cologne-water'. Three pairs of stays were recommended and 'a visit to Mrs. Wise, 31 Saville Row, Conduit Street, Bond Street, will ensure to the lady passenger some valuable advice, and a description of a corset of inestimable utility in a relaxing climate'.

If there was a piano on board, there might be music. But the female passenger was warned not to unpack her own, if she had one, as 'the damp sea air and the motion of the vessel are calculated to seriously damage the delicate machinery of a Broadwood . . . even though it be clamped and fastened and *clothed*, to suit the climate of the tropics'.

No doubt, in the interests of the ship masters and their agents, a generally rosy view of the long sea voyage was given. But there could be more than cumulative boredom to attack the passenger. The weather, discreetly left unmentioned by the handbooks, could often be very bad, and the loss of a ship was by no means an unknown hazard. A storm brought, if nothing more, considerable discomfort. 'The galley was washed away', one passenger recorded, 'the live-stock under the large boat was nearly all destroyed, and seven of the pigs were killed. The deck presented a scene of marvellous confusion; the sailors, attempting to save the live-stock, were thrown down on the deck, and the steward, lying in the water that rushed over it, was holding on to a pig; the animal bit his hand, the steward let go, and the pig was washed overboard by the next roll of the ship'. While all this was going on, the passengers were left to shift for themselves and were without food for most of the day. When they finally entered the saloon, 'the captain apologised for the dinner on the table, on account of the galley having been washed away: it consisted merely of one great cheese, and each person was supplied with a biscuit!'

Fortunately, there was another way to India. This, the overland route, became increasingly popular after 1837. It was not only quicker, but much more interesting. The cost of the journey was about the same as for the Cape route, but the sea passages were by steamer, not sailing ship, and along the way the passengers called in at such interesting places as Gibraltar, Malta, and Alexandria. In the latter city, the passenger was conveyed by donkey to the Hotel de l'Europe, or perhaps to the only other hotel, the Hotel de l'Orient. As this was operated 'on French principles', however, it was assumed that English travellers would prefer the former lodging. From Alexandria, the next stage was by a long, narrow, covered boat—'the only part of the whole trip to India which is positively disagreeable'—to Atfé, where

7

passengers transferred to one of the small Nile steamers. Twelve hours later, they reached Cairo.

There, before Mr Shepheard built his hotel, the choice was between the Great Eastern and, inevitably, another Hotel de l'Europe. This was apparently the better of the two; 'the rooms are cleaner and more spacious—the table is more sumptuously provided—the attendance infinitely better', though there were no 'shampooing, joint-cracking and moustachio-dyeing' in the hotel baths.

If the India steamer had already arrived at Suez, there was little time for sightseeing. But if it had not, then a few days could be spent visiting the pyramids ('particularly good fun'), the Pasha's palace (rather tawdry), the slave market ('alas, no romantic Circassians or voluptuous Georgians'), or a petrified forest. The Sphinx was not really worth the effort. 'To my perception', wrote the author of the *Handbook to India,* 'the colossal head (all that now remains) very closely resembles, when seen in profile, a cynical doctor of laws, with wig awry, suffering strangulation per tight cravat'.

There was unfortunately nothing very romantic about crossing the desert, either. Any passenger who expected 'turbanned travellers, long strings of camels, rude tents, guards bristling with arms' was in for a disappointment. Instead, forty vans, each drawn by four or six horses, in which the passengers sat at the sides, 'transport the living contents of two crowded steamers across the arid and desolate plain which divides Cairo from the Red Sea'. The vans' two wheels were immensely strong 'and capable of bearing, without damage, the violent collision with lumps of stone to which they are exposed in some parts of the road'. Every ten or twelve miles, there was a station where the horses were changed and a meal was provided of eggs, mutton chops, roast pigeons, stewed fowls, good bottled ale, and tea or coffee. At the halfway point, there was a hotel with bedrooms and the chance to sleep for a few hours before continuing to Suez.

At Suez, passengers for Ceylon, Madras and Calcutta boarded a substantial steam vessel of some 2,000 tons belonging to the Oriental and Peninsular company. These vessels were pretty well-found—but would have been the better for more portholes.

Passengers for Bombay travelled by smaller steamers belonging to the East India Company which, in the early years of the service, seem to have been manned by officers who were 'dead against the passengers and dead against steam'. So they 'neglect the one and curse the other to their heart's content'. Sometimes the coal gave out and a bad journey was made worse by the delays of having to proceed under sail. The food offered was almost uneatable, and was inevitably ham and eggs. There was neither soda water nor ice.

Things were to improve immensely on the Bombay run when the Oriental and Peninsular Steam Navigation Company (later to reverse its title and become the P & O) took over, for the bill of fare on their ships was so extensive that it would have been difficult for 'the greatest *gourmet* of the City of London Corporation to say if he could add anything to the *carte*'. In particular, there was plenty of ice, and 'a fusillade of soda water kept up from nine a.m. to nine p.m.'

Even a bad journey came to an end sometime. Soon the traveller would tread the soil of India, 'the land which was the cradle of the human race, the land of poetry, and of the Arabian Nights!' —the 'splendid empire' of those peaceable merchants, the Directors of the Honourable East India Company.

2 *This splendid empire*

When the eighteen-year-old queen succeeded to the throne, Britain's Indian dominion was little older than she was herself. The East India Company, of course, had been in India since the beginning of the seventeenth century, first as traders, and then as conquerors. Robert Clive had really set things moving by making himself ruler of the vast province of Bengal in the middle of the eighteenth century. From then onwards, great proconsuls had pushed out the boundaries of conquest. For more than half a century, it had been a soldiers' world—of defence and attack, victory, defeat, and stalemate. In fact, the British had never been sure of their dominion. Some had never even been sure that they wanted it, either. And it was not until 1818, with the final defeat of the one native power which might have thrown the British into the sea, that a sense of permanence appeared.

With permanence came change. Change in attitudes, change in ideas, concerning Britain's purpose in India, concerning Indians themselves. The British began to think of their conquest as something of a miracle, or, at the very least, as a sign from divine providence that it was their destiny to rule India. But Britain's expansion in India had had another, strictly worldly causation. Those politicians in Britain who had supported the conquerors in India had not been dreamers of empire, but believers in the potential profits of conquest. Progressively, they broke the East India Company's monopolies in the interests of a rapidly industrialising Britain, avid for markets. The Company remained sovereign, but on an eroding sufferance.

Why the British conquered India is fairly straightforward. How they were able to do it—and against what appeared to be great odds—is not. The 'philosophers' of empire who were to proliferate in the last decades of the queen's reign produced their reasons, of which the most generally accepted (because the most stimulating) was a belief in the superiority of the white man over the coloured. It is true that there were some remarkable men among the conquerors who made India into Britain's back yard, but, on balance, there was no more leadership of an exceptional order on the British side than there was on the Indian. In fact, quite a number of Indian leaders were the equals of their British contemporaries, and a few were distinctly superior. The clue lies in the competitive nature of Indian leadership. Ambitious Indians were concerned with establishing their own sovereignty and maintaining it against all comers, their own supporters (adventurers like themselves) included. The contrast between the Indian leaders and the British was a contrast between ambition uncontrolled and ambition disciplined. What gave the British their supreme feeling of confidence was the knowledge that, in times of crisis, *they* could rely on the support of their fellows.

The British had no more military expertise than their opponents. Some of the European-trained armies of the Indian princes were quite as good as the Company's forces, just as well armed, and frequently better generalled. But these armies were usually led by mercenaries whose main aim was to satisfy their own ambitions, even if it meant changing sides or using their strength to set themselves up as independent rulers. The British, when they fought, were out to win not just one battle but a whole campaign. For them, defeat was merely a passing setback, whose effect could be cancelled out in the next engagement. It was this belief that no single defeat would be final which gave victory to small British forces faced with what seemed to be outrageous odds. Once a number of such victories had been won, the British became convinced that even the most powerful of their enemies could be crushed—in the end.

It was also greatly to the advantage of the British that they could not only concentrate resources upon some given area, but could also replenish them once they were exhausted. This was a matter both of economics and of maritime mobility. The British could move reinforcements, human and material, by sea from Britain or around the coasts of India. If things went badly in one place they could compensate from another. Not so the Indian rulers. They had nothing to draw on, for their defeat was someone else's gain. Furthermore, the revenues of the Indian princes were constantly decreasing. The Indian economy, in general, was contracting, while the British—in the first flood of the industrial revolution—possessed a rapidly expanding commerce.

The British, therefore, were equipped for conquest. They also had their sense of solidarity, and a belief that their actions not only satisfied personal ambition and the commercial interests of their employers, but were also to the general advantage of the British nation.

Against such nationalism, racial identity, or what you will, Indians had little defence. Community was divided from community by caste, and men of one religion from those of another by that sharpest of barbed wire, tradition and custom. Some particular hatred might momentarily unite the antagonists, but when it was removed their prejudices revived with even greater intensity. All this made it possible for the British to conquer India, piecemeal. It also made their conquest acceptable—because they were foreign, detached, almost irrelevant to the bitter infighting which preoccupied the Indian leaders. Where power was the only criterion, Indian rulers (who intimately knew the realities of power) felt no shame at acknowledging the rule of men who were capable of exercising it, as long as the capability remained, and as long as it was made evident.

This was the task of the Company's army, a substantial force, only a sixth of whom were Europeans. The British had conquered India with Indian soldiers, and that was how they intended to hold on to it. The European population was very small—about 41,000, in 1837. Approximately 37,000 of these were soldiers, either in the Company's own European regiments or in those of the queen, on loan to the Company. 6,000 were officers. The civil service accounted for 1,000 of the remaining Europeans, and, of those not in the services, there were about 2,000 in Bengal and 500 each in Bombay and Madras. In a limbo, neither European nor Indian, lay the Eurasians—or East Indians, as they were sometimes called—who numbered around 30,000. The native population was somewhere in the region of 150,000,000.

Until 1833, the Company had exercised strict control over European immigration. The authorities did not approve of 'non-officials' such as missionaries, businessmen, and indigo planters, and used their powers of deportation frequently against people whom they regarded as undesirable. Most Europeans in India approved of this. 'Many of the adventurers who come hither from Europe', wrote Bishop Heber in 1824, 'are the greatest profligates the sun ever saw; men whom nothing but despotism can manage, and who, unless they are really under a despotic rule, would insult, beat and plunder the natives without shame or pity'. Deportation, he went on, was 'the only controul which the Company possesses over the tradesmen and ship-builders in Calcutta and the indigo planter up the country'. The Charter Act of 1833 put a stop to that, and the country became wide open to all—even missionaries.

If anything, the opening up of the Company's dominions to unrestricted immigration intensified the disdain with which the army and the civil service looked upon the other members of English society in India. As in England, people engaged in trade were beyond the pale. That paragon of Victorian chivalry, Henry Lawrence, summed up the view in a note in his journal about a Calcutta chemist and his wife, who were fellow-passengers on Lawrence's first journey home. The man, he said, was 'a forward, vulgar, ignorant, malicious and pertinaceously obstinate fellow', and his wife was 'much of a muchness. . . . Of course, they were in no society in Calcutta'. Eurasians were regarded with as little favour, having the additional—and insulting—disability of mixed parentage and guilty liaisons. Thirty years before, no-one would have thought much about it. Many Englishmen had associated with Indian women, 'chiefly Muhammadans of respectable families but in reduced circumstances'. A new spirit of morality, however, partly compounded of racial arrogance and partly of a stricter Christian faith, now frowned not only on any new liaison, but on the product of earlier ones. This meant that higher appointments in the Company's service were no longer open to Eurasians, so, instead, they practically monopolised the positions of clerk and bookkeeper both in government and private offices.

There was, of course, no doubt about who were the leaders of society. Whatever it said in public, the army (on which British dominion depended) never had any doubt in its heart that it was 'infinitely inferior in every respect' to the civil service in rank and rewards. The advice Henry Lawrence, himself a soldier, gave to his brother John was simply that the civil service offered 'the greater field for ability, vigour, and for usefulness'.

On the whole, the civilians had no firm ground for their superiority. Few really bothered to learn the language of the people they ruled with any fluency, and they were thus heavily dependent on their native clerks, who had taken the trouble to learn the language of their conquerors and were, in many cases, not at all unwilling to use their masters' ignorance to their own advantage. British rule in India had, in fact, very early become a tyranny of interpreters. 'I have heard', wrote Colonel Sleeman in the late 1830s, 'some of our highest diplomatic characters talking, without the slightest feeling of shame or embarrassment to native princes on the most ordinary subjects in a language which no human being but themselves could understand'.

The average civilian was promoted according to a fairly routine pattern. He started work as an assistant to the Commissioners of Revenue and Circuit, spending one day in one department and the next in the other. If he was drawn by opportunity or inclination towards the law, he became first an assistant, then a joint magistrate, then full magistrate, then, if he was lucky, a judge or commissioner. This stage was usually only achieved after eighteen or twenty years' service. A young man who leant towards the revenue side would follow a roughly parallel course of seniority until, in due process, he might become a Collector or even a Commissioner of Revenue and Circuit himself.

Between the army and the civil service, there lay a strange ill-defined region in which military men acted as administrators, and civilians claimed the right to direct military operations. Among the soldier-administrators there were many great names, and, on the whole, when educated military officers were appointed to difficult situations and wild regions they contributed an expertise which no civilian could match. There were young men like Captain Kennedy, an ex artillery officer in charge of a district in the Himalayas, who not only commanded a regiment of mountain chasseurs but also discharged, according to Victor Jacquemont, 'the functions of a collector, acting as judge over his own subjects and, what is more, those of the neighbouring rajas, Hindu, Tartar, and Tibetan, sending them to prison, fining them, and even hanging them when he thinks fit'. It was from such men as Kennedy, Jacquemont said, that he learned most 'about the affairs of the land'.

That civilians were placed in positions of such authority as to be able to interfere with the operations of an army in the field was the result of campaigns in north-west India and Afghanistan which began within a couple of years of the queen's accession and continued for the rest of her reign, and afterwards. A new species of civilian, called the 'political officer', came into existence. He was usually skilled in languages, given control of wild frontier areas inhabited by warlike tribes, and entrusted with emergency powers which were basically undefined but included authority to make use of military forces in his area. Relations between himself and the local military commander were often strained. His actions were almost invariably high-handed and independent, lacking in precedent, and—given the unavoidable delays in communication—without the endorsement of 'higher authority'. When the British occupied the Punjab in the forties, it was young men with military training but civilian duties who established a pioneer administration—assuming wide responsibilities, taking unconventional action, and disregarding the formalities of discipline.

Such freedom led, not infrequently, to folly and disaster, as in the first Afghan war. In 1849, the then governor-general, Lord Dalhousie, blasted the pretensions of over-enterprising political officers when he wrote to Henry Lawrence about one of his subordinates, Major Herbert Edwardes. 'From the tone of your letter', he said, 'I perceive it is not necessary to say that you should pull up Major Edwardes—at once. But I further wish to repeat what I said before, that there are more than Major Edwardes . . . who appear to consider themselves nowadays as governor-general at least. The sooner you set about disenchanting their minds of this illusion, the better for your comfort and their own. I don't doubt you will find bit and martingale for them speedily. For I repeat, I will not stand it in quieter times for half an hour, and will come down unmistakably upon any of them who may try it on, from Major Edwardes, C.B., down to the latest enlisted General-Ensign-Plenipotentiary in the establishment'.

Concerning the men who had neither the inclination nor the

patronage to leave the army for the better paid—and often more exciting—work of a political officer, there was not a great deal to say. The training given to officers in the Company's army scarcely fitted them either for efficiency or for heroism. And, like his civilian counterpart, the young cadet soon found himself in debt. At the larger stations, too, social conditions invited him to waste his time. 'In Europe', said Colonel Sleeman, 'there are separate classes of people who subsist by catering for the amusements of the higher classes of society, in theatres, operas, concerts, balls, etc., etc.; but in India this duty devolves entirely upon the young civil and military officers of the government, and at large stations it really is a very laborious one, which often takes up the whole of a young man's time. The ladies must have amusement; and the officers must find it for them, because there are no other persons to undertake the arduous duty. The consequence is that they often become entirely alienated from their men, and betray signs of the greatest impatience while they listen to the necessary reports of their native officers, as they come on or go off duty'.

Even without the social demands of a large station, an officer's military duties were scarcely arduous. The same Herbert Edwardes who later incurred the wrath of the governor-general described the routine of his life in 1841 to a friend in England. 'Well, a black rascal makes an oration by my bed every morning about half an hour before daylight. I wake, and see him salaaming with a cup of hot coffee in his hand. I sit on a chair and wash the teaspoon till the spoon is hot and the fluid cold, while he introduces me gradually into an ambush of pantaloons and wellingtons—if there is a parade. I am shut up in a red coat, and a glazed lid set upon my head, and thus, carefully packed, exhibit my reluctance to do what I am going to do—to wit, my *duty*—by *riding* a couple of hundred yards to the parade.

'Here two or three hundred very cold people, in same condition, are assembled, and we all agree to keep ourselves warm with a game of soldiers, whereupon a very funny scene ensues, and we run about the plain, and wheel about and turn about, till the sun gets up to come and see what the row is about; and then, like frightened children, we all scamper off and make the best of our way home. Then the packing-case is all taken off again and I resume my nap. . . . This, if there is a parade; if not, I take a gallop with the dogs'.

The army had an oriental extravagance about its arrangements. When the Bengal army moved from its base at Firozpur in 1838, it numbered 9,500 combatants, and 38,000 camp followers. One of the officers excelled his fellows by having a train of four horses, eight camels and elephants, and twenty personal servants. Even in actual battle conditions, three elephants carrying, for the use of one officer, a number of double-sided tents with glass doors was thought to be only slightly eccentric. And so it was, for the commisariat and transport arrangements for the rest of the army were a great deal less than efficient. In the Afghan war of 1839–41, the British army suffered one of the most shameful defeats it ever had to bear, from an enemy who carried their commisariat on their backs and their weapons in their hands.

In its fitness for war, of course, an army depends on the mental and physical fitness of its officer corps. But in the British army in India, all chances of promotion were seriously hedged by the tendency of officers to hang on till they dropped (or were killed). The younger officer, avid for promotion, had little chance unless disease weeded out some of his seniors. Even so, a youth joining the army at seventeen could hope for no more than to become a lieutenant at twenty-one, a captain at twenty-nine, a major at forty-four, and—with luck—a lieutenant-colonel at fifty-four. As one soldier who deserted the army for political work put it, when war came the army would be led by 'gallant veterans, who during health and strength were never trusted with command, and whose only guarantee of efficiency was old age—whose very existence was often a token of their never having earned command'. It was as well for the British that, when their own leadership was at its worst, Indian leadership was virtually non-existent.

Because European society in India was divided into hermetically sealed compartments, it is easy to overlook the fact that the majority of the European population in the larger towns and stations consisted of common soldiers and seamen. The latter were constantly changing as vessels arrived and departed, but the

European soldiers of the Company's military establishment remained in India for an indefinite period—which was, in actual fact, assumed to be twenty-one years if death or disease did not intervene. They usually did. The mortality rate among common soldiers was extremely high. Indeed, the life expectation of a European soldier in India was less than half what it was in England. The only compensation was that the rate of pay was higher than in Her Majesty's forces and, if the soldier survived, he received a reasonable pension. But the odds against survival were high. Apart from the natural stresses of an abrasive climate, the soldier's lot was not enviable. Discipline was extremely harsh and, though flogging had been abolished in the native army, white soldiers could still face sentences of from five hundred to a thousand lashes. Such sentences were by no means rare. Three out of every four men in the Company's forces—and the queen's men were no different—could show the stigmata of a back scarred by the lash into lumps of thick calloused flesh and hideous weals. Men often died in their early twenties from the effects of the lash. Flogging depended very much on the whim of the commanding officer, but even this brutal and infinitely degrading punishment was considered merciful when the alternative was a court martial which wielded the power of life and death. A military execution (and they were alarmingly frequent) was a ceremonial occasion. The soldiers were paraded to form three sides of a square, the fourth being the stage for the condemned man and his executioners. From the guard room came a procession moving to the strains of the Dead March, played by the regimental band. The Provost Marshal rode in front, followed by two files of soldiers with their arms reversed. Then came the parson and the prisoner and, bringing up the rear, the execution squad of twelve privates with a corporal and a sergeant in charge. After the procession had made a circuit of the square, it stopped before a coffin, and the parson prayed. Hysteria moved through the rigid ranks; some soldiers wept and others fainted as the condemned man, eyes bound, stood to attention to hear the death warrant read out once again.

Outside the bounds of this harsh and unmerciful discipline, the common soldier had ample leisure in which to do nothing. There was, in fact, nothing for him to do. Drunkenness and fornication were his principal activities. No attempt was made to control the soldiers' relations with Indian women, and some settled down into permanent relationships which contributed not only to the man's happiness but to the Eurasian population. There were even some English wives, whose morals were notoriously lax. But it was 'only just to notice the temptations, restraints, and miseries, to which this class of women are subject, in a country so little calculated to cherish their better feelings, or to provide them with necessary occupation, or common comfort. Unable, from extreme heat, to move out of the little room allotted to them in the "married men's quarters", during the day, and provided, for two rupees a month, with a Portuguese "cook boy", who relieves them from the toil of domestic duties, the only resource of the soldiers' wives is in mischievous associations, discontented murmurings, and habits of dissipated indulgence. Strolling in the evenings through the dirty bazaars of a native town, probably under the auspices of an ayah who may have picked up a smattering of the English language, these unhappy women purchase liquor, to conciliate their careless husbands. On returning late to the barracks, the truant wife frequently finds her partner already in a state of intoxication; mutual recrimination follows, and then succeeds a scene for which we may well weep, that humanity has such'. The children were, more often than not, neglected. Indeed, the child of a European soldier had very little chance of reaching maturity. It was not until 1846 that a scheme was begun to provide schools in the hills for such children, neglected both by their parents and by the army.

For a year or two of Queen Victoria's reign, there was another class of European soldier in India—the military adventurer. While the Punjab remained an independent native state, its army included a number of European officers. The most important of these were not British—Generals Allard and Court came from France, and Avitabile was a Neapolitan. But quite a few of the smaller units in the Sikh forces were led by British officers who had once served in the Company's army but who had left for one of a number of reasons, ranging from dismissal for misconduct to a desire for the higher, and probably more dangerous, rewards offered by employment in the service of a native prince. Some of these men were Eurasians, who could rise to a position denied them in the Company's service. The majority, however, were deserters, and most were Irish, though they very often tried to conceal their origins by calling themselves Americans. One, Alexander Gardiner, traced his 'ancestry' through a father who had settled on the shores of Lake Superior, 'just where the Mississippi breaks out of it'!

The lives of many of these men might have been lifted from an Elizabethan play, and there is a terrible uniformity in the tragedy of their deaths. But some passed into the British service when the Punjab was annexed and were given respect by those who might otherwise have despised them.

And what of relations between the British, this tiny ruling minority, and the immensely fecund majority—the 'natives'? On the highest level, governors-general dealt with princes, with much pomp and ceremony. On occasion, their meetings took on all the attributes of an oriental Field of Cloth of Gold. But it was always a meeting of superficialities, and though a few men— usually political Residents at some native court—did establish relations of mutual respect and understanding with both princes and peasants, they had always been rare and became even more so in Victoria's reign. As a rule, ordinary Englishmen were aloof and often arrogant. Bishop Heber, with his sharply discerning eye, had noticed during his travels in 1825 that the old free and unselfconscious relationship between Indians and British was rapidly disappearing. The English had an 'exclusive and intolerant spirit' which made them, wherever they went, 'a caste by themselves, disliking and disliked by all their neighbours. Of this foolish, surly, national pride, I see but too many instances daily, and I am convinced it does us much harm in this country. We are not guilty of injustice, or wilful oppression, but we shut out the natives from our society, and a bullying, insolent manner is continually assumed in speaking to them'.

The attitude of the British to their native subordinates in the civil administration oscillated between the poles of indifference and abuse. Little or no encouragement was given to those who worked well and hard. As for servants, perhaps the best description of their treatment by the majority of their masters and mistresses is implicit in the reason given by Emily Eden for the devotion of Government House domestic servants—it was, she said, 'one of the few houses in Calcutta where they were not beaten'.

The religion of the British did nothing to promote racial harmony. On the contrary, it menaced the beliefs of Hindu and Muslim alike. The Company itself had from the beginning been so attached to religious neutrality that it had forbidden the entry of Christian missionaries into its territories. Finally, however, forced by reform-minded Christians in Britain, the government ruled that the Company should open its doors to the missionaries. Their proselytising, and that of British officers in the Company's army, was to prepare the way for the revolt of 1857. But even then, no lesson was learned by those who were convinced that the British brought to India not only a higher civilisation but a better religion.

Whether the British had indeed a purpose in India had begun to occupy men's minds some time before the Victorian era began. Some of the men who had consolidated British rule had had their doubts. 'We have ceased', wrote Charles Metcalfe, who had done much to establish the empire in the first decades of the century, 'to be the wonder that we were to the natives; the charm which once accompanied us has been dissolved, and our subjects have had time to enquire why they have been subdued'. But others had no doubts. There seemed to be no point in morbid speculation about the future. The present was there to be faced—and dominated. 'To fear God and to have no other fear is a maxim of religion, but the truth of it and the wisdom of it are proved day by day in politics'. It was a suitable motto for the militant Christians of early Victorian India, representing the aggressive side of their attitudes, and achievements. It also explained much of their popular appeal in a period constantly in need of heroes and in which enthusiasm was easily aroused— for here were men creating a splendid empire with neither doubt nor fear, not content to allow circumstances to control them, men who compelled the world to shape itself to suit their vision.

c

3 Bombay ducks

The newcomer to India found it a land of nicknames. It was the British way of putting everyone in his place, a carefully considered—and highly effective—system of caste. The English who lived and worked in Bengal were known as 'Qui-his', from the usual manner of summoning servants in that presidency (*koi hai* = is there anyone there?) The English in Madras were called 'Mulls', a contraction of 'mulligatawny', the hot pepper soup supposed to be drunk by everyone in the area. The English of Bombay had to carry the name of 'Ducks', presumably by association with the strong-smelling bummelo, a dried fish better known as Bombay Duck. It was just as well that when a civilian was appointed to serve in one of the presidencies he usually stayed there for the whole of his official life. A Duck would never have felt comfortable in Bengal, and a Mull was always considered outside Madras as a pretty low form of life.

Bombay had always been something of a backwater. In 1825, in fact, the Directors described it as 'of little importance to the Company'. But the opening of the overland route was to give it importance, though old habits took a long time to change. It was many years before Bombay had a decent hotel or boarding house. According to a local belief, this was simply because no hotel could have a chance of financial success as long as private hospitality was so lavish. It was just too bad if a visitor had no friends in Bombay and no letters of introduction. 'The Victoria Hotel solicits the patronage of travellers; but, as it is situated in the very dirtiest and very narrowest street of the fort, the additional annoyances of flights of mosquitoes, a billiard table, a coffee and a tap room, place it without the pale of respectable support. The Sanitarium affords shelter to invalids, and is delightfully situated, where the smooth sands and fine sea breeze render it a tempting locality for the convalescent; but the rooms are far too small for family accommodation. In this dilemma, visitors usually pitch tents on the esplanade; and if in the hot season, cause them to be *chuppered in*, as the phrase is, or a

false roof erected with bamboos and date leaves, to secure them
equally from the intense heat of the mid-day sun, and the evil
effects of the evening dews'. On the whole, a tent was quite
the thing. If comfortably furnished and provided with a small
retinue of servants, the expense was 'not greater than will be
incurred at the hotel, and with the advantage of perfect seclusion
and independence'.

The new civilian or cadet, of course, had no need to worry. He
was met, and his accommodation arranged. A cadet would invariably receive 'an invitation from the regiment quartered in the
town, or Fort George barracks, to accept the hospitalities of
the mess, and is put into appropriate apartments by the barrack-
master'.

When a newcomer had settled in, it was time to see the town.
Those who had been led to believe that everywhere in India
was like Calcutta, a city of palaces, were immediately disil-
lusioned. Bombay was no new Rome; it was more like an English
county town transferred to the Orient. Only the Town Hall,
an elegant neo-Classical building, had any distinction. The European houses were usually of one storey, 'with an overhanging
thatched roof', and looked to the disappointed eye of a new
arrival 'for all the world like a comfortable English cow-house'.
Fortunately, the interior was more impressive: 'We stepped
direct, without any intervening hall or passage, into a large and
elegant drawingroom, supported on pillars of faultless proportion.
A large screen of red silk divided this apartment from a spacious
diningroom'.

An unusual feature (to the visitor's eye) was the wide verandah,
its shady overhanging roof supported on low arches and open
to the garden. The trouble was that, once you had seen one
Bombay bungalow, you had seen them all. Even the furniture
all seemed to have been supplied from the same emporium, the
only difference being that the more affluent bungalows had
mahogany furniture instead of jackwood, and silk or damask
on the couches in place of chintz.

As time went on, of course, and Bombay became more affluent,
so too did the houses of the upper levels of English society there.
By 1851, the bungalow, however substantial, was not thought

good enough for senior members of the civil service. Their houses became 'lofty and stately-looking mansions, with facades adorned with spacious porticos supported on pillars of sufficient width to admit two carriages abreast, thus insuring to the occupants a sheltered mode of ingress and egress, equally essential during the heat of the fair season and the damp of the monsoon'. Inside, the ground floor contained dining and breakfast rooms, a library, and one or two suites of guest rooms. 'The staircases are generally wide and handsome, conducting to the reception and family rooms; and not unfrequently, a charming withdrawing room is found on the flat top of the porch by surrounding it with a balustrade, which also serves as a support to a light veranda-like roof'.

Bombay had a pleasant tradition in 'hot weather houses'. During the hot season, the Bombay esplanade was 'adorned with pretty, cool, temporary residences, erected near the sea; their chuppered roofs and rustic porches half concealed by the flowering creepers and luxuriant shrubs, which shade them from the midday glare'. Standing in a line along the sea front, the bungalows were made of 'bamboo and plaster, lined with strained dungaree, dyed a pale straw colour; the offices are placed at a short distance from the bungalow; and the whole is enclosed with a pretty compound, filled with fine plants, arranged in tubs, round the trellised verandahs: in this situation the shrubs flourish well, despite their vicinity to the sea, usually considered so inimical to the labours of horticulturists'. Inside, there was an agreeable simplicity and cool China matting. 'The clean smooth China matting which covers the floors; the numerous lamps shedding their equal light from the snowy ceilings; the sweet perfume of the surrounding plants, and the fresh sea breeze, blowing through the trellis-worked verandahs, render them delightful retreats after the heat and lassitude endured throughout the day. Elegance combines with comfort, in making these pretty abodes so truly pleasant; and a fine-toned piano, and a good billiard table, are the usual additions to varied articles of luxury and convenience'. On the whole, the writer decided it was 'difficult to imagine anything more agreeable than a late dinner in an esplanade bungalow after returning from the evening drive'.

24

Bombay ducks

In the cool of the evening, the ladies and their escorts would venture to take the air. The usual mode of travel was at first a palanquin, a kind of covered litter carried by a number of bearers. Very few people had their own, so they were usually rented by the hour. The palanquin bearers were, however, something of a trial as they had a habit of putting down the conveyance at some spot suitably distant from the passenger's destination and striking for more pay. Palanquins began to disappear in the early years of the young queen's reign, although they were not finally frowned upon until the 1860s.

The more fashionable way of taking the air was in a carriage, and there was a wide variety of styles to choose from. On the esplanade, during the hour of the promenade, 'there may be seen the English landau fresh from Longacre; the smart denner of the military aspirant marked by its high cushions; the roomy buggy of the mercantile Parsee, adorned with green and gold; the richly gilt chariot of a high caste Hindoo, with its silken reins and emblazoned panels'.

There was very little else to do in the hot weather and at the time of the monsoon rains. There would be a band playing on the esplanade, each music stand lit by a lamp—for the dark came down quickly in Bombay. The only other lights were on the carriages, drawn up for a moment so that their occupants might listen to the music. The ladies did not descend and walk about, but the gentlemen 'flitted about from carriage to carriage, paying their *devoirs* to the fair occupants, who were just recovering from the unusual and overpowering heat of the day'. The European children either rode their own ponies or were drawn by servants in little carriages of their own. They were, however, encouraged to take a stroll and were 'led by their servants round and round the band-stand, which', thought one observer, 'would give the little things a decided taste, or dislike, for music in future years'.

The hot weather was particularly trying. Mentally and physically, no-one was at his best. 'A few sickly attempts at dinner-parties' took place, but it was 'impossible to conceive anything more ludicrously forlorn than the pallid faces of both hosts and guests exhibited upon these occasions. Though struggling convulsively to repress the yawns of weariness and languor, every one was haunted by the same insane notion that something was expected of him in the way of conversation, whilst the mind was totally incapable of forming two connected ideas; and even the recognised "beaux esprits" of society, trembling for their laurels, were obliged to succumb to the leaden influence of the weather, and lapse into the universal dreamless silence'. And even though everyone hoped for a shower of rain to bring some relief, when the monsoon actually broke things were hardly better—if certainly different. 'Nothing short of perfect health, and an easy conscience, could enable one to bear up cheerfully through the intense gloom of a season, which may be described as consisting of one uninterrupted succession of thunder, torrents, and tedium'.

The rainy season usually began early in June, and for the first ten days or so brought a welcome change from the stifling heat of the preceding weeks. 'But beyond that, human nature cannot be expected to endure, without the relief of a grumble; and the natural consequence is, that faces become blue as the sky continues black'. Fortunately, even the monsoon had an occasional break, with fair weather, and even some sunshine which 'coming "like angels' visits, few and far between", are rapturously hailed, acting as a sufficient stimulant upon our fainting spirits, to enable them in a measure to hold out during the four mortal months of the monsoon. These "breaks", as they are called, are eagerly taken advantage of for the purposes of sociability, and many a pleasant dinner-party, and sometimes even a "soirée dansante" will be given by spirited individuals, who are determined to brave all the risks of sudden storms, and defalcations of guests, rather than endure any longer the monotony of total seclusion'.

For those who were not compelled to stay in Bombay during the hot season—and that usually meant wives and children—there were the hill resorts of Poona and Mahableshwar. Everyone was rather more relaxed in these pleasant airy places, and the rigid protocol of Bombay was put aside in favour of an 'increased spirit of sociability . . . The little unostentatious dinner, and even tea parties go briskly round, bringing the good folks together on a footing of intimacy which might never be attained in Bombay'.

Poona was a pleasant station, even in the rains, but Mahableshwar had to be evacuated when the rains came—the roads became impassable and rivers swollen that they could not be crossed. The little bungalows, which had given so much pleasure by their simplicity were now 'completely encased in a most comfortable great-coat, consisting of "chuppers", which are large screens of thatch, fastened to frames of poles, and so contrived that they cover up each face of the cottage, and prevent the rain from reaching the walls. The chimney is taken care of in the same manner; the bungalow has no longer any shape whatever; it looks much like the figures of ladies in the loose "polka" great-coat, which has been the fashion of late years, more useful than graceful'.

Still, throughout all that the worst seasons could produce, the men at least had work to do. Whatever their various responsibilities, their lives followed much the same pattern. From March until October, the months which comprise the hot and rainy seasons, he would wear a 'light cotton jacket, like a barber's or a footman's, in the morning'. After rising at an early hour, and whatever the season, he would go for a ride (unless it was raining). In the cold weather he might even join the local hunt. In the hot weather, however, he would hasten home before the sun rose; then 'he usually undresses, puts on his pajamas (the loose Turkish trouser), drinks iced soda-water, lies down on the couch, novel or newspaper in hand, and in all human probability goes to sleep'. Rising again, he would bathe and dress for breakfast at ten. This, whatever the season, consisted of rice, fried fish, eggs, omelette, preserves, tea or coffee—'more in the fashion of a Scotch than an English matutinal recreation'. Suitably defended against hunger, the civilian then left for his office, where he worked until four or five o'clock. After that, it was time for bathing and dressing again as a preliminary to the evening drive, an occupation which had 'no recommendation beyond that of passing the most disagreeable hour of the day in inhaling coolish air, for you meet the same faces, the same equipages, and receive and make the same formal bows, almost every evening'.

27

This was quite understandable, for the entire European population of Bombay did not exceed 450.

While the men were at work, the married ladies either visited each other or settled down to the writing of chits. The writing and answering of these notes, which were sent by the hand of a special class of servant, was one of the great pre-occupations of European society. One authority held that 'every lady of *ton* has to write on an average two thousand chits per annum'. The chit system was greatly dependent on the servants who carried these missives. Very often, they delivered them to the wrong person—with interesting consequences, if they contained gossip and scandal, as they often did. Even shopping was carried out by chit. An answer was always required, except perhaps in the case of a simple invitation to dinner, when 'the word *salaam*, sent by the messenger to his master, serves the several purposes of an acknowledgement of, or a receipt for, the chit, and an acquiescence in the request it contained'.

Chit-writing was mainly a hot weather occupation, as people were too fatigued by the weather to venture out of doors. In the cold weather, Bombay society came to life. 'Our fashionables flock in from all the adjacent parts, to take possession of their handsome winter quarters; and every gradation of sociability from the snug, round-table dinner party to the crowded ball is in full requisition'. For the gentlemen, the day's routine remained the same, but the ladies had a constant round of visits to make and visitors to receive. Morning was the usual time for these, after ten o'clock and before two, when the family took its midday meal, the sacred Anglo-Indian ritual of tiffin. This was no longer the vast meal of the eighteenth century, however, when 'hecatombs of slaughtered animals' graced the table, but a fairly light collation. There might be guests, but it was considered 'an act of glaring impropriety in a lady, to invite any gentleman to stay and partake of this meal, who is not either a relative, or an intimate friend of the family'. This curious though presumably moral attitude could be very hard on the poor visitor who was neither relative nor close friend. Even in the cold weather, the sun can be warm, and a round of visits during which no refreshment was offered could be very frustrating. 'At the last house,' one such visitor recorded, 'we actually listened, with parched throats, to the jingling of glasses and plates, which betokened the preparation of the tiffin table in an adjoining room, without these sounds producing any other effect upon the lady of the house than giving us, by suddenly dropping the conversation, a pretty significant hint to decamp: and accordingly in a state of utter exhaustion we made our parting bows'.

Conversation at these morning visits was often dull. Lady Falkland, wife of the governor of Bombay in the late 'forties, found her guests with little more to talk about than their health and the weather—hardly to be wondered at, as they had driven six miles at the hottest time of the day in the hottest month of the Bombay year for the privilege of attending her ladyship's morning reception. No wonder the Englishwomen in India had a 'washed out look'. In the cold weather, their conversation may have been more lively.

The new overland route, fully functioning by 1838, had made quite a difference to the intellectual climate of Bombay. 'The present rapid communication with Europe', wrote a lady resident in that year, 'has introduced a very superior class of ideas and interests; and among other advantages, are many of a literary kind—reviews, papers, periodicals, and books, arrive before their novelty is dimmed in Europe; thus all intelligence of interest is discussed, and every means of gaining information easily acquired'.

Certainly, rapid transit of goods had made quite a difference to the elegance of the ladies' dresses, which were now only as far behind the latest London and Paris fashions as the time it took for the patterns to reach Bombay and the tailor to make them up.

The cold weather was the time for fine clothes to match the gaiety of release from the rains. Colourful bonnets and gowns were brought out from the cases of camphorwood and tin where they had lain protected from the damp and insects. Vessels arrived from Europe, almost every day, it seemed, with 'their interminable cargoes of millinery and haberdashery; whilst almost every lady is anxiously on the look-out for some particular ship, conveying to her that most coveted of all acquisitions—a box of new finery, selected by her friends at home'. And ladies for whom there was no parcel would besiege the shop of a Parsee entrepreneur called Muncherjee and buy up his entire stock in an afternoon.

Afternoon shopping was only indulged in as a matter of necessity. The morning was the more favoured time. Opinions differed widely on the shops' standards, according perhaps to the sophistication of the traveller or the length of time the resident had been away from England. The invaluable *Handbook of India* was much concerned over 'high charges and paucity of supplies'. One visit was enough to show 'how inefficient they are to gratify taste, or to satisfy the numerous wants of civilised life'.

'The Parsee master, attired in a white cotton garment and pointed head-dress of glazed chintz, meets the visitor at the door, and with something more grave than a nod, yet scarcely graceful enough to be called a bow, ushers him along between a double row of glass cases; less, certainly, but of the same form as those which English gardeners use for raising cucumbers. These are locked; but as soon as the article sought for is supposed to be seen, the Parsee produces from a large pocket in the side of his dress a small bunch of keys, when something remembered to be in fashion or invented ten years ago is laid before the purchaser. Nothing of the kind can carry disappointment farther than a Parsee shop, where, in lieu of the improvements of modern times, where the highest degree of convenience is the object desired by the manufacturer, are to be found articles only of the most cumbrous kind; the mechanism, where any exists, totally deranged, and the intrinsic value consequently lost. The poor Parsee, however, knows little of all this, and prices his various goods with amusing inconsistency, making all pay for his bad debts and damaged wares'.

But there was at least one establishment which gave the lie to the *Handbook*. This was the emporium of Jangerjee Nasserawanjee, where the walls were 'surrounded with glass cases, filled with fine French china, bijouterie, gold lace, sauces, brandied fruits, riding whips . . . A central avenue is flanked with cases containing jewellery, French clocks, and all descriptions of knicknackery.

On the floor have subsided Cheshire and Gruyere cheeses, hams, cases of sardine, salmon and other edibles; and from the ceiling depend bird cages, lamps, and coloured French lithographs in handsome frames'.

There was a good chemist's shop where supplies of soda water —which, when iced, was considered a great blessing—could be obtained. But for many years the main lack was of a good bootmaker. Instead, there were a number of Chinese tradesmen who went from house to house 'with white coats, red slippers, straw hats, flat features, and long plaited hair, holding in their hands little bundles, containing silk and satin shoes intended to fit everybody, and consequently fitting nobody. These worthy Crispins receive orders, and with bad leather, coarse linen, and paste in abundance, essay their execution, the result being that the public pay for their want of skill in the penalty of uneasy or distorted feet'.

There were quite a number of travelling merchants, though their numbers decreased as time went on and more and more 'Europe shops' opened in the bazaar. Most of these merchants —'box-wallahs', they were called—were Muslims, hereditary traders and money-lenders. Part of their stock would be made up of Kashmir shawls and Delhi scarves, chintzes, calicos, crapes and woollens, fine muslins and silks from China. In a small mahogany box they might carry a blaze of jewels, rubies, emeralds, diamonds and sapphires, some well cut, some only roughly cut. The box-wallah, however, dealt not only in fine cloths and jewels but also in 'chow-chow', bits and pieces, commonplace things like soap and pickles, vinegar, cotton socks, eau de cologne, and orange marmalade which was allegedly Scottish but actually made in Surat.

The box-wallah dismissed, the visitors gone, tiffin over, the afternoon was spent decorously at home unless there was the sudden need to besiege a merchant for the latest thing from Europe, just that moment landed. It seems that by the late forties the habit of taking a siesta had become unfashionable on the grounds that this 'pernicious habit' enervated the system and induced a tendency to fever. Instead, the hours were 'most agreeably filled up by the undisturbed exercise of music, working and

31

reading'. At last, five o'clock came and the carriages were ready
for the evening drive along the esplanade.

Afterwards, it was time for entertainment. This took the form
either of private dinners or functions at Government House.
There was a theatre, but it was seldom opened. A concert was a
very rare occurrence. No great singer ever thought of appearing
in Bombay, 'and when a mediocre one arrives, very little encouragement is given, because he or she may not be a Mario or
a Jenny Lind'. Apart from the races, the only public amusement
in Bombay consisted of a series of subscription balls which
were carried on 'with tolerable spirit and liberality throughout
the season; all arrangements being under the control of a selected
number of gentlemen stewards'.

A dinner and ball at Government House displayed clearly the
stratification of Anglo-Indian society. There was a really very
simple division between 'those who belong to the service and
those who do not'. The services, of course, had their own
hierarchies, while the ladies were 'more tenacious of their rank
than we are in England'. The women, said Lady Falkland, 'going
into and leaving the dining room, take precedence according to
the rank of their husbands, as they do in Europe: but I was, at
first, surprised that at the end of the evening no one moved to
go away till she whose husband held the highest official position
rose to depart'. This preoccupation with protocol could lead
to uncomfortable situations. Lady Falkland 'once saw a lady,
far from well, after a dinner-party at Government House, and
wishing very much to go home; who, on my urging her to do
so, hesitated, because another person in company—the wife of a
man of higher official rank than her own husband—did not
seem disposed to move. I took the opportunity of impressing on
the poor sufferer, that the sooner this custom was broken
through, the better. However, she did not like to infringe it,
and so she sat on'. Lady Falkland consoled herself that, whatever the ladies' social position might be in Bombay, 'they would
be but "small folk" in London'.

If the dinner was something of a state occasion, then there
would be as many as two hundred guests at Government House
at Parell. The building had originally been a Portuguese church,

but there was no sign of its ancestry in the spacious rooms. On such occasions, the governor's aides-de-camp were greatly taxed by problems of precedence. The names of partners were very carefully selected beforehand, rigorously adjusted 'with the nicest regard to the distinctions of rank'. This method usually allotted the most charming woman in the room 'to some prosy old civilian or mumbling colonel whose sole merit was his length of service'. Fortunately, there were few elderly Europeans in India. But neither were there many pretty women. Most of the really elderly were army officers. There was one old general of the queen's forces who had been appointed to a senior command in Bombay even though he was nearly blind and deaf, and 'his aides-de-camp were for ever occupied in preventing his falling over the footstools in the drawing-room, when he went out to dinner'.

Acceptance of the non-official Englishmen took some time. The wealthier merchants and businessmen continued to be looked down upon by the official services, though they were not denied entry to Government House. The lawyers of Bombay were something of a class by themselves, being part of the system of British law, and yet mainly concerned with the litigation of the native population (and making a great deal of money out of it, too).

Still, the majority of those seen at Government House and at private parties were the younger military men, adding a touch of exotic colour with their elegant uniforms, and easily outdoing the civilians whose plain coats were relieved only by flowing cravats. The most welcome of guests were, naturally, the ladies, even though most of them were married. The cold weather, however, usually brought out a few unmarried girls to flutter the hearts of the bachelors. As Lady Falkland noted, 'the arrival of a cargo (if I dare term it so) of young damsels from England, is one of the exciting events that mark the advent of the cold season. It can be well imagined that their age, height, features, dress, and manners become topics of conversation, and as they bring the last fashions from Europe, they are objects of interest to their own sex'. But there was very little chance for the bachelors unless a girl's parents, or the relatives to whom she had been consigned, approved of a suitor—and everyone in India always knew just who each young man was, his prospects, and his family background.

A young girl had to be protected from military men, especially from any young ensign with whom she might have come to an 'understanding' on the voyage out. The best catch of all for her was undoubtedly the civilian, known as a 'three hundred a year dead or alive' man because when he joined the service he received a salary of £300 a year, and had to subscribe to a fund which, after a number of years' service, would guarantee his widow a pension of £300 a year.

Failing marriage, a man's opportunities for a healthy sexual life seem to have been restricted. Gone for ever were the free and easy liaisons with Indian women which had aroused no criticism in the early part of the century (and which still occurred in the remoter inland stations). A young man might invite some courtesan to his bungalow, but he would have to be excessively discreet if he wished to maintain his position in 'civilised society'. Bombay, if the majority of travellers are to be believed, was a remarkably moral place, perhaps because of the difficulty of keeping any irregularities secret in a tiny and intimate community. Perhaps, too, as a result of lack of opportunity. 'There are none of those lures and haunts which prove so attractive and fatal to the young Londoner', maintained the *Handbook of India*. 'His Indian contemporary almost *must* spend his evenings in a decorous manner, for not only would he soon become marked if he frequented such scenes of debauchery as there are, which are of the very lowest description, and where common soldiers, sailors, and the absolute blackguards of the place resort; but there is not that field for a "lark" which tempts the London spruce apprentice, and youths of higher degree, to take to the streets in search of such adventures'. Even drinking was frowned upon, not apparently because it was a vice and might wreck a man's health, but because this 'sad propensity risks the degradation of the English character in the eyes of the native community'.

In fact, many of the attitudes which later came to be associated exclusively with Victorian England were already present in India. But Anglo-Indian society had distinct advantages over society in England. Anglo-India had neither ' "parvenus" nor "nouveaux riches" . . . to shock one with their upstart airs', and 'with very few exceptions, no one comes to this country without either having laid the foundation, or completed the accomplishment, of a gentleman's education'. Indeed, 'the man of cultivated mind will perhaps meet with less to shock his fastidious tastes than in the necessarily mixed society of England, where the aristocracy of birth, and the aristocracy of wealth, alike struggle for pre-eminence'.

4 *Benighted province*

The Calcutta-bound traveller missed Bombay even if he came by the overland route, for the steamer from Aden made directly for Ceylon and went on from there to Madras, capital of what the rest of Anglo-India knew as 'the benighted province'. Once it had been the most important of the Company's territories, its tenure menaced alike by Indian rulers and French rivals, but by the time Victoria came to the throne it ranked low in the scale, 'for the very satisfactory reason', wrote Mr Stocqueler, the Baedeker of early Victorian India, 'that the country which forms its limits is in a settled state, abundantly fertile, and making a pleasant progress towards civilisation.' It was called 'benighted' because it had become a backwater and young men believed, with reason, that the future held more adventure in the north.

Madras was difficult to land at because a heavy swell rolled on to the shore. Ships had to stand off in the roads and transfer goods and passengers to boats which carried them over the surf. There were plans for a pier and harbour, but it was to be the end of the queen's reign before they were built.

The Madras roads were full of ships and boats of every kind and shape. 'But none can compare to the catamarans, and the wonderful people that manage them. Fancy a raft of only three logs of wood, tied together at each end when they go out to sea, and untied and left to dry on the beach when they come in again. Each catamaran has one, two, or three men to manage it: they sit crouched upon their heels, throwing their paddles about very dexterously, but remarkably unlike rowing'. To a newcomer, the first sight of a catamaran could be almost unnerving. 'I perceived to my astonishment, a naked figure walking apparently on the surface of the sea, and rapidly approaching us. This was a catamaran man, the bearer of a dispatch from the shore'. As well as official messages, these intrepid boatmen carried the inevitable chits from 'hospitable residents, whose doors are open to the introduced stranger'.

Whether introduced or lacking in credentials, passengers still had to reach the shore. For that often exciting passage there was the masoolah boat. 'Imagine a huge affair, something in shape like one of those paper cock-boats which children make for amusement, or an old-fashioned tureen, or the transverse section of a pear or pumpkin, stem and stern alike, composed of light and flexible planks, sewn together with coir, and riding buoyant as a gull on the heaving wave, the sides rising six feet or so above its surface, the huge empty shell crossed by narrow planks or benches, on which, when seated, or rather roosted, your legs dangle in air several feet from the bottom: further, picture in the fore-part a dozen or more spare black creatures, each working an unwieldy pole-like paddle to a dismal and monotonous chant— and you may have some idea of a masoolah boat and its equipage'. This crude affair was what the visitor to Madras had to commit himself to if he were going to land at all.

'On approaching the surf, the boatmen's monotonous chant quickened to a wild *ulluloo* . . . I looked astern, and there, at some distance, but in full chase, advanced a curling mountain-billow, opening its vast concave jaws, as if to devour us. On, on it came. "*Ullee! Ullee! Ullee!*" shouted the rowers; smash came the wave; up flew the stern, down went the prow; squall went the ladies, over canted the major . . . while those more fortunate in retaining their seats held on with all the energy of alarm with one hand and dashed the brine from their habiliments with the other. The wave passed, and order a little restored, the boatmen pulled again with redoubled energy, to make as much way as they could before the next should overtake us. It soon came, roaring like so many fiends, and with nearly similar results. Another and another followed, till, at last, the unwieldy bark, amidst an awful bobbery, swung high and dry on the shelving beach; and out we all sprung, right glad once more to feel ourselves on terra firma'.

When the travellers recovered themselves, those possessed of letters of introduction left for their friends' houses. Other gentlemen were strongly advised to present themselves at the Madras club and seek election as members. 'This club is an admirable institution. Without insisting upon an aristocratic exclusiveness, it is nevertheless strictly an asylum for gentlemen.

D

It is well and liberally conducted, and the charges come within the means of most persons in the upper circle of society'. There was no alternative, in fact, as the hotels were 'wretched places, affording but little accommodation, and abounding with dirt, bad viands, and worse wines'.

The most striking parts of Madras were the Fort and the Black Town. The first housed some of the offices of government and the latter, as its name precisely states, 'contained the residences of the natives, and the shops of Europeans and natives'. The best European houses were along the Mount Road, 'six miles in length, bordered by trees and villas'. In one of these the traveller with an introduction would find himself a guest. The houses were usually of one storey, with a flat roof and an elegant portico in the neo-Classical style. The hostess would probably be young, though the host was in all likelihood much older—for the man of substance and position had more than an advantage over a young man who still had his way to make. 'India is the paradise of middle-aged gentlemen. When they are young they are thought nothing of; but at about forty when they are "high in the service", rather yellow and somewhat grey, they begin to be taken notice of and called "young men". These respectable persons do all the flirtation too in a solemn sort of way'—and, of course, most of the marrying.

In the pleasant bungalow on the Mount Road, the old style of Anglo-Indian hospitality—a style which never really died out—probably still reigned. Its main constituents were 'absence of unnecessary restraint, abundance of good cheer, and the most unaffected and cordial welcome'.

Guests who were not new to the country followed the custom of taking their own servants with them when staying with friends. At least this meant no extra trouble for the hostess, or (rather more important) her servants. 'The servants fend for themselves in a most curious way. They seem to me to sleep nowhere, and eat nothing—that is to say, in our houses, or of our goods. They have mats on the steps, and live upon rice'. Since the Indian social order was strictly classified by function, each servant had his or her separate work. A lady would have an ayah, a maid, and a tailor. Her husband would have a 'boy'. In addition, there was one man to sweep out the rooms and another to carry water. Another laid the table, and another brought in dinner. There was one servant whose sole duty appeared to be to light the candles, and others who served the meals. Each horse had not only a groom but a grasscutter who, in Madras, was usually a woman. Every dog, too, had his 'boy'. One visitor enquired 'whether the cat had any servants, but I found that she was allowed to wait upon herself; and, as she seemed the only person in the establishment capable of so doing, I respected her accordingly'.

Each servant seemed to have an assistant 'who does all the work that can be put off upon him without being found out by the master and mistress'. Of course, a great many servants were needed, not only to uphold the standing of the establishment, but to be on constant call for those attentions which were considered necessary to civilised life in India. Ladies who had been in India for any length of time had learned never to raise a finger if they could avoid it. They 'lie on a sofa, and, if they drop their handkerchief, they just lower their voices and say "Boy!" in a very gentle tone, and then creeps in, perhaps, some old wizen, skinny brownie, looking like a superannuated thread-paper, who twiddles after them for a little while, and then creeps out again as softly as a black cat, and sits down cross-legged in the verandah till "Mistress please to call again" '.

The trouble with servants, warned the *Indian Domestic Economy and Receipt Book* on its very first page, was that 'laziness, dishonesty, falsehood, with a host of other vices, seem to be inherent in them', which was not surprising 'when we consider the way in which they are brought up'. But the master and mistress had to take some part of the blame. In the first place, they had a distressing habit of taking servants into their employ 'merely on the recommendation of a written character'. This was a very foolish thing to do, as most of them were 'written for the occasion, by a class of persons who earn their bread by writing characters for any applicant who will give them a few annas, or agree to pay a percentage should he succeed in getting the place'. But having found a good servant, the master and mistress might be unable to keep him; in Anglo-India a servant's slightest fault was 'often visited with blows and such abuse as no respectable man will bear, very often too for no other fault than that of not understanding what the master has said, who has given his directions in some unintelligible stuff, from ignorance of the language, that no one could understand'. It was, in fact, surprising that the servants understood anything, for their masters and mistresses spoke to them in a peculiar jargon which one lady christened 'John Company's English'. She herself began to learn the Tamil language, but found it fearfully ugly, 'clattering, twittering, chirping, sputtering—like a whole poultry-yard let loose upon one', and soon relapsed into John Company's English again.

Newcomers found that even the barest civility to servants might not be understood. 'One day I said to my ayah (a very elegant lady in white muslin), "Ayah, bring me a glass of toast-and-water if you please". She crept to the door and then came back again, looking extremely perplexed, and whined out, "What Mistress tell? I don't know". "I told you to bring me some toast-and-water". "Toast-water I know very well, but Mistress tell *if you please;* I don't know *if you please*" '.

Inseparable from the servant problem was the upbringing of children, who spent so much of their life in the servants' charge before being packed off to England (or 'Home'). The children were able to command the widest devotion from the servants, but nurses were not above using a pill of opium to keep them quiet. Often, it kept them permanently so, and the European cemeteries held many graves of children dead in early infancy. If the children survived the combined assault of their nurses and of disease, it was necessary in the interests of their education as well as their health to send them to England. There were even one or two over-Christian mothers who felt that their children were in the gravest moral danger in India from the moment of birth. Think, wrote one of them, 'of our children hearing a language which they generally understand better than their parents, and of our lessons respecting a holy and spiritual God, being mingled in their minds with the silly and abominable fables and images of the surrounding idols!' It was a terrible thought that English children might grow up influenced by heathens, and it was no satisfactory answer to maintain, as most sensible mothers did:

'It is very sad but it can't be helped; and a year at Home will set all to rights'.

Whatever the religious attitude of the parents, it is fair to say that children in India were 'peculiarly objects of passionate love', not only because death or departure for England threatened permanent or temporary separation, but because in the circumstances of an Anglo-Indian household children somehow became 'actually more attractive. . . . Unshackled by the discipline of an English nursery, and the tyranny of a head nurse, both of which tend to engender a spirit of reserve and even cunning, they roam at will through every part of the house, prattling with all the artlessness of fearless childhood, and effectually twining themselves round the affections of every member of the family, and visitors to the house'.

If Anglo-Indian children were seen and heard with more tolerance than they would have been in England, the prevalence of servants kept them out of their parents' way when other entertainment offered. Not that such entertainment was in any way exciting. At dinner parties, the food was mediocre to say the least, and the conversation afterwards positively crushing. 'After dinner the company all sit round in the middle of the great gallery-like rooms, talk in whispers, and scratch their mosquito-bites'.

There was more likelihood of entertainment at the home of some native acquaintance, though most Anglo-Indians do not seem to have had such acquaintances outside the way of business. One senior lady, asked what she had seen of the natives during her years in India, replied: 'Oh, nothing! Thank goodness, I know nothing at all about them, nor I don't wish to: really, I think the less one sees and knows of them the better!' The entertainment in an Indian house would, of course, be regarded as 'interesting' rather than enjoyable. A musician might play the vina, 'an instrument like a large mandoline', but the music that emerged was 'just a mixture of twang and whine'. The dancing girls, too, were a disappointment; though 'graceful creatures . . . sailing about like queens', in spite of their grace and their gorgeous jewellery they were 'tame'. And when they began to sing, it was like the 'bawling of bad street-singers—a most fearful noise and no tune'. These comments, however, came from a woman; perhaps things were more lively when the audience was male. The lady was no more impressed by the food than she had been by the entertainment, or by the house itself (which reminded her of a French *pension*). Most of the dishes were heavy with cayenne pepper, though otherwise quite good, 'but among the Hindoo messes I at last came to something so queer, slimy and oily, that I was obliged to stop'. On the whole Indian India was more amusing at a distance, in letters, for example, written in 'the true Fudge style' and containing such delightful phrases as 'hoping to have the honour of throwing myself at your goodness's philanthropic feet'!

Compared with some of the smaller stations to which a civilian might be sent, Madras was moderately sophisticated. In a small station, there might be only three or four Europeans, who had to rely on travellers or local eccentrics to vary the routine of their lives. Scattered around the country, outside the web of Anglo-Indian society, occasional Europeans were to be found—ex-soldiers of the Company's army, perhaps, pensioners who had settled in the Indian countryside because they knew they would not be happy 'at Home'. (The word 'Home', incidentally, always meant England; 'nobody calls India home—not even those who have been here thirty years and are never likely to return to Europe'). At Rajahmundry, several hundred miles north of Madras, there was 'an old Englishman living as barrack-sergeant—a sinecure for long service. He has been in the place these ten years, and is a very respectable old man. He has a half-caste, dropsical wife, and a sickly nigger-looking child, but seems quiet and contented'.

English soldiers travelling to join their regiments might provide some diversion for the residents of the smaller stations, and gave them the opportunity of induging in good works. A magistrate in a remote district one day discovered seven such, resting on their journey, and tried to find out if there was anything he could do for them. The greatest treat he could possibly give them, they said, 'would be a little tea and sugar to make themselves "a cup of English tea", which was a thing "they had not tasted they did not know when" '. With their tea they were given some tracts, but when asked whether they had a bible, they replied that 'they set such store by it they seldom let it see the light'. So they were presented with another one for general use.

Naturally, common soldiers could not be invited to stay in one's house. Other travellers could, however. Some were welcome, like the young ensign of seventeen, travelling with a company of sepoys who were guarding a consignment of treasure; it was 'a pleasure to see a creature so innocently important and happy'. Others were less welcome and less innocent—travellers who inflicted themselves on some poor official and became a positive nuisance, borrowing a favourite horse, perhaps, or (even worse) going off and leaving all their luggage in their host's spare room until they chose to return, uninvited as before, to claim it. The trouble was that the government would not spend money on travellers' bungalows, making the excuse that 'the residents can always receive travellers'.

The civilian in any station, but particularly in a remote one, had to receive and sometimes return visits from the local aristocracy, great landlords and petty rajas. Conversation on these occasions was often rather stilted, consisting of a series of high-flown compliments and enquiries about His-Honour-the-civilian's health. But occasionally it widened a little. Queen Victoria's accession at least aroused some interest in the native mind. Queens regnant were rarities in India. How was the queen to get *men* to agree to obey her? It proved impossible to explain.

Indians of lower rank were constantly petitioning for appointments on the civilian's staff. There was a routine for this. It was not even necessary to make the petition in words. All that was needed was for the applicant to hang about the gate of the bungalow, displaying some part of the official trappings for the relevant appointment—writing material if the man aspired to be a clerk, a dagger if he hoped to become a messenger. Others insisted on having an audience with the great man, sometimes as often as twice a week if they were the determined kind. On these occasions, the dialogue might be expected to take the following course:

Visitor: Salaam, great chief!
Civilian: Salaam to you.
Visitor: Your Excellency is my father and my mother.

Civilian: I am much obliged to you.

Visitor: Sar, I am come to behold your honourable face.

Civilian: Thank you. Have you anything to say to me?

Visitor: Nothing, great chief!

Civilian: Neither have I anything to say, so good morning; enough for today.

Visitor: Enough; good morning, sar: great chief, salaam!

Even when the visitors were more acceptable, there was no great likelihood of interesting conversation. If they were civilians, most of the talk was of promotion, or, as one impatient blue-stocking of a magistrate's wife put it (à propos of the post of Collector, who was head of the district administration in certain parts of India): 'They sit and conjugate the verb "to collect": "I am a collector—He was a collector—We shall be collectors—You ought to be a collector—They would have been collectors".'

With civilian ladies, it was very hard work to keep any conversation going, even about promotion. They were 'generally very quiet, rather languid, speaking in almost a whisper, simply dressed, almost always ladylike and *comme-il-faut*, not pretty, but pleasant and nice-looking'. Military wives, on the other hand, were always 'quite young, pretty, noisy, affected, showily dressed, with a great many ornaments . . . [and] chatter incessantly from the moment they enter the house'. Their conversation matched their personalities. 'While they are alone with me after dinner, they talk about suckling their babies, the disadvantages of scandal, "the Officers", and "the Regiment" '. When the gentlemen reappeared, they flirted 'most furiously'.

As well as wild animals, hyenas, snakes, and whole martyrdoms of objectionable insects, there were other strange creatures in the countryside around the civilians' bungalows. Among them were the missionaries and their converts—who were usually known by the self-explanatory name of 'curry-and-rice Christians'.

The missionaries' unsubtle evangelism could often undo the more ingenious religious propaganda of others. The civilian official in an out-station would often set up a school and slip in tracts and versions of the bible in local languages among the textbooks. But missionaries openly attacked the Hindu religion, and their aggression frequently put the town in a ferment and resulted in children being taken away from the school.

The government itself patronised the native religions impartially, demonstrating its neutrality in ways that were anathema to its Christian employees. Often it acted as trustee for Hindu temples. This had long been one of the responsibilities accepted by rulers in India, and the British, when they assumed power, took over this responsibility as a matter of inheritance. The Company's soldiers—Europeans included—often attended religious festivals and fired off volleys in honour of some Hindu god. The Company had been condemned by religious reformers in England for thus acting as 'a wet-nurse for Visnu', but it took quite a time before such customs were abandoned, even though many civilians did their best to express their disgust at having, perhaps, to present the gift of a shawl to some idol, or superintend its transportation through the streets. One civilian was even reported to have dragged the idol out of its festival car and had it chopped to pieces by his servants.

Under the pressure of powerful interests at home and the resistance of its employees in India, the Company withdrew its troops from religious festivals. It did not, however, go so far as to encourage Christian missionary activities. For this, too, it was condemned, and by none more loudly that the men who ruled India in the Company's own name.

5 City of palaces

The approaches to Calcutta, the first city of British India,
were depressing. Unlike Bombay and Madras, which the traveller
could observe while still at sea, Calcutta was a hundred miles up
a particularly forbidding estuary. The journey up river might,
of course, take place partly at night, which at least spared the
traveller a view of the flat, endless, featureless plains which
bounded the river. But Calcutta from the water was not a sight
to be missed, and Garden Reach gave the first indication that the
city might be worth the boredom of a journey by daylight. On
the left was the Botanical Garden, hidden behind a screen of
cypress trees, on the right a long succession of villas 'situated
amidst verdant lawns and park-like pleasure grounds, sloping
gently down to the water's edge'. Once past the Reach, the great
pile of Fort William came into sight, with a forest of masts in
the river before it. There would be merchant ships flying the flags
of many countries. Lean, well-trimmed American vessels which
brought great blocks of ice in their holds. Chinese ships, with an
eye painted on either side, so that the vessels could see their
way. Great awkward country boats laden with produce; the green
goose-shaped budgerows used by Europeans for river travel;
and 'airy little bauleahs, with their light venetian'd rooms, which
seem fitted for the water-bowers of lovers on some of the lakes
of those sunny isles which poets are wont to sing of, and where
the breezes are never stronger than can be borne by silken sails'.
Behind all these, the 'lines of stately mansions reposing under the
still calm sky, like some Grecian capital of old, bespoke the City
of Palaces, the proud metropolis of British India'.

This was no static picture, no elegant aquatint world without
movement or smell. On the contrary, Calcutta was famous for its
stenches. The newcomer was frequently shocked to find a loathsome, half-decayed corpse banging against the anchor cable. The
Hindus burned their dead—but only if they could afford the
fuel. The poor usually left partially burned bodies by the side
of the river until they were borne away by the tide. So many

bodies infested the river that the police kept a fleet of boats and men whose job was 'to remove, by sinking, all offensive objects found floating in the river, which they do possibly after the spectacle has passed through the whole fleet'. If the wind were blowing off the land, then newcomers were also greeted with the smell of the open drains which helped to make Calcutta one of the most unhealthy places in India.

But there were thousands of small boats dashing in and out amongst the anchored ships and the landing stage (the *ghat*) was crowded with the most colourful people. 'Females bearing pots or jars on their heads, and children, resembling little black monkeys, astride on their hips; bhisties, or water-carriers, filling their bags from the turbid tide, well seasoned with coconut husks, defunct Brahmins, dead dogs, etc; puckalls, or bullocks, bearing huge skins of the same pure element; palankeen bearers, gabbling (to me) unintelligible abuse, in eager competition, pushing into the very river, and banging their portable boxes one against the other in their struggle to secure fares amongst the frequent arrivals from the shipping; baboos, parroquet-venders, chattah-bearers, sailors, lascars, and adjutant-birds'—all were there. In fact, Europe and India 'commingled . . . in confusion'.

The newcomer was known in Anglo-India as a 'griff' or 'griffin'. If he had not been met, he would find himself besieged by potential servants brandishing a variety of testimonials from long-dead or non-existent Englishmen. Certainly, a new arrival needed servants, but he was well advised to wait a little.

An army man would be given accommodation in Fort William if he applied to the Town Major. The Fort itself had no architectural pretensions, though it had been built according to all the best tenets of military engineering. It remained a fort in the strict sense, and it was said to be large enough to shelter the 'whole Christian population' if it ever came to the crunch. The only trouble was that there was no water supply inside the fort. Water for the 'whole Christian population' would have had to be brought from a tank (or pond) *out*side the ramparts. The fort, however, was amply stocked with weapons and powder. Mounted on its walls, against the unlikely possibility of attack, were some six hundred guns of various calibres. The arsenal held a floating stock of sixty thousand firearms and twenty thousand swords, and the magazines, which were alleged to be 'bomb-proof', could accommodate five thousand barrels of gunpowder. Unfortunately, the principal powder depots were not in the fort itself, but outside the town, and most of the magazine space within the fort was given over to millions of rounds of small-arms ammunition.

The griff's quarters inside the fort were hardly luxurious by anyone's standards—except perhaps those of a traveller who has been cooped up on board ship for weeks or months. The barracks allotted to unmarried officers consisted of a single corridor with rooms leading off it. These were small, but each was designed to act as parlour, bedroom and bath. 'For the latter indispensable accessory to an Indian toilet, provision had most liberally been made, by enclosing a corner of the room with a parapet a foot high, and by piercing the outer wall to let the water off. Naked and comfortless as any quarter in England, the appearance of this one was not rendered more prepossessing by the circumstance of the walls being adorned with sundry deep indentations, stains of suspicious colour, and a profuse sprinkling of ink, all of which told of the choleric temperament of a former occupant, probably some "jolly cadet", who . . . impatient of the stupidity of a bearer, or *khidmutgar*, for being ignorant of *his* language, had perchance striven to render himself intelligible by hurling, in rapid succession, at the head of his domestic, an empty brandy bottle, a bootjack, and an inkstand'.

The barracks were exceptionally noisy. 'The passage was sounding and reverberating, and each occupant of a quarter had much of the benefit of his neighbour's flute, fiddle or French horn, whether "i' the vein" for harmony or not; shoe brushings, occasional yells of servants undergoing the discipline of fists or cane, jolly ensigns and cadets clattering up and down, cracking horsewhips [and] whistling'—all served to contribute to the clamour. Visually, too, there was considerable variety and disorder. 'On the ground might be seen a goodly display of trays, with egg-shells, fish-bones, rice, muffin, and other wrecks of breakfast; sweepers—certain degraded menials . . .—squatting near and waiting for the said remnants, hookahs . . . in course of preparation for those who indulged in the luxury of smoking'.

Fort William was not considered a healthy station. A young soldier arriving there in 1852 wrote in his memoirs forty years later: 'The men were crowded into small badly-ventilated buildings, and the sanitary arrangements were as deplorable as the state of the water supply. The only efficient scavengers were the huge birds of prey called adjutants, and so great was the dependence placed upon the exertions of these unclean creatures that the young cadets were warned that any injury done to them would be treated as gross misconduct'.

The traveller did, however, have an alternative to this kind of accommodation. Unlike Bombay and Madras, Calcutta had a number of quite reasonable hotels and boarding houses. Spence's, near Government House, was said to be the best, though there were differing opinions as to its merits. In 1842, a German traveller found its comfort and service pleasant and its charges not too high. Ten years later, the future Lord Roberts found it dreary—although this may have been because he discovered that, by staying there instead of going directly to the artillery depot, he had lost not only a day's pay but a day's seniority.

Another hotel, the Auckland, was described by the great war correspondent, William Howard Russell of the London *Times,* as a large house in which there had been made 'an attempt to combine a tailor's, a milliner's and dressmaker's, a haberdasher's, a confectioner's, a hardwareman's, a woollen merchant's, a perfumer's, a restaurateur's, a spirit and wine merchant's, a provision dealer's, a grocer's, a coffee-house keeper's establishment, with an hotel, and with a variety of other trades and callings. I should say from my own experience, the hotel suffers in the amalgamation; but it is a great advantage to have at your feet all you want, although, I must confess, I could not manage to get a chop one morning for breakfast below stairs. Mr D. Wilson, who created this establishment by his energy, ability and industry, has made a large fortune; and judging from the zeal with which he advertises all over India, is bent on making it larger'.

But the traveller's best solution, failing a private house, was a club. In Calcutta, the finest was undoubtedly the Bengal Club. This had been founded in 1827 and had occupied a number of houses in the centre of the city before it moved to its final premises in 1845. The Bengal Club had not been the first club to open in Calcutta, but it was the one which most closely resembled the great London clubs. Before its final move to the Chowringee, the principal thoroughfare of British Calcutta, it had occupied a building on the esplanade overlooking the port and its shipping. There it had contained reading rooms, a library, and dining rooms, all of which were 'fitted up in the most convenient and elegant manner'. The new building was even more luxurious and impressive. In fact, all the great houses along the Chowringee and the adjacent roads looked like palaces. They were built in the style of the Classical mansion, which the aristocracy of Europe had elevated into a symbol of power and success. Palladio inspired it, and lesser architects adapted his plans to suit the availability of materials and the demands of the tropics.

Unfortunately, on closer inspection, the great palaces of the men who ruled India had their flaws. The houses were too close together, for one thing. In an open park, each would have had its special grandeur, but the fact of their being close together and surrounded by high walls seemed to detract from their elegance. It did not improve matters to find next to these great mansions a 'batch of miserable native huts, which are about as much out of place as a row of pigsties would be in the middle of Regent Street'. Even the ambience was decidedly vulgar. 'Instead of the caparisoned elephant, and the golden umbrella, and the decorated palankeen with its liveried out-runners, we see the primitive-looking native bullock-cart, as it creaks along the dusty road— the wretched, dilapidated *carhanchy*, or hack-carriage of Bengal, filled with some half dozen fat natives, and drawn by a pair of lean and wall-eyed ponies, threatening every moment to part with at least one of its wheels, and groaning beneath the mass of ghee-inflated flesh that it carries'. On foot, there were none of the gorgeous figures artists insisted on putting in their illustrations of 'Life in India', no princes in 'jewelled turbans and silken raiment but plenty of coolies, with no turbans at all and a lamentable deficiency of raiment'. It was something of a let-down. Could this really be the 'city of palaces'?

Even when night fell, there was little glamour added to the scene, for Calcutta was most wretchedly lighted—at least at the beginning of the queen's reign—and it took a long time for it to improve. The only street lighting was from 'sordid oil-lamps, supplied with material of so inferior a description that even the inside of the lamp is scarcely illuminated, and placed at the respectable distances of the corners of streets, or other wide intervals, which make them appear as few and far between as did the angels' visits of the poet's illustration'.

The streets were not patrolled by watchmen, nor were they paved. The open drains were 'execrable', and helped Calcutta maintain its reputation for all-the-year-round unhealthiness. According to one well-worn saying, the capital of British India was 'bad for new arrivals in the hot weather, in the rains for old Indians [i.e. Anglo-Indians], and in the cold weather for everybody'.

For part of the year the great mansions might be shining white, having been coated with a layer of *chunam*, or lime. But in the monsoon, they had 'a somewhat desolate aspect of uninhabited grandeur; for the walls and the pillars were black and weather-stained, large patches of green damp were visible about the base, and down the sides of the house you might trace the course of the water, that had been, almost incessantly for the last two months, streaming down from the conduits on the roof. The house, too, was shut up; between the pillars of the spacious verandah . . . large green blinds, made of thin pieces of split and painted bamboo, were let down to exclude the glare'.

Indoors, the houses had magnificent rooms. The reception room was inevitably hung with chandeliers, which were usually protected by great bags of some red material. 'Besides these, were suspended from the beams two large punkahs, most elaborately moulded and gilt, with deep fringes attached to the bottom, and semi-circular spaces cut at the top of them, to give a clear berth to the above-described chandeliers, which would otherwise have been smashed to atoms at the first swing of these formidable ventilators'. The furniture was, as a rule, heavy and expensively luxurious, with lots of marble tables, mahogany-framed sofas covered in damask, writing tables, an alabaster cupid or two, and at least one bronze stag. There would also be a piano and numerous elegant-looking albums, some of music, others with such titles as *The Book of*

51

Beauty or *The Book of Royalty*. Just to indicate that the household was by no means frivolous, there would also be a volume of the *Calcutta Christian Observer*—though the first 'very favourable impression of the religious character of the lady of the house' which this conveyed was often belied by the fact that it bore the 'most unequivocal symptoms of having been unread'. In other words, the pages would still be uncut.

The governor-general's house was a real palace, although foreign visitors were inclined to find it unpretentious. The approach was 'up a colossal flight of steps, so spacious that a large number of the inhabitants of the town can assemble in it to greet an arriving [governor-general]. Immediately on entering you find yourself in the great marble banqueting hall, capable of holding with ease more than a hundred guests, and so lofty that palm trees are frequently introduced on the occasion of great entertainments, and the tables of the guests are laid beneath their spreading branches. There are white pillars down the whole length of this noble chamber; and at the end of the vista, an admirable finish to the general effect, is the throne room.

'But the marble hall is only the vestibule to an apartment of greater dimensions—the ballroom, where as many as two thousand guests are sometimes received, and the general look of which is that of a Royal state room. The plan of the whole house is curious, and is exactly suited to an Indian climate. From four corners of a central block of buildings, in which are the reception rooms just mentioned, and others of lesser magnitude, long corridors radiate, communicating at a considerable distance with four wings, each of which virtually constitutes a separate and detached house. Each of these wings is so built that from whatever side the wind comes —north, south, east, or west—a thorough draught can be obtained through every room.

'In one of these wings the [governor-general] has his own establishment, his private rooms, and offices of state. In the same wing, and immediately adjoining it, are the political secretary's room, the aide-de-camps' room, and waiting room; while on the floor below are the private secretary's office, and rooms for the staff of under-secretaries and clerks, whose services are in perpetual requisition to deal with the mountains of papers which daily come before the [governor-general]. So far as its ornaments and fittings are concerned, the whole house is a curious miscellany of trophies and historical associations. The council room and some of the corridors are lined with portraits of . . . Warren Hastings, Wellesley and others. The marble hall abounds with busts of Roman emperors, the busts captured from a French man-of-war and ranged along the walls; while chandeliers of rare beauty hang in each of the principal apartments, also some taken from the French'.

Such was Government House when Lord Auckland announced the accession of Queen Victoria, but it had changed—and not for the better—when a new governor-general arrived eleven years later. 'I find the house superb', wrote Lord Dalhousie, 'the furniture disgraceful; an ADC's bed absolutely broke down to the ground with him the other day from sheer age; the plate and table equipage very poor. I can't afford to spend money on plate, but I think the deficiency in plate and in the inferiority of table decoration would be very much remedied, if I had the means of setting off the table with plants, as is done at Buckingham Palace and elsewhere in London'. However, he noted regretfully that 'at present John Company has no more cash than his neighbours, and I can't ask much at present'.

At least the governor-general's yacht was in better condition. 'Nothing can be more luxurious', Dalhousie was pleased to say, 'than this style of travelling, in a yacht, all green and gilding, with no crew, towed by a steamer, with sofas and punkahs, and bed-rooms and luxuries of all sorts; one sits as much at ease as in a room, with the advantage of catching every breath of air which can find its way to you in this incipient frying-pan'. The yacht was the governor-general's usual means of transport to Barrack-pore, his weekend retreat about fifteen miles from Calcutta, where the air was believed to be somewhat cooler than in the capital. It was certainly more salubrious.

The Barrackpore house was genuinely unpretentious. Though the rooms were large, the house itself was small, so the governor-general's family could have it very much to themselves. The aides-de-camp, secretaries, and other essential supports of the Company's ruler, slept in small thatched cottages built around

E

the park. Even guests were accommodated away from the main house, in separate guest bungalows. Lord Dalhousie found that the furniture was still 'not smart', but at least it was 'not so scandalous and blackguard as that at the Government House' in Calcutta. Obviously no improvement had been made since Emily Eden, some years before, wrote in her journal that the furniture and hangings were shabby, and the furniture 'worse than that of an average London hotel'. The governor-general and his family did not suffer over-much, however. A vast fleet of boats accompanied his yacht from Calcutta, and four hundred servants were thought an adequate number to sustain him in the manner to which he was accustomed.

The park surrounding the Barrackpore house was—almost— like home, 'a pretty pleasure-ground, beautiful garden, an aviary, a menagerie, and all situated on the bank of the river, and sur- rounded by a park quite home-like in its character, and as English as anything can be, where you have banians, and cocoa- nuts, and palms, and mangoes, for oaks and elms, larch, and beech'.

Calcutta, despite all strictures, was an impressive city. Well- travelled visitors frequently likened it to St Petersburg, and with reason. The public buildings, taken as a whole, *were* elegant —architecturally, at least—and they were often kept in better condition than some of the private mansions. The native city was avoided as much as possible, though it was interesting enough to drive through if only the crowds had not made it so difficult for the horses to pursue their way. For the romantic visitor or the newly-arrived resident, there were always a few natives with 'wild, handsome countenances', or perhaps a Chinese with 'twinkling eyes and yellow face and satin dress' stalking among 'these black, naked creatures'.

Some of the richer Indians lived in houses outside Calcutta. Dwarkanath Tagore, perhaps the first Western-style Indian capitalist (who had visited England and been received by the queen), owned a villa in the English style five miles from the city. It stood isolated in a small park which was also in the English style, and was apparently 'a favourite resort of young married couples, who are often invited by the hospitable owner to spend the honeymoon there'. The furnishings of the two-storeyed house were entirely European in taste. So, too, was the owner, for his dinner-table held 'the richest wines and even roasted joints of the sacred animal'—the cow. When Captain von Orlich visited the house in 1843, however, musicians and nautch girls arrived to entertain the guests after dinner. Their dancing was not much admired, but the Captain, who had an eye for a pretty figure, noted that they had delicate feet and hands, and a 'fine contour'. But soon 'their movements became so offensive, that we requested that the dance might be concluded'. It was very regrettable, the Captain felt, that 'the notions of morality and decorum entertained by the Indians, even when they have acquired that degree of refinement which our host undoubtedly possessed, are still so different from ours, that they are quite insensible to that impropriety which so much shocked us'.

It was not the first time that a visit to Dwarkanath Tagore's villa had been productive of moralising. Before Captain Orlich's experience, the governor-general, Lord Auckland, accompanied by his sisters, had accepted an invitation there and had found elephants on the lawn and ices in the summerhouse. On the whole, the party had had a most enjoyable time. The trouble came afterwards. Much of Calcutta society did not approve of their governor-general hobnobbing with the natives.

Life in Calcutta was not particularly exciting. There were balls at Government House, of course, and many private dances and dinners, for Anglo-Indian society was a gregarious society. People who did not mix were regarded as odd (or worse) and did not stand much chance of promotion. If they were old and distinguished, however, any anti-social tendencies—as long as they were not too bizarre—were considered as merely eccentric.

Members of Anglo-Indian society liked to be assured that it was still alive, for death had a habit of coming very swiftly. And yet death was treated with a certain calculated indifference. When, for example, a communication arrived at one of the great mansions on the Chowringee, announcing the death of a certain Mr Collingwood, an exchange such as the following might ensue:

'Mr Collingwood', returned Mrs Parkinson; 'it really is quite shocking; he dined with us the day before yesterday—cholera, I suppose—dreadful!' and Mrs Parkinson endeavoured to look quite overcome, but was not particularly successful.

But Mrs Poggleton pretended nothing at all: she leant forward, held out her hand for the undertaker's circular, looked rather pleased than otherwise, and said, 'Dear me! if it is not the gentleman with that pretty carriage, I declare!'

'Small use to him a pretty carriage now', said Mrs Parkinson, 'the only carriage that he needs is a hearse'.

'Oh; but', exclaimed Mrs Poggleton, with more eagerness than she had manifested throughout the conversation, 'I have been dying a long time for that carriage, and now I shall be able to get it. What a nice thing to be sure!'

Upon this Mrs Parkinson lifted up her hands, and pretended to be immeasurably shocked, muttering to herself, but quite loud enough for everybody to hear, that life was a span, and death hanging over us, and that the world might be destroyed tomorrow, for anything she knew to the contrary, with sundry other moral reflections of this kind, equally original, and expressive of virtuous emotion.

Though society was close-knit, it was by no means free from hatreds. These even blew up into duels, though duelling was no longer quite the approved way of settling points of honour. Attempts had been made to stop duelling in the royal armed forces by lobbyists of the Association for the Discouragement of Duelling, who presented a memorial to the queen in 1843. Within a year, the Articles of War had been so amended that any officer accepting, sending, or carrying a challenge was liable to be cashiered; the seconds suffered in proportion. These regulations had some effect, if not all that had been intended, but they were slow to influence quick-tempered men in India.

The ladies, who had little to occupy their hands but embroidery, had less to occupy their minds. Cultural life in Calcutta was not at its height during the first twenty years of the queen's reign. Books were scarce, and greatly over-priced for many years

—a novel, at one time, cost three guineas a copy. The books which new residents inherited, left behind by some nabob of the previous century, were usually books which had not excited the nabob either. They scarcely offered light reading, for they all seemed to be sermons, or commentaries on the Gospels. Fortunately, the Americans brought in the holds of their ships not only bags of ice, but cheap (pirated) editions of English books. Their range was not very wide, but there were many novels, and even such a bluestocking as Emily Eden insisted: 'the more trash the better'.

There were newspapers, fortunately, and they had been freed from censorship in 1835. Mostly, they were mouthpieces of the various special-interest groups (particularly merchants) who owned them, but they also willingly gave space to disgruntled members of the civil service or the army who wished to attack the government, or even specific persons. Though the person attacked had no anonymity granted to him, his attackers hid behind such high-sounding pseudonyms as 'Brutus' and other Classical personalities. Herbert Edwardes, however, caused something of a sensation in the 1850s by contributing a series of letters under the name of 'Brahminy Bull'. In 1847, members of the civil service were ordered not to contribute to newspapers, but this order had little effect. Scandal and abuse always make news, especially in such a small society as that of Anglo-India.

Scandal, in fact, was the lubricant of much of the social mechanism, particularly for the women. 'In other parts of the world they talk about things, here they talk about people. The conversation is all personal, and, as such, you may be sure tolerably abusive'. What did they find to say about one another? 'The veriest trifles in the world. Nothing is so insignificant as the staple of Calcutta conversation. What Mr This said to Miss That, and what Miss That did to Mr This; and then all the interminable gossip about marriages and no-marriages, and will-be marriages and ought-to-be marriages, and gentlemen's attention and ladies' flirtings, dress, reunions, and the last burra-khana [big dinner]—'.

Calcutta did offer more European-style diversions than the other cities of Anglo-India. There was a theatre, an elegant building opened in 1840 and called the Sans Souci. There were visiting companies, and even an operatic performance or two—though according to mentions in diaries and letters they never seem to have been very good. There was racing around the course in front of Fort William. Racing began very early in the day, at sunrise, in fact, and the meetings were usually over by ten o'clock, 'thus enabling all classes to attend and enjoy the sport without trenching on upon their daily avocations'. The horses were usually Arabs from the Persian Gulf, with an occasional entry from New South Wales; later, Australia came to supply most of the mounts. The men also went shooting outside the city, or hunting. For the less bloodthirsty, there were cricket and racquets.

For all its gossiping and scandal-mongering, Calcutta society was really very moral. Emily Eden had already found it so in the early years of Victoria's reign. 'People are very domestic in their habits, and there are no idle men. Every man without exception is employed in his office all day, and in the evening drives. Husbands and wives are always in the same carriage. It is too hot for him to ride or walk, and at evening parties it is not considered possible for one to come without the other; it is quite out of the question. If Mr Jones is ill everybody knows that Mrs Jones cannot go out, so she is not expected.'

There were a number of men who had grown old in the service and who chose not to keep up with the new-fangled protocol of society. They lived as they had always been accustomed to, richly—even grossly—and to hell with everybody. But even men of the older generation kept their old-fashioned outspoken manners for the time after the ladies had left the table. Then, 'all was grossness and sensuality'. William Knighton, writing in 1855 of just such an old Anglo-Indian (whom he called Ducklet), was greatly relieved 'when he moved an adjournment to the drawing-room, where we found Mrs Ducklet dozing over a volume of sermons, and the fascinating Julia performing sacred pieces on the piano. It was now half-past ten o'clock, and we had sat down to dinner at half-past seven!'

Within twenty years of Victoria's accession, the old men had long since died or gone Home. William Howard Russell noted

that 'the good old hookah days are past; cheroots and pipes
have now usurped the place of the aristocratic silver bowl, the
cut-glass goblets, and the twisted glistening snake with silver or
amber mouthpiece . . . The race of Eurasians is not so freely
supplied with recruits . . . There is now no bee-bee's house—a sort
of European zenana'. Had things changed for the better? 'There
are now European rivals to those ladies (the native kept women)
at some stations. It was the topic of conversation the other day
at mess that the colonel of a regiment had thought it right to
prohibit one of his officers from appearing publicly with an
unauthorised companion at the band parade; and the general
opinion was that he had no right to interfere. But the society of
the station does interfere in such cases, and though it does not
mind bee-bees or their friends, it rightly taboos him who enter-
tains their white rivals'.

But that, of course, was 'up the country'.

6 Up the country

Outside the great centres of Anglo-Indian life there remained the wild and lonely places, where perhaps one British official would rule a vast area and great numbers of people, without seeing a fellow-Englishman for months. The new frontiers still dominated much of British India.

In the less remote districts there were larger colonies of civilians and soldiers, known simply as 'the station'. For displaying Anglo-Indian society, this was the ideal frame—but the visitor had to get there first.

There were a number of ways of travelling 'up the country', by land, by river, or by a combination of the two. In the early fifties, it was just becoming possible to make part of the journey by rail. But this had its disadvantages. One was the possibility of being set on fire by sparks from the engine; the fuel was wood, not coal. In fact, the danger was so acute that, on one occasion, 'as a detachment of Sikh soldiers were going up country, one of them had his clothes set on fire by the embers. All his comrades were dressed in cotton-quilted tunics, with their pouches full of ammunition; and in their alarm they adopted the notable device of pitching the man out of the window in order to get rid of the danger to which they were exposed'.

It was usual for civilians or single officers to travel by land. A regiment of soldiers, however, customarily went by river, which was a very slow and tedious journey. The land traveller could ride his own horse, and usually did so for at least part of the journey. For the rest, there was the palanquin, or the *palki-garee*, a palanquin on wheels—rather like a coffin on springs—which could turn out to be very comfortable, for with the doors closed and a lamp beside one's head it was possible to have a pleasant hour or two's reading before sleep.

Travel needed forethought and careful arrangement. The post office was responsible for the travel service from about 1843 onwards. To organise a journey, or 'lay a dak' (the word 'dak' means 'post'), it was necessary to inform the head postmaster well in advance, so that he could make arrangements with postal officials up the country for the supply of bearers at authorised stopping places along the route. Unfortunately, the post office was organised to handle only a small number of the most frequented routes. Travellers elsewhere had to try and arrange matters for themselves. The usual thing was to buy a palanquin and have it fitted up as comfortably as one's means would allow. The cost of a palanquin was about £10—a substantial sum in terms of the time—but it could usually be re-sold at not too much of a loss at the end of the journey. 'Fitting up' usually consisted of a minimum furnishing of books, plus 'shaving and washing apparatus, a canister of biscuits, a bottle and glass, a drinking cup, a little additional night clothing . . . The clothes of the traveller and such articles as he does not immediately require, are carried in tin boxes, or wicker baskets, called pettarahs, by separate bearers, who run ahead or alongside of the palanquin; and these pettarahs may be procured in any number at the chief towns and stations at a very slight cost'.

The traveller was advised, as far as money was concerned, to take only silver, and particularly 'a considerable number of the smaller coins of eight and four annas, as gratuities to boatmen who ferry you across the small nullahs or rivers, and to the palanquin-bearers . . . at each stage; for in many parts of the country these latter people are paid so irregularly, or kept so much in arrears, that their very subsistence depends upon the bounty of the dak traveller'. The usual number of palanquin-bearers was eleven; two pettarah-bearers and a torch-bearer were also needed, for much of the journey was made at night to avoid the heats of the day. The torch-bearer fed his flambeau 'every now and then with oil which he poured out of a bamboo, shaped like a quill toothpick'.

Mrs Colonel Mackenzie, who made such an up-country journey in 1847, found it delightful. 'Whenever we woke there was something to see or hear; sometimes a jackal prowling near, sometimes the merry chatter of the bearers, and sometimes the wild, but not unmusical, shout in chorus, by which they give notice of their arrival at the chouki [stopping place]'. But Captain Richard Burton, later to become famous for his translation of the Arabian Nights—and the *Kama sutra*—was not so enthusiastic. 'After a day or two', he said, 'you will hesitate which to hate most, your bearers' monotonous, melancholy grunting, groaning chaunt, when fresh, or their jolting, jerking, shambling, staggering gait, when tired. In a perpetual state of low fever you cannot eat, drink, or sleep; your mouth burns, your head throbs, your back aches, and your temper borders on the ferocious. At night, when sinking into a temporary oblivion of your ills, the wretches are sure to awaken you for the purpose of begging a few pice, to swear that they dare not proceed because there is no oil for the torch, or to let you and your vehicle fall heavily upon the ground, because the foremost bearer very nearly trod upon a snake. Of course you scramble as well as you can out of your cage, and administer discipline to the offenders. And what is the result? They all run away and leave you to pass the night'.

In northern India, part of the journey (at least as far as Cawnpore) could be made in flats pulled by steam vessels. These flats had sixteen cabins, ranged on either side, and were divided by size into three classes. The journey to Cawnpore took about three weeks and, in the cold weather, could be most enjoyable. But at Cawnpore the service ceased, and there was no alternative but horse or palanquin.

As most travelling, particularly in the hot weather, was done at night, it was essential to have somewhere to rest during the hours of sunlight. Along the principal routes, at regular intervals, a benevolent government had supplied rest-houses, or dak bungalows. On the whole the government's benevolence was strictly limited to erecting a building. For other comforts, all depended on the person in charge. Young Lieutenant Roberts found the *khansamah*, or steward in charge, like 'mine host' at Home. He 'declared himself at the outset prepared to provide everything the heart of man could desire; when, however, the traveller was safely cornered for the rest of the day, the menu invariably dwindled down to the elementary and universal "sudden death", which meant a wretchedly thin chicken, caught, decapitated, grilled, and served up within twenty minutes of the meal being ordered. At dinner, a variety was made by the chicken being curried, accompanied by an unlimited supply of rice and chutney'.

In between times, there was no surcease for the traveller's pains. 'The hours lag long and wearily; the punkah, of limited dimensions, with a deranged flounce and with unsymmetrical ropes, waggles with a quaint and threatening aspect, and affords but little mitigation of the burning heat . . . We lie recumbent on the cot, which has the authorised and popular number of legs, of which the chairs cannot be said to boast;—we have dozed;—we have read the regulations that hang upon the walls forty times at least;—we have drunk tepid beer, and warm soda-water has allayed our thirst;—we have recorded our names in the book of fate and of the Bungalow'. It was almost a relief when the sound of the palanquin-bearers was heard outside. The sun had set and it was time to journey on.

All dak bungalows were not quite such temporary purgatories for empire-builders. In some, the khansamah had made such an impression on the catering that satisfied travellers even left written testimonials behind, which were carefully preserved. The khansamah in charge of the dak bungalow at Kishnaghur in Bengal, for example, had received such encomiums as 'Peter is a brick'. Better still, there was 'a very poetical effusion' from Mr Cadet Brown:

> 'So I will praise Peter wherever I go,
> And always speak well of his Dak bungalow;
> If I always gets food just as good as he gives,
> In time I shall get jolly fat—if I lives!'

This was rare praise indeed. So were stewards of Peter's quality.

Some people, of course, were able to travel in considerable state. When the governor-general, Lord Auckland, made his tremendous journey across upper India—which lasted from October 1837 until March 1840—he moved with an armed camp as vast as a city. But he was the governor-general, after all, and had to make an impression on the natives. There were lesser figures, however, who still moved in some style. A collector, with his wife and child, considered it modest to travel with an elephant, ten palki-garees, two palanquins, six horses, and sixty

house-servants, as well as about eighty porters and palanquin-
bearers.

When a traveller finally reached the up-country station, he
found that it presented a very different appearance from Calcutta
and the other great urban centres on the coast. It was usually
placed a few miles from some native city, so as to overawe it and
not be dominated by it. The layout of the little town was much
the same everywhere. There were bungalows, naturally, and
'that square white-washed edifice, with an excrescence at one
end, looking for all the world like an extinguisher on a three-
dozen chest!—what is it? You may well ask. It is the church! a
regular protestant building! protesting against everything architectural, aesthetic, ornamental, or useful; designed and built according
to a Government prescription. Next to it is our assembly-room
and theatre; just beyond you see the hospitals; then comes the
racket-court, and to the left is the well-stocked burial-ground.
This is the course, where the live splendour of [the station]
resort when shades of evening close upon us. There is the band-
stand, and this is the station bath. On the extreme right are
the barracks, for you must know that Europeans man the guns
of our battery that is quartered here. That is the artillery-mess,
and opposite lives Stickerdoss, who sells Europe-goods, and
can accommodate you with anything, from a baby's bottle to a
bolster'.

The bungalows were only faintly reminiscent of Calcutta's
great mansions. They were white-washed, and had columns holding up the projecting verandah. But their roofs were high and
thatched; sometimes they had a double roof to give extra protection from the sun. In the hot weather, the doorways would
be filled in with grass curtains which, when doused with water,
produced a slightly cooled breeze. To help keep down the
temperature, there was a remarkable device known as a thermantidote. This was an enormous machine, made of wood. It
was about seven feet high, four or five feet wide, and between
nine and twelve feet long. It was hollow, and circular in shape,
ending in a funnel which was fixed to the window of the house.
Inside the cylinder there were four large fans, fixed to an axle
which was driven from outside. When the fans revolved, air

was driven into the house. The air was cooled in the cylinder; a circle about four feet in diameter was cut out of each side of the thermantidote and filled with a mat made from a grass called khas-khas, which gave off a fragrant smell when wet. The mats were kept wet by means of a perforated trough above, which it was a servant's duty to keep filled with water. On a simpler level, there was also a device rather like a paddle-wheel which could be used to direct air on to the wet grass screens in the doorways.

A low wall surrounded each bungalow, enclosing what was known in the special language of Anglo-India as 'the compound'. Inside the compound, as well as the bungalow there were the servants' quarters, the stables, and a cow-house. There was also the garden, to which a great deal of attention was devoted. Water was drawn from a well (of which there would usually be two). Irrigating the ground was a rather complex piece of engineering. The water was raised by bullock power and then emptied into a channel which, in turn, fed many smaller channels all over the garden, each flower and vegetable bed having its own. Because of the plants and trees, the fact that it was an *Indian* garden could never be disguised, but it was always possible to grow roses which reminded one pleasantly of Home. The trouble was that the very English desire for a garden could have its disadvantages, even lethal ones. The gardener and his assistants often flooded the flower-beds, and the water that remained there became a splendid breeding ground for mosquitoes.

Inside, the typical bungalow was very sparsely furnished. There would be a few basket chairs from the bazaar; perhaps, too, a vaguely Sheraton one made up by some local carpenter or purchased—as most of the fittings of an Anglo-Indian bungalow were—from the effects of someone who had died. Clothes were kept in tin boxes, to defend them against the avid white ants which ate practically everything and were particularly fond of cloth. In the hot weather, there would be no carpet on the floor. The punkah was kept going all the time, except when the punkah puller fell asleep, the rope fastened to his big toe. The bed was no splendid fourposter, but only a string frame on four short legs.

The Anglo-Indian household everywhere woke early. The civilian took his exercise before breakfast, and the soldier made his first and only appearance on the parade-ground. After breakfast, the civilian departed for his office or the court, while the officer usually spent the rest of the day in the most pleasant form of idleness he could achieve. Some devoted their days to music or drawing, 'which of course they prefer in the society of ladies'. Military men also spent a great deal of time in gaming for very high stakes, though as time went on this came to be frowned upon as un-Christian—which did not make a great deal of difference. The hot, dull vacancy of everyday life demanded compensation.

Unfortunately, there were few compensations. For the majority of people, the petty dissipations of society formed the only resort. 'These are the men who drink but are not drunkards, bet and play cards but do not gamble ruinously; eat and drink and sleep and gossip and shilly-shally through their day, trying with all the singleness of purpose they possess to steer a dexterous course between the burden of existence on the one hand, and the vacuum of literally doing nothing on the other'.

The army mess was usually on its best behaviour when there were guests, but at other times its manners could be pretty coarse. 'I had always thought of a mess as the abode of luxurious refinement', wrote one rather naive young man in the 1850s. 'I find it a bad tavern. I had not expected to hear literary conversation at a mess-table, but still less such appalling ribaldry as I did hear in the fortnight during which I belonged to the mess. I am not likely to be prudish in these matters; I have spent all my life at Winchester and Oxford, and at both places have been in company with boys and men who were noted for this style of conversation; but I am quite certain that a man saying, at a wine party, such things as are common at the 81st mess, would have been kicked out of the room as a gross offender—I do not say against morality, but against gentlemanly behaviour. They pride themselves on a very subtle distinction between dinner and after-dinner. A man is supposed to be reasonably decent while the cloth is on the table, but may compensate himself by the utmost licence of blackguardism directly it is off. I stayed in the mess for a fortnight, but could not stand it any longer; so now I live alone'.

The up-country station often showed the tension between the two types of Englishman who now ruled India. The militant Christians were growing in numbers and they did not reserve their criticism just for the heathen. On the contrary, it was more often directed at their fellow-countrymen and their standards of behaviour. The white man's burden was slowly being gathered together, and those whose backs appeared too weak to take the strain—or who were obviously unwilling to shoulder the load— became the target for abuse. A man who kept a native mistress was not only beyond the pale on moral grounds; 'when a man in office is under the power of a native woman, she invariably takes bribes, and he gets the credit for doing so; for she of course gives out that the Sahib shares in her extortions. . . . Now, putting the principles of morality out of the question, it is evident that an officer who thus places himself into the hands of a Heathen woman, is wholly unfit for any situation of authority'. As far as drinking was concerned, Mrs Colonel Mackenzie (who was very much a muscular Christian) exclaimed: 'How many are as fit for work, as clear-headed, as even-tempered, as fit for meditation and prayer, after dinner as before! . . . I have long thought we should abstain from wine and beer (for many ladies in India drink both) in order to redeem the time—to keep our bodies in *subjection,* and . . . be able to minister more largely to the wants of others'.

This preoccupation with other people's souls did not inhibit the Anglo-Indian vice of retailing scandal. Except for the possibility of converting the heathen, there was nothing else to do. Most of the gossip derived from the women servants, who met frequently to exchange intelligence about what was served at the last dinner to which their mistresses had not been invited, or what the judge's wife was up to, or how the doctor was able to afford such expensive dresses for his wife. These tales and more, suitably embroidered or even invented, served to fill the time while the memsahib was having her hair brushed or her feet shampooed.

Later in the morning there were more serious, or at least more practical, matters awaiting the memsahib's attention. The provision cupboards had to be inspected, because servants could *never* be trusted. Inventories of stores had to be checked. Everything that could be weighed had to be weighed. The level of the liquid in wine bottles had to be marked, as men servants were known to have a penchant for the sahib's brandy. The routines of the household had to be observed and tours of inspection carried out. The kitchen had to be visited.

Only the most determined and conscientious of wives carried through this programme. The weaker ones, clearly, did not. Many were so overcome by their first sight of the kitchen where their food was prepared that they never summoned up the courage to enter it a second time. 'If your eyes are not instantly blinded with the smoke, and if your sight can penetrate into the darkness, enter that hovel, and witness the preparation of your dinner. The table and the dresser, you observe, are Mother Earth. . . . The preparation for your dinner must therefore be performed in the earth's broad lap, like everything else in this Eastern land. As a matter of course, you will have curry, the standing dish of the East. There are the slaves busy at its preparation. The chase for the fowls has terminated in a speedy capture. Already the feathers are being stripped, and the mixture of the spicy condiments is in course of preparation. . . . Simplicity is the prevailing feature in an Indian kitchen. A spit, two native saucepans, a ladle, and a knife, comprise all the requirements of an Eastern cook. His grate is extemporised at a moment's warning with a lump of mud and a cruse of water'. The Indian cook had a talent for extemporising, and as long as one did not see him stirring the rice pudding with his fingers or straining the soup through his turban-cloth, the results were reasonably satisfactory. If a London chef had been set down in an Indian kitchen 'and there told to prepare a dinner, consisting of every delicacy in fish, flesh, and pudding, for twenty people, by seven o'clock p.m., his first emotion would have a direct tendency to suicide. . . . Nothing that he would call a spit, a grate, an oven, or any one convenience would meet his wildered eye; and he might as well go to the Highlands to look for knee-buckles, as there to search for a dripping-pan, or a roller; sieves, dredgers, cullenders and such like would be just as plentiful as blackberries are in Hyde Park, and even a dishclout would be very difficult to procure. Yet the indigenous cook will, out of this nettle, deficiency, pluck the flower, good dinner'.

The ordeals of inspection did not take up the whole of a memsahib's day by any means. The lady with intellectual pretensions might read instructive works, though they often turned out to be only 'improving', in the precise Victorian sense—formidable books with formidable titles, like *The Fulfilment of the Scriptural Prophecies,* or collections of sermons. Books were expensive in Calcutta and even more so in the outstations. Anyone who came into possession of a novel had to keep the fact secret if she was not to be subjected to constant importuning. Most bungalows boasted a book or two of poems, prominently displayed. Bulwer Lytton became quite popular and Lord Byron, strangely enough, retained a considerable following. Anglo-Indians were much given to writing verses, though these were seldom published in book form. They were usually used to bulk out the enormous letters that everyone wrote. Most of them had a fashionable touch of melancholy, for one of the continuing themes of Anglo-Indian poetry was exile, a terrible nostalgia for the green fields, simple flowers, and soft rain of England.

And are my days all happy now?
Youth's dream is life's reality?
Are there no clouds upon my brow
Because there are none in the sky?

And do I love the matin scream
Of gaudy parrots in the glade?
Or nightly mingling in my dream
The little bul-bul's serenade?

Sing not to me thou merry bird;
Thy song is but an Eastern tale,
I'd give it for the simplest word
Of England's gentle nightingale.

As well as reading, and writing poetry, the Anglo-Indian wrote endless letters. There were always relatives at Home anxiously awaiting a really long screed, full of information about everything from local scandal to descriptions (usually inaccurate) of native customs.

F

Some ladies newly arrived in India took up natural history with uncritical devotion. Young women always seem to have been told before they left England that the insects of India were either not properly classified or totally unknown. In their boredom with life, they determined to rectify the situation. It was 'impossible to go "*à la chasse*" oneself, so I employed the beggar-boys, who at first liked the amusement and brought me a great many'. But they had a habit of becoming tired of collecting *rare* insects and either gave up altogether or only brought horrifying beetles, instead of the beautiful insects that were constantly appearing at dinner and settling in the soup.

It was often a little difficult for the amateur coleopterist to take a purely scientific, and therefore detached, attitude to what were, after all, pests. 'Attracted by the lights, they fly into the room in countless numbers. There is every variety. The long, graceful green mantis alights on the table, and begins stretching out its arms as in an imploring attitude. There are myriads of moths, with wings which seem made of delicate gold and silver tissue; some look inlaid with mother-of-pearl'. These were intriguing, but unfortunately there were also likely to be 'a long, dark yellow, hornet-shaped insect, with no end of joints, which makes you shudder as it flies by; blister flies, with either ruby or emerald-coloured bodies; large beetles, "armed to the teeth" in black, strong, shining armour, and with horns like formidable spears. These beetles are so strong that, when placed under a wine-glass, they move it before them as they advance along the table'.

The men had some latitude in their choice of entertainment, even if the choice was limited. Women seldom indulged in any kind of sport. Though it was not entirely unknown for a lady to accompany the gentlemen on a tiger hunt, it was still thought to be a little 'fast'. But it could be a most delightful experience. In the cold weather, the jungles were quite beautiful, the trees covered with creepers and blossoms of different colours. Peacocks could not only be heard, giving their peculiar shrieking call, but would actually be seen in great numbers. In front of the hunter's elephants, herds of spotted deer would start out of the undergrowth. But such enjoyment of nature could have its disturbances. A lady might be distracted from admiring the wild roses when a great wild hog appeared and charged the elephant. When the gentlemen shot it and the elephant trampled it to death, it was a disgusting sight which quite marred the day.

After their morning ride, most of the men on the station gathered at the coffee shop for a cup of steaming coffee and a good gossip. Their subjects were usually very much the same as those which occupied the ladies in their bungalows. They might discuss the authentic revelation that the 'prime York ham' which had been presented with such a flourish at the judge's dinner the other night came not from York, but from a ravine near the local river; the native vendor of swine had actually been seen handing over his produce to Mrs Judge on her verandah. Even more entertaining was an eye-witness account of the dance at the Collector's, when the heat was so great that 'Mrs Chunam, who, as it is declared, has elevenpence out of the shilling of Hindoo blood floating in her veins, and who delights to veneer as much of herself as is exposed to public view, for the purpose of the whitening of her otherwise shady complexion—the heat, we understand, was so great that the veneer cracked and peeled off in flakes; and further, that her dress happening to subside from off her shoulders, a lovely olive rim, where the veneer had not been applied, became visible for the general edification'. Or the gentlemen might agree that one of the ladies danced like a 'paviour's rammer', or argue over the song which another of the ladies had favoured the company with. It was all about a 'bonnie coo', and the man who had been present maintained that it was 'a hymn, or at any rate a roundelay'—although one of his hearers immediately placed a bet that it was, in fact, 'a Caledonian melody of an agricultural character'.

Whatever laughter the dinner-parties might afterwards raise in the coffee shop, they were the foundation of social life on the station, especially when some visiting notable passed through. The senior civilians competed strongly for the honour of his presence at table. The district magistrate might be the most expert at catching travellers of renown. 'A governor was once entrapped in his snare, to his unlimited satisfaction; while last year, he skilfully made capture of a bishop, but for whose appropriation popular rumour avows that he betokened symptoms of repent-

71

ance'. But visitors of any tolerable rank were made more than welcome, if only because they had unfamiliar faces and, perhaps, brought news from Calcutta and the great world outside the station. Travellers were advised to avoid embarrassment for themselves and any friends they might have at a particular station by warning their friends in advance, so as 'literally to give them the start of the three-cornered billets which come tumbling down' on any new arrival.

At dinner parties there was a ritual which was seldom contravened. The host and hostess occupied the centre of the table. At either end were the unfortunate young men who, as the most junior among those present, had to carve the ritual dishes of turkey and ham. It was not unknown for the unhappy dissector of the turkey to consign 'a pound and a half of stuffing into the lap of the adjoining Mrs Koofter'. Greater disasters than that were possible, too. 'The flounce of the punkah becomes partly disengaged and, after flapping about remorselessly like an unreefed sail in a gale of wind, succeeds in whisking off the protecting wire-gauze top of the lamp, and launching it on the apex of Miss Goley's head, occasioning the blowing-out of the lamp, and the consequent oleaginous effluvium that proceeds from the expiring wick. . . . Then the punkah has to be stopped to undergo reparation; and frantic and awful is the heat that is engendered thereby.

'Then, after an interregnum of considerable duration, the second course is produced, succeeded by a pause "more fearful than before".

'The sweets have vanished, and at last the dessert, indicative of a concluding climax; the decanters are circulated, and the fair hostess telegraphs . . . the signal for departure and a move (in the right direction) is made.

'Then the gentlemen are doomed to a further session, which terminates in the production of coffee, when the gong tells its tale of midnight. The piano is heard in the adjoining room: some faint voice warbles a doleful strain, the "Burra Beebee" [senior lady] rises, and a general dispersion ensues'.

The dinner would have included iced wines, and probably an iced pudding. Only Calcutta and the coastal cities could make use of the ice imported from America but, inland, there was a traditional method of manufacture which was used to the full. During the cold weather, 'small earthenware vessels of shallow build, resembling saucers in shape, are filled with water, and placed in an open field, upon a low bed of straw. At dawn of day there is a coating of ice upon each vessel, of about the thickness of a shilling. This is collected by men, women, and children . . . who receive for each morning's, or hour's work, a sum of money, in cowries, equal to about half of a farthing. When collected, it is carried to an ice-pit, and there stored.

'The expenses are borne by a subscription, and the amount for each ticket depends entirely on the number of subscribers. In some large stations, an ice-ticket for the hot season costs only three pounds. In smaller stations it will cost six pounds. The amount of ice received by each ticket-holder is about four pounds, and is brought away each morning at daylight, in a canvas bag, enveloped in a thick blanket, by the ticket-holder's own servant.

'It is then deposited in a basket made expressly for the purpose. In this basket is placed the wine, beer, water, butter, and fruit. The bag of solid ice is in the centre of all these, and imparts to each an equal coldness. These four pounds of ice, if properly managed, and the air kept out of the basket, will cool an inconceivable quantity of fluids, and will last for twenty-four hours —that is to say, there will be some ice remaining when the fresh bag is brought in'.

If the station included a regiment—and not all stations did— there would be amateur theatricals, put on by the junior officers. Among the more puritan Christians, a strong disapproval of this type of entertainment developed, though no such disapproval was felt when another type of contemporary distraction was offered—a Thug's demonstration of the methods he had used to murder innocent travellers. This may have been because the British were justifiably proud of having stamped out the terrible cult whose adherents robbed and killed in the name of the Hindu goddess, Kali. By the time Victoria came to the throne, the campaign against the Thugs had been going on for twelve years, with considerable success. But there were still many Thugs around, sheltering from the British in the native states, who had to be persuaded to move against them. It was always possible that a local jail might contain a few Thugs awaiting transport to another district.

The Thugs used a scarf to strangle their victims, and were quite happy to demonstrate how they did it to anyone who cared to watch. 'Some of them pretended to be travellers, and the others joined them and flattered them, and asked them to sit down and smoke, and then pointed up to the sun, or a bird; and when the traveller looked up, the noose was round his neck in an instant, and of course, as a *real* traveller, he would have been buried in five minutes'.

In a highly formal society—formal at least in its public face —the worship of God had a special significance. Church attendance was not only a social duty but an expression of solidarity. This was, however, scarcely the solidarity of Christians as Christians, nor was the church a meeting place for men and women of all colours united in worship. When William Howard Russell enquired as to the identity of a man riding in a very smart carriage, complete with liveried servants, he was told: 'That is the chaplain of the station, who marries, and baptises, and performs service for the Europeans'. 'Does he go among the natives?' 'Not he; he leaves that to the missionaries, of whom there are lots here'.

More often than not, the chaplain was quite a decent fellow, and if you visited him in his bungalow you would probably find 'a hearty welcome and some excellent bitter beer. His sanctum will recall your college days—gowns, guns and hunting-whips promiscuously combine: here a MS sermon lies complacently by a cookery-book and a *Bell's Life;* while there a packet of letters and a prospectus of the races, with the hospital report and a receipt for milk-punch'.

The inhabitants of the station had as little as possible to do with the natives, but contact could not be entirely avoided. The civilian had his court to contend with, the officer his sepoys. Others managed to avoid encounters even if they were supposed to have a duty to the natives. The station doctor, for example, often treated only Europeans, though he was paid 'head money' for every native soldier in the garrison. The ladies knew nothing whatever about any natives other than their own servants. Even ladies who indulged in missionary activities usually confined their evangelism to their domestics, while those few who took an earnest interest in 'the Hindoo way of life' wrote the mass of Indians off as quaint, heathenish and childish, in fairly equal proportions. But every station seems to have had a pet raja.

At Cawnpore, for example, there was the Nana Sahib who was very popular with the inhabitants of the station. He was the adopted son of a distinguished prince who had, at one time, ruled a great state; defeated by the British, he had settled in luxurious exile at Bithur, a few miles from Cawnpore. For thirty-three years the British had paid him a lavish pension. When he died in 1851, the British refused to transfer the pension to his 'son'. This did not seem to upset the Nana Sahib greatly. He entertained generously, and, whatever his religious beliefs, had no prejudices about serving beef and pork. His palace was full of European wares, deployed in such confusion that they were the cause of much innocent, and sometimes badly concealed, amusement. During the early period of his contact with Europeans, the same confusion reigned over his dinner table. A guest might be 'sat down to a table twenty foot long (it had originally been the mess table of a cavalry regiment), which was covered with a damask table-cloth of European manufacture, but instead of a dinner-napkin there was a bedroom towel. The soup . . . was served up in a trifle-dish which had formed part of a dessert service belonging to the 9th Lancers—at all events, the arms of that regiment were upon it; but the plate into which I ladled it with a broken teacup was of the old willow pattern. The pilao which followed the soup was served upon a huge plated dish, but the plate from which I ate was of the very commonest description. The knife was a bone-handled affair; the spoon and the fork were of silver, and of Calcutta make. The plated side-dishes, containing vegetables, were odd ones; one was round, the other oval. The pudding was brought in upon a soup-plate of blue and gold pattern, and the cheese was placed before me on a glass dish belonging to a dessert service. The cool claret I drank out of a richly-cut champagne glass, and the beer out of an American tumbler, of the very worst quality.'

As time went on, the Nana Sahib became more sophisticated

and his parties were well attended. The Nana was extremely charming, his manners courteous, his gifts munificent—and it would have been bad manners to refuse such elegant shawls and jewels. The Nana, of course, was assumed like most native princes to indulge in nameless orgies in the Indian-style part of his palace, in rooms decorated with pornographic pictures. It made him all the more attractive (though no one would have admitted it).

7 Navel of the world

In the same year that ushered in the Victorian age, another royal heir succeeded to a throne. Taking the reign-title of Bahadur Shah, a fifty-two-year-old poet became King of Delhi. It was an empty title for the descendant of the great Mughal emperors who had once ruled all India. In 1803, the last emperor had become a pensioner of the British, who did not depose him but kept him in his palace out of sentiment, while ignoring him out of policy. It was a foolish decision, and relations between the British and the king remained a constant irritation until, in 1857, the palace became the focus of rebellion.

But for twenty years there was no sign of the events to come. It remained the ambition of young British civilians to serve in the Delhi Territory, as the administrative area was known, and the office of Resident was coveted and intrigued for by men already high in the Company's service. Before the annexation of the Punjab, it had been the frontier post of British India, a watchtower on the marches. The Resident, with his army of spies collecting information, was a figure of tremendous consequence in affairs of state. Until the Grand Trunk Road reached Delhi in 1850, Calcutta had been three months' journey away. The Resident had almost untrammelled authority.

The Delhi Territory stretched from the Jumna to the Sutlej, from the city itself northwards to the foothills of the Himalaya. It had been the centre of a vast empire whose remains—buildings, sentiments, administrative systems—lay everywhere in whole or partial decay.

The city itself exercised a vivid hold on the imagination of the British. The source of its fascination was partly history, partly situation. History provided a vast assemblage of buildings, some in active use, most in the melancholy of ruin. At the period of the aquatint, of the romantic turn of mind, Delhi had provided all the elements of romance. Its relics of past empires had inspired not only sentiment but scholarship. Culturally, it had been, and remained, pre-eminent. Men who were not interested in the ruins of the past might enjoy the present beauties of Urdu and Persian literature.

For nearly six months of the year, the weather was fine, cool and stimulating. The half-desolate countryside was full of wildfowl, deer, and pig. The hot weather, however, was unpleasant and the heat brought dust, sweeping in clouds across the sandy plains. Then, days were spent in darkened rooms, but the nights in gardens under the moon.

Some six miles outside the city walls lay the Shalimar gardens. The Mughal emperor, Shah Jahan, who built the Taj Mahal at Agra as a memorial to his love for his wife, had beautified them with pavilions and pools. Aurangzeb, the last of the great emperors, crowned himself in the shadow of their tall trees. When the British occupied Delhi, they found the Shalimar a wilderness, a tangle of palm and citrus trees, clogged with undergrowth, rustling with snakes, the air sharp-edged with the cry of parakeets, peacocks, and kingfishers. But they recognised its virtues as the emperors had before them, and saw that the gardens would offer an escape into privacy and freedom after the formality and responsibilities of the day. The undergrowth was partly cleared, the pools restocked with gold and silver fish, the old pavilions refurbished, their marble made clean and bright.

The number of Europeans in the Delhi Territory was small. The officials were usually out on tour, only one or two being left in Delhi itself to be responsible for the administration. There was an ever-changing body of military officers, commanding the regiments stationed in the cantonments. There was the commandant of the palace guard, whose tour of duty was very much longer. There were officers detached from their regiments for civil duty. The jealousies of all Anglo-India had full play in Delhi. The regular officers hated those who had been clever enough to insert themselves into the civilian administration; this attitude often had a sound financial basis, since detached officers received not only their regimental pay but a civilian allowance as well. There was also the traditional antipathy between the queen's officers and the Company's. Company officers belonging to a regular regiment also looked down on officers of irregular forces. These were usually regiments which had been raised during the

Maratha wars by adventurers, and had become part of the Company's military establishment. The men of these mainly cavalry regiments were often men of good family, and a different type altogether from the Company's ordinary soldiers. They displayed their difference by wearing exotic uniforms. One regiment dressed its men in long yellow coats with wide belts of red cloth, trousers to match, and dark red turbans. The officers' uniforms were often even more exotic, and the officers usually favoured long flowing beards. They were the butts of a great deal of rather feeble humour.

Admitted into the society of Delhi were such non-officials as bank managers, but shopkeepers, of whom there was a growing number, were not. Nor were the members of what was known as the uncovenanted civil service, men who had been appointed in India (not London) and were often of mixed blood. But society accepted the professional classes, the doctors and the professors at the Delhi College, and finally the chaplains, the missionaries, and the journalists who ran the two Delhi papers, the *Gazette* and the *Sketch Book*.

Delhi also possessed another division of society which can only be called 'aristocratic Eurasian'. It included men of French, German and Portuguese origins, as well as British. Their fathers had sometimes been adventurers, profiting from the anarchy which preceded the British capture of Delhi. Others had been officials of the Mughal government. Some had been British officers who had married women of noble Indian families and themselves become Indianised. The head of this group, until his death in 1841, was undoubtedly Colonel James Skinner, the son of a Scots father and a Rajput mother. He had fought for one of the Maratha princes, then joined the British—who gave him the Order of the Bath and a valuable estate. Emily Eden found him 'very black' and said that he talked broken English, but added that he was 'one of the people whose lives ought to be written for the particular amusement of succeeding generations'. Colonel Skinner's English may have been faulty, but he spoke Persian with great fluency and wrote his memoirs in that language. Miss Eden also retailed a highly coloured story about Skinner's brother Robert. 'He suspected one of his wives of a slight *écart* from the path of propriety—very unjustly, it is said—but he called her and all his servants together, cut off the heads of every individual in his household, and then shot himself. His soldiers bought every article of his property at ten times its value, that they might possess relics of a man who had shown, they said, such a quick sense of honour'.

Colonel Skinner possessed houses on his estates outside Delhi, but he had a town mansion near the Kashmir Gate. It followed the Classical style, with high colonnades. Inside, there were marble floors and marble baths, and behind were the women's quarters. There, his entertainments were lavish and much appreciated. In the cold weather, there would be excursions into the Delhi countryside and explorations of ruins. In the evening, in tents of oriental size and magnificence, there would be fine food, good conversation, and the hookah to smoke—a habit which persisted in Delhi long after it had died in Calcutta. Skinner was known to be a Christian, but his family seem to have remained Muslim by faith. He built a church, which looked rather like a small version of St Paul's with the dome painted bright pink, and opposite it a mosque for the rest of the family.

Anglo-Indian society in Delhi was very restricted. There was a great shortage of unmarried ladies, and dances were usually only worth holding when there were visitors. There was, however, an annual ball held in the Assembly Rooms to celebrate the queen's birthday. Fortunately, the great figures of Anglo-India—governors-general and commanders-in-chief—made occasional visits to Delhi to see the sights and to be seen. At such times there was a torrent of entertainment which left everything even drier than before when the great man's entourage moved on.

The houses of the Europeans, though some of them outwardly conformed to the Palladian pattern which had received its *cachet* in Calcutta, also took their inspiration from Mughal tombs. There was a large central chamber with a high domed roof, which was admirable for the occasional dance but was normally divided by a curtain. It was cool in summer, but badly ventilated because it contained no windows. Most of the houses had a *taikhana,* or underground room, an idea borrowed from Mughal mansions. One such had been designed by an officer in the Engineers for his own use, and he had turned it into a thing of luxury. The room was about thirty feet underground, and the walls were decorated to look like marble. Long corridors led to other rooms which the designer had covered with his own drawings of Delhi landmarks. In spite of its comforts, however, the room had to be artificially lit, increasing the oppressive atmosphere which must have made the hot weather in Delhi so debilitating.

At the centre of Delhi life from the time of the queen's accession until his own death in 1853 stood Sir Thomas Metcalfe, younger brother of Sir Charles Metcalfe who had himself once dominated Delhi and had ended his Indian career as acting governor-general. Sir Thomas did not have the dynamic personality of his famous brother, but he was a man of culture and taste. He was a great builder. In addition to the mansion known as Metcalfe House on the banks of the river Jumna, he adapted a Muslim tomb as a country retreat. Though this was very elegantly furnished, it was no more than a *tombe ornée*. But Melcalfe House was one of the sights of Delhi. It had the conventional Classical colonnade. Around all four sides of the house there was a verandah twenty or thirty feet wide. The furniture was a little heavy, much of it being made of marble, but of great elegance. Metcalfe had a library of some 25,000 volumes, and the walls of the house were covered with fine engravings.

Metcalfe's great hero was Napoleon I, and he had a special gallery dedicated to him. The walls were hung with engravings of Napoleon and his generals as well as plans and views of his greatest battles. In a corner was Canova's bust of the emperor, and there were personal mementoes, such as a signet ring with Napoleon's cipher. When Metcalfe died, it was said that he had been poisoned by the king's chief wife because of his part in persuading the government not to recognise her son as heir. Metcalfe House itself was sacked during the Mutiny and its treasures destroyed or dispersed.

Because of the special character of Delhi, there was considerable social contact between the British and the Indian aristocracy. Though the position of the king was often criticised in Calcutta and by visitors to Delhi, there was an atmosphere of easy tolerance. Among the local characters was a Maratha chief, Hindu Rao, who had moved to Delhi in 1832. He lived in a vast fortress-like mansion that had been built by one of the Residents, on the Ridge. He gave lavish entertainments, at which the then Resident was usually present. When Hindu Rao died in 1855, his funeral offered almost as much enjoyment as the decorations of his house had done while he was alive. 'They dressed up the old gentleman's corpse in his most magnificent costume, covered his arms with jewelled bracelets of gold, with costly necklaces of pearls and diamonds hanging down to his waist, placed him in a chair of state, sat him bolt upright—just as he used to sit when alive—and thus, attended by his relations, friends, and suite, he was carried through Delhi to the banks of the Jumna, where the body was burnt with the usual rites, and the ashes thrown into the river'.

The meeting of two aristocracies, that of the British and that of old Delhi, could best be seen when the Resident gave one of his afternoon receptions. In the cold weather, these would be held in the gardens. On the river front of Metcalfe House there was a terraced pleasaunce. Gardeners had seen to it that there was not a leaf out of place or a blade of grass untrimmed. 'Long lines of English annuals in pots bordered the broad walks evenly, the scentless gardenia festooned the rows of cypress in disciplined freedom, the roses had not a fallen petal, though the palms swept their long fringes above them boldly, and strange perfumed creepers leapt to the branches of the forest trees. In one glade, beside an artificial lake, some ladies in gay dresses were competing for an archery prize. On a brick dais close to the house the band of a native regiment was playing national airs, and beside it stood a gorgeous marquee of Kashmir shawls with silver poles and Persian carpets; the whole—stock and block—having belonged to some potentate or another, dead, banished, or annexed. Here those who wished for it found rest in English chairs or oriental divans; and here, contrasting with their host and his friends, harmonising with the Kashmir shawl marquee, stood a group of guests from the palace.

'A perfect bevy of princes, suave, watchful, ready at the slightest encouragement to crowd round the Resident, or the Commissioner, or the Brigadier, with noiseless white-stockinged feet. Equally ready to relapse into stolid indifference when unnoticed. Here was Mirza Mughal, the king's eldest son, and his two supporters, all with lynx eyes for a sign, a hint, of favour or disfavour. And here—a sulky sickly looking lad of eighteen—was [Jivan Bakht, the queen's] darling, dressed gorgeously and blazing with jewels which left no doubt as to who would be the heir-apparent if she had her way. Prince [Abu Bakr] however, scented, effeminate, watched the proceedings with bright eyes; giving the ladies unabashed admiration and after a time actually strolling away to listen to the music. Finally, however, drifting to the stables to gamble with the grooms over a quail fight.

'Then there were lesser lights. [Ahsanullah Khan] the physician, his lean plausible face and thin white beard suiting his black gown and skull-cap, discussed the system of Greek medicine with the Scotch surgeon, whose fluent, trenchant Hindustani had an Aberdonian twang. . . . A few rich bankers curiously obsequious to the youngest ensign, and one or two pensioners owing their invitations to loyal service made up the company'.

Though Mughal princes and Hindu bankers might attend the parties at Metcalfe House, it was a little difficult for its owner to have easy social relations with the old king. There were difficult questions of protocol. Inside the great palace of the Red Fort, the descendant of the emperors who had made Delhi 'the navel of the world' was still a king with all sovereign rights. The palace was really an entire city, secluded behind its red walls. From the outside, it seemed barely to have been touched by the ravages of time and events. An occasional cannonball had chipped some of the sandstone and marble here and there, but nothing more. Inside, however, much of the glory had vanished. The Persian conqueror, Nadir Shah, had looted the Peacock Throne and most of the valuable ornaments in 1739. The silver roof of one of the audience halls had been taken away in 1764. In 1788, a Rohilla adventurer had dug up the marble floors in his search for treasure and had pillaged the imperial library of its finest possessions.

Little was done to keep the vast number of palace buildings in any reasonable state of repair. Such little money as was available to the king from the pension paid by the British went towards the upkeep of an immense number of imperial poor relations. Visitors always commented on the fact that large areas of the palace were neglected, and the rumour grew that the palace was in fact a vast slum. It seems likely, however, that the private apartments of the king and princes were not only in good repair but comparatively luxurious. None of the British was ever able to penetrate them to find out, and their impressions of the outer courts and parts of the zenana became accepted as descriptions of the entire palace.

The misery affected others than the king and his immediate family. The palace housed a large number of distant relations, the descendants of past emperors. Originally, these people (and their ancestors, in many cases) had been confined by the Mughal emperors within the palace bounds, in order to prevent them from being set up as pretenders to the throne. But when the British arrived, they refused to leave the palace; there was certainly no chance of their making a living outside its walls. These people were called *salatin*. They occupied a special quarter of the palace, where they lived in numerous huts, naked and half starved. Relatives nearer the king fared better, but there was never enough money to go round and the king was constantly trying to squeeze more out of the British.

This added another area of irritation to relations between the Resident and the king. The position was clearly anachronistic, but there seemed to be a general unwillingness to do anything about it. In the meantime, the king carried on with his court rituals, and continued to attend festivals and ceremonies with all the splendour he could afford. Lord Dalhousie wanted to use the Red Fort as a powder magazine, and would gladly have despatched the king to another of his palaces. But the authorities in England were more cautious. Dalhousie had to be content with making it clear to the old king that he would be the last to hold the title, and with sneering at him—if only in a private letter— for taking a 'confection composed of pearl, coral, and ruby . . . for raising the spirits' when he was ill. 'Could you believe that', asked Dalhousie, 'half way through the nineteenth century?'

But there was more to the court of Delhi than an old man

writing elegant poetry and playing the charade of being a king.
Bahadur Shah, himself a stylish poet, gave his patronage to
greater ones, as well as to painters and musicians. Delhi was
the last refuge of a traditional culture, which Englishmen had
once looked on with respect, but which they now chose to consider
as obsolete as confections of 'pearl, coral and ruby'. Dalhousie
merely articulated that indifference to Indian culture which was
the hallmark of the Victorian in India.

8   *Unto the hills*

In the nineteenth century, the British in India lifted their eyes up unto the hills—and went there to recover their strength. Before they had really established their rule in India, they had found themselves confined to their enclaves on the coast; they went no further than the adjacent countryside in an attempt to gain some respite from the hot weather. But by the time of Victoria's accession, the British conquest of India had opened up the high hills, and the practice of going there was firmly established. To leave the sweltering plains produced, in many, a sense of ecstasy. 'The scene was grand, and the effect upon the mind almost overpowering; but soon this feeling of exultation subsided into an extreme exhilaration of the animal spirits, as involuntary as though we had swallowed a tolerable dose of laughing-gas, and recklessly bid defiance to the grovelling cares of the world below'. And the first weeks merely confirmed that here was paradise. 'You luxuriated in the cool air. Your appetite improved. The mutton had a flavour which you did not recollect in India. Strange, yet true, the beef was tender, and even the "unclean" [pork] was not too much for your robust digestion. You praised the vegetables, and fell into ecstasy at the sight of peaches, apples, strawberries, and raspberries, after years of plantains, guavas, and sweet limes. You, who could scarcely walk a mile in the low country . . . wandered for hours over hill and dale without being fatigued. With what strange sensations of pleasure you threw yourself upon the soft turf bank, and plucked the first daisy which you ever saw out of England! And how you enjoyed the untropical sensation of sitting over a fire in June!—that very day last year you were in a state of semi-existence, only "kept going" by the power of punkahs and quasi-nudity'.

Each of the great centres of Anglo-Indian life had its hill station, sometimes more than one. The English in Bombay, for example, had Poona and Mahableshwar. Until 1819 Poona had been the capital of the Maratha prince who became the adoptive father of Cawnpore's pet raja, the Nana Sahib. The hot-weather residence of the governor of Bombay was at Dapoorie, eight miles from Poona. Lady Falkland found it extremely pleasant, a simple place consisting of a number of bungalows in an extensive garden which, in the rains, became 'daily more beautiful. Trees and plants seem to revive, creepers burst into blossom, running over large trees, and hanging in graceful festoons, or garlands, which are seen peeping through the thick foliage'. There were disadvantages. In the rains, at any rate, there was no respite from pests, and the garden of Eden did not lack its snakes. Lady Falkland, however, soon became 'accustomed to the sound of a snake coming to an untimely end, and have sometimes been awakened in the morning, by the servants killing one in the verandah'.

Dapoorie was all very well for the governor and his lady, but it was rather inconvenient for people staying at Poona, who were expected to make morning visits to pay their respects, and to attend dinners and balls. The distance that had to be covered required a 'considerable portion of fascination in a host and hostess to reconcile their guests to such an expedition on a wet night, or when the thermometer stands above 88°'. Still, few men in the hierarchy of Anglo-India had a greater 'portion of fascination' than a governor.

Even with the best will in the world, the roads could make very hard going for carriages. This meant that everyone might be late and the hostess might find herself wondering if anyone would come at all. At last, however, carriages would be heard. 'But out of them came people perfectly useless at balls—a middle-aged colonel, or a collector, who I knew made a point of never dancing. Then wheels approached again, and a troop of young hussars advanced. I began to think all womankind had been drowned. At last, some ladies appeared. I always knew, by the expression of the aide-de-camp's face, who was about to enter: he was all smiles when flounces, feathers, and fans were at hand; while his face lengthened at the sight of swords, spurs, and sabretaches'.

Safe arrival did not mean that the tribulations of the hostess (and her guests) were over. The ballroom might be invaded by blister-flies; if one of these insects were crushed against the skin a large and painful blister immediately developed. 'Some of these little tormenters climbed up into flounces, hid themselves in folds of net, visited the mysterious recesses of complicated trimmings; some crept up gentlemen's sleeves, other concealed themselves in a jungle of whisker, and there was something very attractive in a bald head, the owner of which, in removing the insect, was sure to blister his hand, or skull, or both. One heard little else all the evening but "Allow me, sir, to take off this blister-fly, that is disappearing into your neck-cloth", or "Permit me, ma'am, to remove this one from your arm" '. But the dancers were not to be discouraged. 'They polked and waltzed over countless myriads of insects that had been attracted by the white cloth on the floor, which was completely discoloured by their mangled bodies, at the end of the evening'.

The main problem at Poona (and most other hill stations) was the difficulty of finding accommodation, 'for in addition to the three or four regiments always stationed in Poona, and the numerous visitants from Bombay; all the civilians and engineers, flock in with their families, from their respective districts, too happy to exchange their tents and jungle life for comfortable bungalows and a regular holiday-making in Poona. The best houses are frequently engaged from the previous year; but woe to the unwary man who has delayed providing himself with a shelter before the season begins!' A number of people had opened hotels, but all proved unsuccessful owing to 'the exorbitance of the charges, and the total disregard of comfort and cleanliness in the arrangement of the establishment'.

The Poona station, though larger than most because of the presence of so many soldiers, was very much like any other down in the plains. Everything, however, was really designed to suit the garrison—even the church, which the architect had designed in such a way that there were plenty of seats for the military but very few for the civilian. If the churchgoing civilian did not arrive early, there was very little chance of finding a seat, or even standing room in the aisle. 'This very economical arrangement', one visitor decided, nevertheless had 'its peculiar advantages; inasmuch as it greatly tends towards filling the Scotch church which is immediately opposite; and doubtless the engineer who superintended its construction had some such object in view'.

The presence of so many soldiers meant that each regiment vied with the others in giving balls and dinners. The expense of the entertainments, and of furnishing the mess with plate, usually fell heavily upon the junior officers. Most of them, in fact, laid the foundation of debts that followed them throughout their service. These 'accumulating rapidly from year to year, by the fearful interest charged upon borrowed money, reaches at length to a height of inextricable involvement, which dooms the victim to a perpetual residence in India'. Most of the senior officers in the Company's regiments were married men who only used the mess on rare occasions. Other officers were almost permanently absent on other duties, on the Staff, perhaps, or as political agents. This left the young subalterns to carry the burden. It was nothing rare to find that the junior officers, 'thus shackled by heavy mess expenditure, have actually not received one rupee of their pay for several months! The small surplus remaining from the inevitable items of Mess Bill, Military Fund, Library, and Band, being totally absorbed in the extra charges for "guest nights", balls, and "contributions for new mess kit" '. Even the delights of a good amateur theatre and fancy dress balls could not prevent many of the young officers from seeking other employment which would release them from the costs of regimental life.

Madras, like Bombay, had its military hill station. At Bangalore, the air smelt 'of hay and flowers, instead of ditches, dust, fried oil, curry and onions, which are the *best* of the Madras smells'. Furthermore, the station had 'an English church, a Heathen pagoda, botanical garden, public ballrooms, Dissenting meeting-house, circulating library, English shops, and Parsee merchants, all within sight of each other'.

Bangalore was not quite a hill station. It was not really high enough up for that, and though the climate was very pleasant for someone coming up from the humid heat of Madras it had its dangers. Though the gardens of the bungalows were sometimes very beautiful, they were also damp, and a sharp attack of fever often resulted from a walk down the 'sweet shady walks which all smelt of ague'.

At Bangalore, as at Poona, most of the British were military. The wives rode about 'in habits made according to the uniform of their husbands' regiment'. The more superior, senior ladies 'seem never to become Indianised. . . . Some of them keep up schools for the English soldiers' children, girls especially—superintend them, watch over the soldiers' wives, try to keep and encourage them in good ways, and are quite a blessing to their poor countrywomen'.

From Bangalore it was possible to go up to a real hill station in the Nilgiri hills. In about 1850 a line of what were called 'transit coaches' was established between the two places. 'The carriages were what were known as "nibs" and were two wheeled and water proof with venetians and glass windows. They were drawn by bullocks which were changed every five miles. . . . If not pressed for time this was a pleasant way of travelling, with a chance of some shooting *en route*. A servant could be carried on the covered seat by the driver, and there was room for a portmanteau, gun-case, etc. in the well of the conveyance'.

The station in the Nilgiri hills was Ootacamund, or Ooty, as it became affectionately known in the late 1840s. When Captain Burton visited it, he found it delightful, at least for a time. But many things began to annoy him, once he had recovered his usual jaundiced attitude to all things Indian. The architecture he found particularly repellent. 'The style bungalow—a modification of the cow-house—is preferred: few tenements have upper stories, whilst almost all are surrounded by a long low verandah, perfectly useless in such a climate, and only calculated to render the interior of the domiciles as dim and gloomy as can be conceived.' If the diminutive, scantily furnished rooms, 'with their fireplaces, curtained beds, and boarded floors, faintly remind you of Europe, the bare walls, puttyless windows and doors that admit draughts of air small yet cutting as lancets, forcibly impress you with the conviction that you have ventured into one of those uncomfortable localities—a cold place in a hot country'. In the rain, Burton found the country impassable, 'the cantonment dirty, every place wretched, everyone miserable'.

The ladies at Ooty were the usual Anglo-Indian assortment, from the elderly, delighting in scandal to the youthful, like the 'young lady who discourses of her papa the Colonel, and disdains to look at anything below the rank of a field-officer'. The men were no improvement—'misanthropes and hermits who inhabit out-of-the-way abodes, civilians on the shelf, authors, linguists, oriental students, amateur divines who periodically convert their drawing-rooms into chapels of ease rather than go to church, sportsmen, worshippers of Bacchus in numbers . . . We have clergymen, priests, missionaries, tavern-keepers, school-masters and scholars, with *précieux* and *précieuses ridicules* of all descriptions'.

Burton could not even find a good word for the dances, though a hill station was the only place in India where there were often more women than men. After the ladies had retired at the early hour of 3 a.m., worn out with their exertions, the men would settle down to a substantial hot meal, followed by singing and 'a little horseplay in different parts of the room', until finally, with 'very pallid complexions', they wound off 'along a common road, leading, as each conceives, directly to his own abode'.

There was sport to be had, and a pack of hounds. There was bison, though hunting it required 'a cool head and a steady hand'. It was usually shot 'with ounce or two ounce iron or brass balls, and plugs made by the hill-people, who cut a bar of metal and file it down to the size required with the rudest tools and remarkable neatness'. The ibex was another favourite quarry, though it was 'addicted to scrambling down and rolling over tremendous precipices', which meant that the hunter either lost the beast or had to risk his neck to retrieve the carcase.

In the north, there were a number of 'sanatoria' in the foothills of the Himalayas. There was Mussoorie, for example, which quite inexplicably reminded Fanny Parkes, when she visited it in 1838, of 'the back of the Isle of Wight'. There was an excellent family hotel run by a Mr Webb, with a ballroom and five billiard tables.

The most important of the Himalayan hill resorts was Simla, which was to become the summer residence of the governor-general and, because of that, the Anglo-Indian Olympus—though it was also to be known by many less complimentary names. The heyday of Simla came after the Mutiny, but it had been known and liked since the area became part of British India after the Gurkha war in 1815. The first house built by a European in Simla was erected in the 1820s, and the town had grown and continued to grow because, as one visitor wrote in 1828, 'the temperature of Simla seems peculiarly adapted to the European constitution. We have reason to be thankful that we are here far elevated above the atmospheric strata that have hitherto been subjected to the cholera, a disease now raging in Calcutta'. When Emily Eden arrived in Simla ten years later, she could reflect that: 'There we were, with the band playing the "Puritani" and "Masaniello", and eating salmon from Scotland, and sardines from the Mediterranean, and observing that St Cloup's potage à la Julienne was perhaps better than his other soups, and that some of the ladies' sleeves were too tight according to the overland fashions for March &c; and all this in the face of those high hills, some of which have remained untrodden since the creation, and we 105 Europeans being surrounded by at least 3,000 mountaineers, who, wrapped up in their hill blankets, looked on at what we call our polite amusements, and bowed to the ground, if a European came near them. I sometimes wonder they do not cut all our heads off and say nothing more about it'.

But it was another hill people who were actually about to cut off English heads. While the Eden sisters were in Simla with their brother, the governor-general, British forces were on their way to put a long deposed ruler of Afghanistan back on his throne. At first, the British appeared to be successful, but, in the end, British troops were massacred, envoys murdered, and their weakness revealed for all to see. At Simla, they heard only of the victories. The ladies who had refused to dance until their husbands returned from Afghanistan weakened, and gave in. After all, the triumph of British arms had to be celebrated.

In Emily Eden's time in Simla there was a remarkably beautiful young woman who formed a focus for stares and criticism. The newcomer was only seventeen and had eloped with an army officer whose surname was James. Mrs James and her husband —'a smart-looking man with bright waistcoats and bright teeth' —came up to Simla to stay with her mother, and everyone found her very attractive. Miss Eden considered her 'very pretty, and such a merry unaffected girl'. She even felt quite sorry for her, married to a man fifteen years her senior, with very little money, and a lifetime in India before her. Simla society would have been incredulous had they been able to look into the future of 'little Mrs James'. A few years later, she made a second elopement and left for Europe, there to embark on a career which was notoriously scandalous. Under the name of Lola Montez, she became, for a year, the virtual ruler of Bavaria, having entirely captivated the king. Her life ended in New York in 1861.

Simla began to find itself more than just another hill resort during the governor-generalship of Lord Dalhousie, who spent a great deal of time there despite the fact that in 1849 he remarked that the place was 'overrated in climate and everything else'. This sourness may have been induced by his going down, on his arrival, 'with an influenza—a genuine Piccadilly influenza'. He also found that there were too many festivities, 'balls here, balls there, balls to the Society, balls by the Society, amateur plays, concerts, fancy fairs, investitures of the Bath &c., &c. I quite sigh for the quiet of Calcutta'. Nevertheless, he built a new road over the mountains and was able to claim that 'most of it has been done by free labour, which the native tributary states are bound to contribute, and its cost in actual outlay has thus been inconsiderable'.

Sir Charles Napier, when commander-in-chief, took a dislike to hill stations and the custom of going there for months on end. His orders restricting officers' leave were much resented in the army. Napier's point was that, if the British soldier had to remain in the plains, his officers should too. In the usual Anglo-Indian manner, Napier was heavily attacked by anonymous authors and, in particular, in a humorous periodical called the *Delhi Sketch Book*. The standard of the verse was not very high, but the feeling behind it was much to the point:

> And all leave to the hills
> Has been stopped, and one grills;
> In the plains, like a Shadrach in his furnace flame;
> While all the time he [Napier] swears
> That public affairs
> Prevent him from doing, *as he'd like to do*, the same!

93

Society in Simla revolved round the governor-general. As one visitor wrote: 'An officer aspiring to get a civil or military appointment, who desired to get to some place where, by currying favour with the great, he might create an influence for himself sufficient to secure that object, would select Simla'. The gentlemen, and their wives, adopted various methods of attracting attention. One lady was very good at sketching portraits, and she drew the governor-general—without his knowledge, of course —in every conceivable attitude, on horseback and on foot. These sketches were placed in a prominent position during a ball, and very soon the name of the artist was being passed about. 'The wife of another civilian, however, maliciously neutralised the effect these sketches would probably have had, by falsely saying, loud enough for his Lordship to hear, "Ah! she said she would do the trick with her pencil!" The consequence was, that when the lady's husband begged his Lordship would accept this collection of portraits, as well as a few sketches of the house inhabited by the Great Man, his Lordship—as delicately and gracefully as the circumstances would admit of—"declined them with many thanks"; just as though they had been so many unsuitable contributions to some popular periodical'.

Another amateur artist was more successful by appealing to a typical love of animals. She sketched in full colour a likeness of the commander-in-chief's favourite charger, and presented it to him. 'And the next *Gazette* made known that Captain C— was a Major of Brigade'.

By the time of the Mutiny, Simla was acquiring an enduring reputation for 'bright ladies and gay gentlemen'. There appear to have been some wild spirits around, some high living and high gambling and a great deal of not so harmless flirting. Yet at the same time such ladies as Mrs Colonel Mackenzie were visiting the Simla church to take drawings of the new stained glass window for the Bishop of Calcutta. The window had been causing trouble. There were some people who objected to it on the grounds that the natives would regard it as an object of worship, an idol, while others thought that the figure of the Redeemer with a lamb was not only irreverent but calculated to distract the congregation. The Bishop had even received a letter which talked of the inexpediency of having 'these figures in the midst of a heathen population'.

Still, Simla was pleasant even for Christian ladies. The Mall was crowded with people, and the women were wearing finer bonnets than Mrs Mackenzie had seen for many a day. The servants who carried the *jampan*—a kind of armchair supported on two sticks, which was the normal transport for ladies—wore livery. 'Most of them are in plaid tunics and trousers edged with red, looking like magnified little boys; but others are in long robes, generally black down to their feet, with deep red borders, and red caps; so that the first man having a wand in his hand, they look like a company of magicians'. No wheeled carriages were allowed at Simla, and the only alternative to the *jampan* was horseback. The favourite ride was round a hill called Jakko where, thoughtfully, a macadamised road was provided.

The time inevitably came when there must be a return to the plains. Even though this meant that the cold weather had arrived, it was still something of a wrench to leave Simla, 'poor, dear Simla', as Emily Eden called it when she turned back for her last view of it. Wives went back to their husbands and a more discreet existence, until the next time. Men went back to their lonely outposts and cuffed a servant or two, to let off steam. The average season at Simla was 'a very pleasant one . . . enlivened by several exciting incidents—to wit, a duel, a police affair, a court martial, and an elopement'.

9 *The wild and lonely places*

As the frontiers of British India expanded towards their 'natural' limits, they came to enclose many wild and dangerous areas which had to be governed, not according to the normal procedures of settled administration with their narrow laws and regulations, but with a mixture of harshness and sympathy.

One such area was the Punjab, which had been made into a strong kingdom by the genius of Ranjit Singh who, despite everything—despite even the military weakness of the British, revealed so clearly in the great debacle of the Afghan war—had maintained a wary friendship with the new power. But in 1839, Ranjit Singh had died. Anarchy struck the Punjab, and the next six years took on the improbable quality of an oriental romance. There was a queen-mother and a boy king, an effeminate vizier, and an arrogant, turbulent army trained by French and Italian generals. The army was ruled by committees and, finger on the trigger, tried to play kingmaker. Many of its leaders were intriguing with the British. In an attempt to protect her son, the Rani—whom Henry Lawrence described as 'a strange blend of the prostitute, the tigress, and Machiavelli's Prince'—tried to relieve the pressure by pushing the army towards a foreign war. On 11 December 1845, the Sikh army surged across the river Sutlej. Then, sobered by their own temerity, they waited—'an army listening in silence to the beating of its own heart'.

This first Sikh war was to do no credit to British arms. Officered by a Peninsular general of outstanding stupidity, the British almost lost the war as a result of a pathological belief in the virtues of the bayonet and a majestic disregard for the usefulness of artillery. After the Sikhs had been defeated at Firozpur, the governor-general, Sir Henry Hardinge—who had been an officer under Wellington in the Napoleonic wars—exclaimed from the heart: 'Another such victory and we are undone!'

Finally, the Sikhs *were* defeated, and a regency was set up in Lahore with Henry Lawrence holding 'peaceful viceregal authority over the province'. To supervise the administration, there was a swarm of young officers, 'Mr Lawrence's young men', as they came to be known. They scoured the countryside, looking for oppressions from which they might free the people. They found many (as they would have done in British India itself), and if persuasion failed they took the law into their own hands with no legal authority whatsoever. 'What days those were!' one of them recalled. 'How Henry Lawrence would send us off to great distances; Edwardes to Bannu, Nicholson to Peshawar, Abbott to Hazara, Lumsden somewhere else, etc., giving us a tract of country as big as half of England, and giving us no more helpful directions than these: "Settle the country; make the people happy; and take care there are no rows!"'

They were very muscular Christians, these men, very conscious of doing God's work. The way in which Herbert Edwardes subjugated Bannu shows the kind of thing they were expected to do, and did cheerfully in the knowledge that, trusting God, they were bound to succeed. In 1847 Edwardes was a lieutenant, not yet thirty years old. Bannu was a wide valley, high in the northern hills. It was full of wild tribesmen and there was a fort in every village. The Sikh method of collecting taxes had been to send an army every three years to burn such crops as they did not eat and to drive the cattle off. Afterwards, the villagers returned to the homes from which they had fled, and waited for the next visit from the tax-collector. Edwardes, with a small force (of Sikhs), descended on the valley and began to negotiate with the tribal leaders, who were almost shocked to find a Sikh army that did not plunder. In the end, they were persuaded to pull down their forts. By the end of the month, Edwardes wrote, 'in spite of being preached against in the mosques, in spite of two open attempts at assassination, and a third plot to murder me in a gateway, I had carried that measure out, and left but two Bannuchi forts standing in the valley and these two by my permission'.

By the end of the three months he spent in the valley, Edwardes had achieved more. 'A new town had been founded, which to this day is flourishing; a military and commercial road, thirty feet broad, and twenty-five miles long, had been undertaken and has since been completed through a formerly roadless valley, and is now, under the protection of ordinary police, travelled by the merchant and traveller in ease and security; tracts of country from which the fertilising mountain streams were diverted by feuds, had been brought back to cultivation by the protection of a strong government; others, lying waste because disputed, had been adjudicated, apportioned, occupied, and sown once more; through others a canal had been designed and begun; while a people who had worn arms as we wear clothes, and used them as we use knives and forks, had ceased to carry arms at all; and, though they quarrelled still, learned to bring their differences to the war of the civil court instead of the sharp issue of the sword'.

Others were less successful—or fortunate. The Sikhs, hating a state of disguised subjection, decided to try again to defeat the British. The war began in 1848 with the murder of two of 'Lawrence's young men', and ended eight months later in another terrible battle, which the British won by the barest margin. The two young men were avenged. Edwardes, who led the avenging force, had their bodies exhumed and reburied under a suitable monument. On it was inscribed, in Edwardes's words, an epitaph which sums up the beliefs of the iron men of the Punjab.

On this, the farthest frontier of the British Indian Empire,
which their deaths extended,
lie the remains of

PETER VANS AGNEW   WILLIAM ANDERSON
of the   and   Lieut. 1st Bombay
Bengal Civil Service   Fusilier Regt.

Who, being deputed
by the Resident at Lahore, whose Assistants they were,
To relieve Dewan Moolraj
(Viceroy of Mooltan under the Sikh Empire),
at his own request,
of the Fortress and Government which he held,
were assaulted and wounded by the Garrison
on the 19th of April, 1848;

and being basely deserted by their Sikh escort,
were, on the following day,
with a signal breach of national faith and private hospitality,
most barbarously murdered
in the Eedgah, under the walls of Mooltan.
Thus fell these two young public servants,
full of youth, rare talents, high hopes, and promise of utility;
even in their deaths doing their Country honour.
Covered with wounds, they could not resist,
but hand-in-hand awaited the onset
of a bloodthirsty rabble:
calmly foretelling the day when
'thousands of Englishmen
should come there to avenge their death,
and destroy Moolraj, his army, and his fortress'.
History records how the
prophecy was fulfilled.
After two separate sieges,
The Fort of Mooltan was surrendered to the British troops,
and the bodies of the two murdered officers
(which had been treated with the most savage indignities)
were, in all righteous vengeance,
carried through the breach
made by the British guns,
and buried, with military honours, on the summit
of the Citadel.
'Thousands of Englishmen'
stood round the grave.
Dewan Moolraj
was brought to trial at Lahore, convicted of
murder, and sentenced to be hanged;
But was recommended to mercy, and
finally ordered to be transported for life.
His Rebellion
was followed by an insurrection of the
Sikh people, and brought on
the Second Sikh War;
which resulted in the Annexation of the

Punjab to British India,
and the restoration of peace,
after many years of anarchy
(with a brief interval),
to the countries between the Sutlej
and the Indus.

Thus did an overruling Providence
bring good out of evil.

There were other young men to take the place of those who died. Some of them were hard men. John Nicholson was one of these, a violent, manic figure, a homosexual bully, an extreme egotist who was pleased to affect a laconic indifference to danger. 'Sir', he wrote to his superior officer, 'I have the honour to inform you that I have just shot a man dead who came to kill me. Your obedient servant, John Nicholson'.

This 'autocrat of all the Russias', as he was known to his colleagues, even exasperated that other iron man, John Lawrence. Lawrence did not believe that the Punjab could be ruled 'by rosewater expressions or by buttermilk management'; when he became lieutenant-governor of the Punjab, other Europeans regarded it as a delightful Sunday pastime to wait after church in Lahore and see him, before driving home, 'hammering his coachman'. But even John Lawrence—who became the archetype of the great Victorian administrator, just as Nicholson did of the great Victorian hero—had some saving graces, including a certain irreverence for those objects of material value which were the symbols of Victorian success.

Among the possessions of Ranjit Singh had been the famous Kohinoor diamond. Ranjit had acquired it from another ruler, the worthless Shah Shuja, whom the British had tried so unsuccessfully to replace on the throne of Afghanistan. Shah Shuja had gone to Ranjit for help, and the Sikh ruler had nagged his guest and starved his family until Shah Shuja parted with the diamond. It was an immense stone—the name means 'mountain of light'—and immensely valuable. After the end of the second

Sikh war, its custodian handed the jewel over to John Lawrence, who wrapped it up in a cloth, put it in a pillbox, put the box in his waistcoat pocket, and promptly forgot all about it. About six weeks later, the governor-general sent a message to say that Queen Victoria had ordered that the diamond should be sent to her. At a meeting with his brother Henry, John said: 'Send for it at once'.

'But *you*'ve got it', Henry reminded him.

John recalled in a flash where he had put it, but gave no sign of confusion or anxiety. 'Ah, yes, of course; I forgot about it', he said, and calmly went on with the business of the meeting. At the first opportunity he slipped away and sent for his personal servant.

'Have you got a small box which was in my waistcoat pocket some time ago?'

'Yes, sahib. I found it and put it in one of your boxes'.

'Bring it here'. An old battered tin trunk was produced. 'Open it and see what is inside'.

The servant did so, undoing all the folds of cloth with great care while John Lawrence held his breath in suspense.

'There is nothing here, sahib, but a bit of glass'.

The bit of glass is now in the British imperial crown.

In the mainly masculine world of the Punjab, wives played only a small part. Few of the young men were married, but those who were often had wives almost as tough as themselves. There was something very exciting about life in camp, as well as freedom from scandal and all the other snares of 'the station'. Honoria Lawrence, Henry's wife, always accompanied her husband when she was allowed to. From the very earliest days of her marriage, Honoria had decided to stay with him whatever the discomfort. Her first introduction to roughing it in India had been in a survey camp. She felt it was her proper place, as she and her husband were 'all in all to each other', and she kept a journal describing life in the camp. It resembled nothing she had ever known before in sheltered England. Not only were there white officers on the staff, but Eurasians and natives as well. Then there were grain merchants who ran a kind of bazaar, elephants to carry the camp equipment, and flocks of sheep, goats

H

and poultry to provide mutton, milk, and fowls for the pot. In the centre of the encampment was the Lawrences' tent, where the great man himself sat 'with his legs over the arm of the chair, without jacket, waistcoat or cravat', receiving the village notables and listening to complaints. Or he might consult with a native assistant, 'very old and thin, his skin shrivelled up and looking altogether like a burnt rag that you could blow away. He wears the usual turban and vest, but adds a pair of spectacles. He talks a little English, and is a complete copying machine, writing out the official letters and working the multiplication. He calls Henry his "sucking father", and is very irate if his work is found fault with. "One, two thing I do: no mistake. Multiply, sine and co-sine" '.

In the foothills of the Himalayas, fires had to be kept alight to ward off tigers and wild elephants. Honoria, however, was convinced that 'a lady who has nerves, who shrinks from driving over rough and smooth, or riding through a jungle' had no business in the countryside and ought to stay in the large stations.

To the south of the Punjab lay the province of Sind, whose rulers, the Amirs, had been attacked and conquered during what Sir Charles Napier, who was in charge of the conquest, called 'the tail of the Afghan storm'. As always, there were what the Victorians regarded as sound moral reasons for the conquest. The government of the Amirs was 'hated by its subjects, despotic, hostile alike to the interests of England and of its own people, a government of low intrigue, and so constituted that it must fall to pieces by the vices of its construction'.

Sir Charles Napier, 'a small dark-visaged old man . . . with a falcon's glance', believed in standing no nonsense. When the Amirs asked what terms he would give them in return for submission, he told them: 'Life, and nothing more. And I want your decision before twelve o'clock, as I shall by that time have buried my dead, and given my soldiers their breakfasts'. Napier had not really approved of the war, but he found it 'a very advantageous, useful, humane piece of rascality'. In England, a great empire builder of an earlier generation wrote that: 'Coming after Afghanistan, it put me in mind of a bully who had been kicked in the street and went home to beat his wife in revenge'. Napier's public comment took the form of a sardonic pun. He sent a Latin one-word telegram to the governor-general—*Peccavi*, I have Sin[ne]d.

Napier did not approve of civilians, who had, he said, 'worn out originally vigorous appetites and feeble minds while enjoying large salaries and the adulation of black clerks'. He virtually told the governor-general to keep his hands off Sind and himself established, instead of a civilian government, an administration on semi-military lines which later reached its apogee in the Punjab. He gave the chiefs and nobles back their swords, with the words: 'Take back your sword. You have used it with honour against me, and I esteem a brave enemy. But if forgetful of this voluntary submission you draw it again in opposition to my government, I will tear it from you and kill you as a dog'. His principal weapon was fear. He hanged criminals, with placards round their necks, as a warning to others. He refused to abolish flogging in the forces under his command, though the government had done so years before. If the notables behaved themselves they were allowed, on some suitably auspicious occasion, to bow to a picture of Queen Victoria, which was kept 'covered with a curtain from the view of private men and retainers'. He was generally known among the tribesmen as 'Satan's brother'.

Behind the harshness there was a reformer. Slavery was abolished. Suttee, the practice of burning widows—prohibited in British India a decade before—was stopped, and when those who practised it complained that it was their custom, Napier replied: 'My nation has also a custom. When men burn women alive we hang them, and confiscate all their property. My carpenters shall therefore erect gibbets on which to hang all concerned when the widow is consumed. Let us all act according to national customs'.

In another wild and lonely place—the hilly country of Orissa in eastern India—a wild tribe known as the Khonds practised human sacrifice. This had first been observed in 1837. The sacrifices were made to the spirit of natural fertility which in one part of the country took the form of an elephant, and in another that of a bird. The victims were known as *meriah* and were carefully prepared for the sacrifice. They were usually bought, in exchange for fixed numbers of such useful items as goats or pigs, cooking pots or spears, and there was quite a trade in people kidnapped from the plains. When the time for sacrifice came round, the victim—who might have been kept for years in considerable comfort—was disposed of by slow and revolting stages.

The custom of sacrifice was too well established to be stamped out in a swift and forceful campaign, even if the British had had the strength to mount one. In any case, the government was often over-cautious, for fear that in attempting to suppress one evil they would create another and cause suffering to a greater number. Gentle but firm persuasion seemed the only alternative to a long drawn-out punitive campaign over dangerous and difficult terrain, haunted with disease, and menaced by men who knew the jungles and forests like the backs of their hands.

There always seemed to be men willing to take risks. In Orissa, one was Captain Campbell, and another Lieutenant Macpherson—whose friends in later years felt that Campbell had been awarded not only too much of the credit for the venture, but too much of the promotion as well. Campbell's campaign combined persuasion with a modicum of force. It lasted for sixteen years, with an interval of five years between 1842 and 1847 when Campbell was away fighting the Chinese in a war primarily designed to expand the opium trade. (In their reforming endeavours, the Victorians saw nothing incongruous in engaging in a long and mainly peaceful campaign to suppress one evil while, at the same time, fighting a war to increase another). Before he left for China, Campbell had won some success with the Khonds. He had called the chiefs together and told them of the horror the Great Government felt at the thought of human sacrifice. If it continued, he said, the government would demand a life for a life. Campbell had recently commanded troops in a successful war against one of the hill rajas, and the chiefs, remembering this, agreed to his demands.

When Campbell returned from China, he found that there had been some backsliding. He also had to move a mountain of suspicion—he was said actually to be collecting *meriah* victims

for himself. The report was that he intended making a sacrifice
to the water spirit because a reservoir he had built had run dry.
It was even rumoured that, as a special treat, he occasionally
fed his elephants with human flesh. Campbell's reply was to
invite inspection, not only of his camp, but of his personal tent.
Though its fittings were by no means luxurious, they caused
considerable comment. 'It is the house of god!' his visitors
exclaimed.

Persuasion continued, strengthened now and then with a small
show of force. Between 1837 and 1854 over 1,500 potential
sacrifices were rescued. Most of them were handed over to
Christian missionaries in the plains. But though the custom of
human sacrifice slowly disappeared, the beliefs behind it remained. In 1853, Campbell learned that worship of the fertility
spirits continued. The old invocation had been replaced, however, with another:

'Do not be wrathful with us, o goddess, for giving you blood
of beasts instead of human blood! Vent your anger on this
gentleman [Campbell], who is well able to bear it.'

10 *At the edge of the abyss*

In Northern India in 1857, as the hot weather approached, people commented on its mildness. They were eating strawberries in Lucknow as late as the end of April, and even in Calcutta the punkah did not come into use until May. Everywhere, the routines of Anglo-Indian life ran smoothly. On Sunday the churches, pleasantly cool, were full of officers in summer uniforms, civilians in black coats and white trousers, ladies in light sprigged muslins. Life was comfortable, or as comfortable as it could be made. Delicacies from Europe were now easily obtainable, and so were the foods that made the British feel they were at Home —tinned Cambridge sausages, Cheddar cheese, Portuguese sardines. But these were costly, especially in the up-country stations, and the substantial Anglo-Indian breakfast was more likely to consist of devilled turkey, Irish stew, fresh fish, or a pigeon pie, with tea, beer, and iced claret.

Yet there were ripples in the great dark sea that surrounded the little islands of white life. For months there had been rumours of disaffection in the Bengal army. Tales were told of secret meetings in the sepoy lines, where the terrible news that the British intended to turn all the sepoys into Christians was discussed and discussed again. In the countryside, too, there was a strange unrest. It was said—by whom, nobody knew— that British rule was coming to an end, and that it would happen on the centenary of the battle of Plassey, which had begun it all on 24 June 1757. From village to village, they were passing the flat cakes of flour and water known as *chapatis*. A messenger would arrive bearing them, saying that they had been brought to his own village and must be passed on. No one knew their meaning, no one dared disobey the summons to pass them on.

The news reached British officials. What could it mean? Some argued that it was a method of carrying away disease. In one part of the country, in fact, cholera broke out after the chapatis had circulated. One official believed that their message was the message of the fiery cross, but his superior, to whom he reported these fears, replied that it was probably a case of 'a dyer's vat having gone wrong' and the dyer was trying to propitiate the gods'. When the Indians were questioned, they said the chapatis meant that something was coming but they did not know what it might be. Others replied that they believed it was by government order.

There was every reason for tension. Behind the bland face of Anglo-India lay a different reality—the great world of India, the India of the village, of the princely state, of the native army. As the British had conquered India and begun to impose their own kind of government, they had stamped on many toes. Princes had been dispossessed of their rights and pensions, land-owners found their estates confiscated because they had no written titles to their land—in a country where such things were unknown. Many of these acts were, to some extent, justified, but to the people who suffered the consequences there did not appear to be any justification but that of power. Because Indians had already been adjudged by the British as morally despicable, little attempt was made to mollify their feelings. The dispossessed, and those who felt that their turn might very well come next, felt deeply aggrieved; some were already conspiring against the British before the Mutiny broke out. Chief among the conspirators were Ahmad Ullah, 'the Maulvi of Faizabad', advisor to the ex-king of Oudh who had been dethroned and whose state had been annexed in 1856; the Rani of Jhansi, whose state had been annexed in 1854; and the Nana Sahib, darling of the British at Cawnpore. But the real threat lay with the sepoys of the Company's army, whose loyalty, in spite of mutinies in the past, had never really been questioned. In 1806, sepoys had rebelled at Vellore, in Madras province, because they had been instructed to shave off their beards, wear a turban, and give up caste-marks. The men thought this was a deliberate attempt to turn them into Christians. In 1824, a sepoy regiment refused to move for action in Burma because it felt its caste endangered by the refusal to supply special transport for its cooking utensils, and caste usage compelled each man to have his own set. Guns opened fire on them on the parade ground where they had assembled, and next morning six of the ringleaders were hanged and hundreds more condemned to fourteen years' hard labour on the public roads. Five more were later executed and their bodies hung in chains as an example to their fellows. In 1852, another regiment had also refused to cross the sea to Burma. This time the men were merely marched away to another station. A number of smaller mutinies and near-mutinies had taken place. All resulted from fear of caste-pollution and the attempts of over-zealous officers and missionaries to convert the sepoys to Christianity.

It was not only princes, landowners, and sepoys who felt themselves threatened. Ordinary people, too, had suffered under the heavy hand of government. When great estates were sold up, peasants were uprooted as well. Taxes fell heavily on those least able to support their weight. A man could not travel without having to pay a toll to cross a river. Salt, so essential in a tropical country, was a government monopoly, its price inflated by tax. Justice, through the process of law, was too costly to seek. Even oblivion was expensive, for the government exacted its dues on opium and liquor. A traditional society, conscious that something was in the air, turned to traditional magic to protect itself. There was a wide sale of charms against unstated evils. Magical symbols began to appear upon the walls. Prophecies were heard throughout the land. The agents of the dispossessed moved freely around, spreading and embroidering rumours. Religious mendicants whispered of the horrors the British were planning.

Naturally, the agitators looked to the sepoy army as fertile ground. Each of the three presidencies into which British India was divided—Bengal, Madras and Bombay—had its own army. The Bengal army was not, in fact, recruited in Bengal, but farther west. Many of the sepoys had their homes in Oudh, an area which was already seething with discontent over the deposition of its king and annexation by the British. The Oudh sepoys had had many privileges in their own country—'that great nursery of soldiers', as someone called it. The sepoys could, and often did, ask for and receive the British Resident's support against the native government. With annexation, such privileges had disappeared and, with them, prestige. 'I used to be a great man when I went home', an Oudh cavalryman told Sir Henry Lawrence. 'The best of the village rose as I approached; now the lowest puff their pipes in my face'. Fear of the British and of their inexplicable actions had prepared the sepoys to believe anything, however wild. The old order was undoubtedly being destroyed, and it was by no means improbable that the white man intended to destroy the old religion as well. The situation was emotionally explosive, and it needed only the feeblest of sparks to set it off.

In January 1857 a new weapon was scheduled to be introduced into the Bengal army to replace the old musket affectionately known as 'Brown Bess'. Ironically enough, many senior officers in both the Company's and the queen's forces had resisted the introduction of the new rifle. Most of the men commanding stations were over sixty, set in the ways which many of them had learned under the Iron Duke years before. They were great believers in the virtue of 'cold steel', the bayonet and the sword, but they seem to have felt a similar nostalgia for that inefficient arm, the musket. Their attitude inspired one critic to parody that old Irish song whose first line runs 'Believe me, if all those endearing young charms'.

> Believe me, if that most endearing old arm,
>   Which we miss with so fondly today,
>   Which never did Afghan or Sikh any harm,
>   Was to shoot straight for once in a way,
>   It should still be the weapon for Guardsmen and Line,
>   Let the windage increase as it will;
>   And we'd think the performance sufficiently fine,
>   If one ball in five hundred should kill.

The new Enfield rifle had to be loaded with a greased cartridge, the end of which was bitten off before loading. Soon the rumour grew that the grease was made from beef fat or hog's lard, and that an attempt was being made deliberately to break the caste of the Hindus and to insult the religious prejudices of the Muslims. The cow is sacred to Hindus, and the pig is an unclean animal to Muslims. It is difficult for Westerners to understand the sepoys' response to such rumours, because there is nothing in the West so everyday and so fundamentally sacred as the system of caste. The sepoy envisaged pollution so great that it amounted to a threat of damnation and an interruption of the divine order whose consequences would be terrifying beyond belief.

The greased cartridge rumour had its first effect at Berhampur in Bengal, on 26 February 1857, when the 19th Native Infantry refused to use the cartridge. There were no British troops there, so its officers marched the regiment to the military station of Barrackpore, near Calcutta, to be disbanded under the eyes of a British regiment which was hastily brought back from Burma. That a regiment of Europeans had to be brought from such a distance merely emphasised the thinness of the British presence in northern India. Most European troops from Bengal itself—and the command stretched from Calcutta to the Afghan frontier—had been moved into the Punjab when it was conquered and annexed eight years earlier, and which had been acquired complete with the troubled Afghan frontier. At Calcutta there was one infantry battalion, and another was stationed about four hundred miles away at Dinapur. One regiment was stationed at Agra, and one at Lucknow. Altogether, in an area as large as France and Germany combined, there were only four battalions and a few batteries of artillery totally manned by Europeans, and therefore reliable. The queen's forces had been considerably reduced because of the demand of the Crimean war. In the spring of 1857, there were no artillery or engineer units, and only four regiments of cavalry and twenty-two infantry battalions in the whole of India. Altogether, there were about 40,000 Europeans of the Company's and royal armies, and the immense total of 300,000 Indians, an overwhelming majority of almost eight to one.

As the hot weather approached, European troops were being moved to cooler stations in the foothills. Officers were going on leave. The commander-in-chief, General Anson—who had seen no fighting since the war against Napoleon over forty years before—had retired with his staff to the hill station of Simla, nearly a thousand miles away from Calcutta, the governor-general, and the civil government.

At Barrackpore, news of the imminent arrival of the 19th Native Infantry had its effect on the sepoys stationed there. On 29 March, a young soldier fired the first shot in the great Mutiny. Convinced that the British would turn against all sepoys, he put on his uniform and, seizing his musket, walked down to the quarter-guard, calling on his comrades to follow him. At the guard, the sepoy ordered the bugler to sound the call for 'assembly'. The bugler would not, but the men on guard did nothing even when the sepoy fired at an English sergeant-major. The shot went wide.

The adjutant, Lieutenant Baugh, now appeared on the scene, having been alerted by a European corporal. He had loaded his pistols, buckled on his sword, mounted his horse, and ridden down to the guardroom where, as he arrived, another shot was fired. It missed Baugh but brought down his horse. The situation now developed into tragic farce. Baugh fired at the mutineer—and missed. He drew his sword, and he and the sergeant-major rushed at the sepoy. The sepoy seems to have been a much better swordsman than either of the Europeans, for he wounded them both. He might even have succeeded in killing them if another sepoy had not restrained him. But the guards now turned on the two Europeans, striking them with the butts of their muskets. One even fired at close range—and missed.

News of what was going on finally reached the officer commanding the station, General Hearsey. He and his two sons had their horses saddled and then galloped to the guardroom. There they saw a crowd of sepoys, mostly unarmed, and a number of European officers milling around in great confusion. The mutineer was still holding his musket and calling on the other sepoys to join him. Hearsey, a battle-worn sixty, did not hesitate. Told that the mutineer had a loaded musket, he said 'damn his musket' and galloped forward, revolver in hand. The mutineer raised his musket to fire—then turned it on himself instead. But he only succeeded in wounding himself slightly, and was taken prisoner by the guard, now loyally carrying out its duty. This first mutineer's name was Mangal Pandy, and soon all mutineers came to be known as 'pandies'.

11 *Up among the pandies*

On Saturday night, young Lieutenant Gough sat on his verandah in the harsh darkness of an Indian May. The city of Meerut, away from the military lines, bubbled with more noise than usual, but it was quiet on the lieutenant's verandah, except for the perpetual hum of insects which forms the background to night in India.

Lieutenant Gough thought back over a day which was the most disturbing he had ever spent. It had been dark and heavy, with low clouds, and a dry hot wind had blown across the parade ground. There had been some 4,000 men there, drawn up to form three sides of a hollow square. What a sight they had been—the shining brass helmets and leather breeches of the Bengal Artillery officers; the black horsehair plumes of the Dragoon Guards; the olive green of the 60th Native Rifles; the silver-grey of his own 3rd Cavalry; and, of course, the scarlet coats and white collars of the Native Infantry. To the casual eye, it might have been just another of the ceremonial parades which the commander loved to mount. But no eye at that parade had been casual. All had been wary, some angry, many a mirror of fear. The Indian troops carried their arms, but everyone knew that their ammunition pouches were empty—by order. The British troops had their rifles, the new Enfield rifles, loaded, and they pointed them at their Indian comrades.

On the fourth, open side of the square stood eighty-five sepoys. They were clad in their uniforms, but their feet were bare and they carried no weapons. Around them stood a guard of British soldiers, themselves wary and hard of face. A British officer read aloud from a paper, but the dry wind seemed to blow his words away like fallen leaves. An Indian officer, with no flicker of emotion, translated into Hindustani, and the words appeared to touch all the sepoys present. Then there was silence —and afterwards soldiers ripped the buttons from the sepoys' uniforms and the coats from their backs. Armourers with tools and shackles came forward and slowly began to fit fetters on the condemned men.

Among the condemned were many who had served the British government in harsh battles and strange places, and had never before wavered in their allegiance. As the fetters were placed upon them, they lifted up their hands and implored the general to have mercy on them, but seeing no hope there they turned to their comrades and reproached them for standing aside and allowing them to be disgraced. There was not a sepoy present who did not feel indignation rising in his throat. Many of them were in tears, but what could they have done in the face of the loaded field guns and rifles, and the glittering sabres of the Dragoons? For a moment, it had seemed to Lieutenant Gough as if the sepoys were about to attack the British with their bare hands; but the prisoners were marched off and the tension eased.

Gough had gone down to the temporary jail and had been deeply shocked by the grief of the men, who had begged him to save them. Now, in the dark of the verandah, he wondered what would happen next. It was just over a fortnight since the eighty-five men had refused to use the new cartridges, and only a day since the court martial—of native officers—had found them guilty of mutiny. Gough's reflections were shattered by a rustle in the darkness, as a figure approached silently, almost furtively. But it was no thief. A whisper identified it as a native officer of his own troop who had come, he said, to discuss the troop's accounts. Gough found this puzzling. It was a Saturday night, a night for leisure, not for routine business. Then suddenly the true reasons for the visit came pouring out. The lieutenant-sahib must know that tomorrow, Sunday, the men would mutiny —all of them, even the cavalry, the sahib's own men. They would break open the jail and release their comrades. Murder was planned, murder and fire.

After the man had left, Gough went to the Mess and informed his colonel. His story was greeted with laughter and contempt, and he was told that he should be ashamed of listening to such an idle tale. But Gough was convinced, and he made another attempt—he went to the brigadier commanding the station. His reception was no better here. If no one else was worried, why should Lieutenant Gough concern himself?

The next day was 10 May, and all Gough could see when he

went out on his verandah was a sea of flame on the horizon. Galloping down to the cavalry lines, he found 'a thousand sepoys dancing and leaping frantically about, calling and yelling to each other', and blazing away with their muskets in all directions. By nightfall, Meerut was a city of horror. British officers had been cut down by their own men, women had been violated—not by men, but by sticks of burning tow and thatch thrust far into their bodies.

Everywhere there was chaos and confusion. Senior officers seemed struck with paralysis. There were as many British as native troops in Meerut, and the British had artillery, yet nothing was organised. Some of the younger officers did what they could, but the mutineers broke open the jail and, unhindered, set off for Delhi, some forty miles away to the south-west.

No one pursued them. Next morning, the first of them reached Delhi. Some went to the palace of Bahadur Shah, titular king of Delhi and last sad remnant of the once powerful Mughal empire. They proclaimed him emperor of Hindustan. Others joined their fellows in the three native regiments stationed in Delhi and persuaded them to kill their officers and then hunt to death the Europeans in the city. A last message went out on the telegraph line: 'The sepoys have come in from Meerut and are burning everything. Mr. Todd is dead and we hear several Europeans . . . We must shut up'. Delhi was in the hands of five thousand rebel soldiers; the English who had survived the massacre fled the city. The Indian Mutiny had begun.

In spite of all the warnings, the British were caught by surprise, which in most cases they compounded with ineptitude. For a time, British rule disappeared from large areas of northern India, and men and women were freely tortured and murdered. The story of the Mutiny is one of many heroisms—some great, many small. But perhaps the most remarkable courage of all was shown by the women. Used to a life in which they were wholly pampered by their menfolk and by their servants, under stress the majority of them showed a toughness and determination no one would have suspected to exist behind the facade of the 'gently-nurtured' lady of Victorian convention. Nowhere was this courage shown by as many as inside the besieged Residency at Lucknow.

Until 1856, Lucknow had been the capital of the kingdom of Oudh. When Oudh was annexed, the king had been sent off to a comfortable exile in Calcutta, but he left behind hundreds of functionaries, tradesmen who had depended on the court for their livelihood, and pensioners who would have to wait for the British to investigate their claims. Many of these men and their families were starving. Furthermore, three-quarters of the state's forces had been disbanded. And lastly, there were new taxes and new laws which pressed heavily upon the people. A tax on opium raised the price to such a level that there were many suicides among addicts who could no longer afford the drug. The people of Oudh were very ready for rebellion.

On 20 March 1857, Sir Henry Lawrence, well-tested in the service of the Company, was appointed to the charge of Oudh. The situation in Lucknow and the countryside was immediately clear to his unprejudiced eye—the materials of revolt lay everywhere. Lawrence's reports to the governor-general were precise and accurate, but there was to be no time to rectify the wrongs, no time for the British to do anything but fight for their lives.

By early April, the new cartridges were having repercussions in Oudh, and incidents had occurred among the sepoys. Lawrence did his best, by a mixture of firmness and conciliation. He was temporarily successful in reminding the sepoys of their loyalty, but the emotions that had been roused were not capable of being calmed by reason or crushed by inadequate strength. And the strength was inadequate. The number of European troops in Oudh was ridiculously small and widely scattered, and the men were outnumbered by nearly ten to one. Lawrence began preparations to meet the crisis he could foresee. He began to fortify the Residency.

Lucknow was an extravagant and magnificent city. William Howard Russell was astounded by it. 'A vision of palaces . . . domes azure and golden, cupolas, colonnade, long facades of fair perspective in pillar and column, terraced roofs—all rising up amid a calm still ocean of the brightest verdure. Look for miles and miles away, and still the ocean spreads, and the towers of the fairy-city gleam in its midst. Spires of gold glitter in the sun. Turrets and gilded spheres shine like constellations. There is nothing mean or squalid to be seen. There is a city more vast than Paris, as it seems, and more brilliant'.

The Residency area, which included a large number of offices as well as the houses of officials, stood to the north of the city on a raised plateau backing on to the river Gumti. Further up the river was an old fort, in which there was a garrison. The houses and narrow streets of the city embraced the Residency area closely; militarily, it was almost indefensible.

News of the rising at Meerut arrived at Lucknow on 13 May. Five days later, after outbreaks of arson and in the face of disturbing rumours of more trouble to come, work began on fortifying the old fort, the Machchi Bhawan, and preparations in the Residency were speeded up. By the end of May, the revolt had begun in earnest, but the European force was able to prevent a massacre. It even chased the mutineers into the countryside—which was also in revolt. By early June, British rule in Oudh no longer existed. 'Every outpost, I fear, has fallen', wrote Lawrence on 12 June, 'and we daily expect to be besieged by the confederated mutineers and their allies'. The British in Lucknow withdrew into the Residency.

On 9 June, Mrs Katherine Bartrum had arrived at the Residency from the tiny out-station of Gonda. Her husband, Captain Robert Bartrum, was the station surgeon. Katherine was twenty-three, a shy dark-haired girl, daughter of a Bath silversmith. Happy in Gonda with her masterful husband and little son, Bobbie, who was fifteen months old, she resisted being sent off to Calcutta because she believed it was better to die with her husband than to leave him. Never 'very brave', she claimed, the news of fresh outbreaks made her tremble. 'I could neither sleep, eat, or do anything', she wrote to her sister, 'but look to my husband for protection against foes which I fancied near at hand'. But she gained courage and no longer expected Bobbie, 'the merriest little fellow you ever saw', to be snatched from her arms and murdered before her very eyes.

Nevertheless, she and Robert slept with a loaded pistol and a sword under their pillows, and Katherine consoled herself with her husband's promise that, 'should things come to the worst, he would destroy me with his own hand rather than let me fall into the power of those brutal Sepoys'.

When the order came from Sir Henry Lawrence for women and children at the out-stations to go into Lucknow, Katherine still did not want to leave. Robert was adamant. If only for the sake of the baby, she must go to the safety of the Residency. 'God alone knows', she wrote later, 'how bitter was the struggle to feel that it was my duty to leave him'. Robert accompanied his wife and the wife of a civilian for the first sixteen miles of the eighty-mile journey to Lucknow. Then they parted, the two women and the child on the backs of elephants, to continue to Lucknow with an escort of sepoys, and the men back to their stations.

The two women were far from sure of the sepoys. 'Sometimes they made our elephant stand still whilst they lay upon the ground laughing and talking; but whenever I asked them for water for baby to drink, they would give it to me'. On one occasion Katherine saw the men of the escort loading their muskets. When she asked what they were going to do, they replied: 'Oh, there are so many bad people about, we are going to fight for you'. Finally, the party caught up with another, larger one. As the seven women, twelve children, and four officers moved on through a countryside which was full of marauders and burning buildings, they became even more doubtful of the loyalty of the sepoy escort. In the end, when they sighted Lucknow, they fled from the escort and arrived at the Residency exhausted, covered with dust, and full of anxiety as to 'the fate of those dearest to us, whom we had left behind'.

The Residency came as something of a shock to Katherine Bartrum. The house she was assigned to was 'a most uninviting looking place, so dirty, having neither a punkah to cool the air or a scrap of furniture to set it off'. She knew no one nearby, and never even met most of the few people she did know elsewhere in the Residency area. She was alone, 'left for the first time to take care of myself, separated from dear Robert, and ignorant of what had become of him'. As well as being separated from her loved one, Katherine was also—unprecedentedly—without servants and, above all, without the space and privacy she had

I

always been accustomed to. 'On that first night we slept, fifteen in one room, packed closely together, so that each might feel the benefit of the punkah, which Mrs Boileau with her usual energy and forethought, had managed to have put up during the day. We had to endure intense heat (for this was the hottest part of the year), mosquitoes and flies in swarms. How great a change after the comforts of our own homes!'

Robert escaped from Gonda when the sepoys mutinied, and his letter telling his wife of his escape was full of comfort. 'I trust that grace may be given us both to support this spirit [of perfect dependence upon the Almighty], and that if we do not incur danger the effect may not pass from us; but that I may be a more fitting companion to you in the road that leads to life'. Katherine was to receive only one more letter from her husband.

'Each day brought in fresh fugitives from the out-stations, and fearful were the tales they told of the cruel scenes they had witnessed, and from which, through the mercy of God, they had escaped'. The place to which they had escaped was to provide its own cruel scenes as the weeks dragged on. Many of the children were already beginning to look sickly, through the effects of close confinement in the intense heat. Bobbie was still 'fat and bonnie', but Katherine Bartrum could not overcome her fears for him.

By 27 June, it was clear that the siege of the Residency had begun in earnest. It was now impossible to get food cooked, and Katherine had no means of doing it herself. However, the wife of an English soldier was found to bring hot water for breakfast and tea. Katherine found herself 'fully occupied in nursing, and washing our clothes, together with cups and saucers, and fanning away the flies which have become a fearful nuisance'. So bad were they that sometimes, when food was placed on the table, they swarmed to cover it, black and loathsome.

Because the other occupants were too ill to keep the room clean, Katherine undertook the task. 'So long as God gives me health and strength I will do my best to add to the comfort of others, even if I afford them amusement by giving them occasion to call me the servant-of-all-work'. Her day was very simple. She was up as soon as it was light to wash and dress the children and tidy the room that was both bedroom and living room. After breakfast, which was never appetising, the rest of the day was occupied with such domestic chores as were necessary and possible. Time dragged so much that 'it was almost a blessing to have no servants, because it gave us so much occupation that we had less time to dwell upon our troubles and anxieties concerning those absent from us'. When the children at last fell asleep, 'we used to gather round a chair, which formed our tea-table, sitting on the bedside, and drinking our tea (not the strongest in the world) by the light of a candle which was stuck in a bottle, that being our only candlestick, and then we talked together of bygone days, of happy homes in England where our childhood had been spent'.

Soon the blows began to fall. On 29 June, Mrs Hale died— 'she was taken ill at three o'clock in the afternoon with cholera, and though everything was done for her by the medical men and those around which skill and kindness could suggest, it was all in vain; at 6 p.m. all pain left her, and we saw that she was rapidly sinking; the dews of death began to gather on her brow and she soon became unconscious'. It was the first time Katherine Bartrum had seen death in any shape. Mrs Hale left a little daughter. 'Poor little lamb, how unconscious was she of her sad loss: a motherless babe amongst strangers and her father far away'.

After an unsuccessful sortie against the mutineers, the garrison found itself immured in the Residency. Food was rationed, each person receiving 'attar, or flour, which we made into chupatties; rice; dall, or peas; salt and meat'. There were no proper cooking facilities, so all were cooked together, with ship's biscuits, in 'a saucepan with some water and made into a stew; but as the saucepan was of copper and could not be relined during the siege, the food when it was turned out was often perfectly green—hunger alone could make it enjoyable'. The children suffered most. The heat was intense and there were no coolies to pull the punkah. When the besiegers attacked the Residency, all the lights had to be put out and the children lay and trembled in the darkness.

On 2 July, the garrison blew up the Machchi Bhawan fort. No one had warned the women that this was to happen, and they all jumped to the conclusion that the sepoys had penetrated into the Residency. The room 'was so thick in dust when we had lighted a candle we could scarcely see one another; the bricks and mortar had fallen from the ceiling and the poor little children were screaming with terror.' But all was well—though a stray shot killed Sir Henry Lawrence soon after.

So it went on. Katherine was standing by the door one morning watching a child play with a round shot when the little girl was struck in the head and killed instantly. The only news was of injury and death. There was smallpox to add to the dangers. One of the women in Katherine's house died of smallpox, leaving 'a little girl who looks as though she would not long survive her.' Another woman and her child were dying, too. 'I have been listening to her during the night; she frequently exclaims, "Lighten my darkness I beseech Thee, O Lord", and many such beautiful expressions'. The woman's mind was failing. 'She wanted to sit up, and asked me to bring her boxes and pack them up as she was going on a long journey and must have everything prepared. I did what she wished, sorted her things and put them back in the boxes. "Thank you", she said, "now I am quite ready: the doolie is here but the bearers have not come" '. What a mournful scene it was, thought Katherine, 'that poor young thing and her child dying far away from all she loved'. The baby had been born ten days earlier, during the siege, and died two days after its mother.

By early August, there were only three adults left in Katherine's room, 'and we looked at each other, as much as to say: "Who will be the next to go?" ' But little Bobbie, who had almost died of cholera, recovered, and someone was even able to provide a little milk for him. There was nothing to be done but pray, cook what food there was, fan the flies away, and read a psalm for comfort in tribulation. 'How touchingly applicable were many of those beautiful psalms to our own case. Never before had been breathed forth with such earnestness those words, "O let the sorrowful sighing of the prisoners come before Thee: and preserve Thou those that are appointed to die" '.

Katherine's hands were so painful with the unaccustomed work and the diet, that she had to have the doctor to lance the boils which covered them. The doctor brought Bobbie a little sugar, which he said he had stolen. He was in 'a sad state of anxiety', for his wife was in Cawnpore, from which there was no news. There was no news from Robert Bartrum, either. And of relief, no sign. 'Are we forgotten altogether by our friends in England, that reinforcements never appear?'

As time went on, Katherine became more and more worried about her child. Food was becoming even more scarce, and there was no wood for a fire. 'One of the soldiers broke down some railings for us; but it is a difficult matter to chop them up, since I have only my dinner knife to do it with, and this will be worn out should the siege last much longer'.

Rations were once again reduced. The weary days went by, days punctuated only with tragedy. Would it never end?

Then, on 23 September, 'such joyful news! A letter is come from Sir J. Outram, in which he says we shall be relieved in a few days: everyone is wild with excitement and joy. Can it really be true? Is relief coming at last? And oh; more than all, will dear Robert come up? And shall we meet once more after these weary months of separation?'

The sound of firing was heard in the city beyond the Residency. Were the distant guns those of the relieving force? On 25 September the answer came, 'and at that moment the noise, confusion, and cheering were almost overwhelming'. The relieving force had broken into the Residency. Was Robert with it? 'I was not long left in suspense, for the first officer I spoke to told me he was come up with them, and that they had shared the same doolie on the previous night'. With her son in her arms, Katherine rushed out to find him, scanning every face along the way, but she was told that her husband was with the heavy artillery and would not be in until morning. 'I could not sleep that night for joy at the thought of seeing him so soon, and how thankful I was that our Heavenly Father had spared us to meet again'. Next day there was disappointment. A gentleman told her that he had shared the same tent as Robert the night before, and that he would be along soon. But still he did not come. 'So I gave baby his breakfast and sat at the door to watch for him'. But still he did not come.

Next afternoon, the doctor came on his usual visit, looking kind

and sad. ' "How strange it is my husband is not come in! " "Yes",
he said, "it *is* strange! " and turned round and went out of the
room. Then the thought struck me: Something has happened
which they do not like to tell me! But this was agony too great
almost to endure, to hear that he had been struck down at our
very gates. Of this first hour of bitter woe I cannot speak. . . .
My poor little fatherless boy! who is to care for us now,
baby?'

Robert had been killed on the threshold of the Residency. At
first, Katherine could not understand why God had 'forgotten to
be gracious', but she pulled herself together and thought of her
son, hers and Robert's. 'Poor little fellow, how often had I said
to him, "Papa is come: now baby will get quite well". He
could not understand why I was so sad, and would clasp his little
arms round my neck and kiss away my tears. Now he was doubly
dear to me: all I had left to make life endurable'. Robert 'had
fought the good fight, he had finished his course'; she knew
that he would 'rise again at the last day'. Now there was only
the child to live for.

The relief was no relief. The force which had been strong
enough to break in to the Residency was not strong enough to
break out again. The ordeal was not yet over. Although the
weather was becoming cooler, sickness and famine still haunted
the Residency. It was difficult to keep clothes and body clean,
as there was no soap; 'we have to use the dall, or pease, by grinding
it between two stones and making it into flour, and this is a good
substitute for soap; but we have so little of it, that it is a question
sometimes whether we shall use it to wash with or to eat'. The
renewed siege was not, however, to last so long. In the second
week of November more troops arrived to hold the way clear
long enough for the garrison to be evacuated. 'November 17—
Heard that we are to leave Lucknow tomorrow night, with just
what we can carry. Well! I can only carry my baby, and my
worldly effects can be put into a very small compass, since they
consist merely of a few old clothes. My heart fails me at the
thought of the terrible march, with no one to look after me or
care for me but God. I have lost my kind friend Dr Darby, who
has been wounded; and they say he will not recover. He promised

to take care of me on the journey to Calcutta, but now I am utterly friendless'. Even yet, the ordeal was not over.

Katherine and her child were placed in a doolie, a kind of palanquin, to cover the five miles to the British camp. The bearers lost their way. 'It immediately occurred to me that they were taking me to the sepoys: I sprung out of the doolie, and ran with my child in my arms, screaming across the plain until I heard voices answering'. The voices belonged to British soldiers, and they helped her to the camp. 'I had been on my feet with my baby in my arms for upwards of three hours, walking through deep sand and wet grass, and my dress had become so coated with mud, that it was with difficulty I could get on.' At last, here were welcoming faces, milk for Bobbie, and a cup of tea for Katherine. When there was time for thought, even the kindliness and the safety seemed to intensify Katherine's sorrow, 'but the God of the widow and the fatherless will not forsake me'.

In the security of Calcutta, on the eve of sailing for home, Katherine Bartrum's tragedy played itself out. Bobbie had grown very delicate, and the doctors in Calcutta had assured her that only a sea voyage would restore him to health. Instead of rushing home by the overland route, therefore, they were making the four-month voyage by way of the Cape. As the time came to board the ship, Bobbie became weaker. On 11 February, they boarded the *Himalaya*. By then, the child was very ill, 'but I *cannot* spare him, and I do not think God will take away my little lamb when I have nothing else left'. Katherine was frightened. A friend who had also survived the ordeal at Lucknow kept watch with her. 'Look', she said, 'how bright his eyes are growing'. But Katherine had turned her head away, 'for I *could* not see my child die'. On 12 February Katherine Bartrum sailed for England, alone.

Katherine Bartrum passed through the valley of the shadow. So, too, did Lieutenant Gough of Meerut, who won one of the new Victoria Crosses and died a general. But others, like Robert Bartrum and his son, did not, and their bones became part of the earth they had walked upon as kings.

12   *Bloody assize*

When news of the outbreak at Meerut reached Calcutta there had been panic. The majority of the European inhabitants of the City of Palaces were non-officials—businessmen, and the like. They were known by the more worldly soldiers and civilians as 'ditchers', because most of them had rarely travelled outside Calcutta and seldom even went beyond the old defensive line known as the Maratha Ditch. They knew nothing about Indians, except those with whom they did business, who formed a growing middle class not very different from themselves. Safe, as they thought, in their great houses, they relied upon the government for their protecton. But suddenly the government's power was in doubt. At Barrackpore, only a night's march from the centre of the city, men whom they had once looked upon as the trusted guardians of life and property had turned into potential despoilers and murderers. There was, too, a fear, 'dominant over all, that the vast and varied population of the Native suburbs and bazaars would rise against the white people, release the prisoners in the gaols, and gorge themselves with the plunder of the great commercial capital of India'. And to make it worse, the governor-general, Lord Canning, did not appear to grasp the extent of the danger. By 28 May, a correspondent of the newspaper *Friend of India* was recording that: 'Men went about with revolvers in their carriages, and trained their bearers to load quickly and fire low. The ships and steamers in the rivers have been crowded with families seeking refuge from the attack, which was nightly expected, and everywhere a sense of insecurity prevailed'.

The governor-general's appearance of calm reassured no one. On 25 May he had given a ball at Government House to celebrate the queen's birthday, even though rumours had been rife in the bazaar that, on that day, attempts would be made—what kind of attempts no one quite knew—to convert all Hindus to Christianity. The celebratory *feu de joie* for the queen was not abandoned, but it was fired from muskets, not from the new rifles. Some Europeans, fearing that the gathering would be used as an opportunity to murder all the leading members of the community, stayed away. One young lady hired two English sailors to sit up in her house and protect her on the night of the ball, 'but they got tipsy, and frightened her more than imaginary enemies'.

A few days later, the sound of fireworks set off at the marriage of a princess of Mysore brought all the menfolk out with their guns. 'I never came across such a set of old women', complained Lord Canning.

Canning refused offers from the Masonic Lodges, the trade associations, and the French and Armenian communities, to enlist in a volunteer corps. This convinced most people that the governor-general was incompetent, and there were calls for his instant dismissal. In October 1857, when it at last seemed that the British had taken a grip on the Mutiny by recapturing Delhi, Queen Victoria's loyal Calcutta subjects sent her a petition. This alleged that Lord Canning, by his moderation and his interference with the rights of British subjects, had been 'a principal cause of the great calamities which have desolated this land, has strengthened the hands of the enemy, weakened or destroyed the respect before entertained for the name of Englishman in the East, imperilled British rule, exposed the Capital of British India to massacre and pillage, excited the contempt of all parties, estranged from the Government of India a large and loyal body of Christians, and in every way proved himself unfit to be further continued in his high trust'. And all because Canning had turned his face against indiscriminate violence and sought to restrain British officers and civilians from indulging in a reign of terror.

But a reign of terror there certainly was. The distance between panic and bellicosity is only a sense of shame. The British in Calcutta and elsewhere, smarting with the realisation of their own fears, turned in hatred against all Indians. Something had to be done to erase suggestions of cowardice—which had been admirably summed up in an announcement in a Simla paper, after many of the menfolk had deserted the ladies and taken refuge in the ravines surrounding the town: 'The ladies of Simla will hold a meeting . . . for the purpose of consulting about the best measures to be taken for the protection of the gentlemen. The ladies beg to inform those who sleep in the *khuds* [ravines] that they sincerely compassionate their sufferings, and are now preparing pillows for them stuffed with the purest white feathers. . . . Rest, warriors, rest'.

Demands for vengeance were strongly supported by people even further removed from danger than those who lived in Calcutta. In newspapers in England, opinion had switched from incredulity —surely a collection of damned niggers could hardly present a threat to the Empire?—to outrage. Stories of atrocities, of Englishwomen boiled alive in butter, of children barbecued on bayonets, filled the most staid of journals. A letter in *The Times*, obviously published with approval, declared: 'Not one stone in Delhi should be left standing upon another. . . . Every sepoy should be a pauper, his house in flames, himself fleeing from man who hunts like a wolf'. Soon, however, *The Times* was editorialising in more ponderous terms: 'This blind and indiscriminate exasperation is resolving itself into the mere hatred of a dark skin'.

Europe accepted the solidarity of the white-skinned races. In Paris, the emperor Napoleon III immediately agreed that Britain's India-bound reinforcements should be permitted to use the overland route through France to Marseilles.

In England, it became a wet-afternoon amusement for country house parties to sit around the billiard table devising tortures for the leaders of the revolt. The palm was awarded to an ingenious gentleman who proposed that the chief villain 'should be forced, first, to swallow a tumbler of water in which all the blue papers in a seidlitz-powder box had been emptied, and then a tumbler with the contents of all the white papers in a state of solution'. In the better clubs, too, it was common to chuckle over the exquisite punishments devised by psychopaths like General Neill, who 'had forced high Brahmans to sweep up the blood of the Europeans murdered at Cawnpore, and then strung them in a row, without giving them the time requisite for the rites of purification'.

'Have you heard the news?' said a celebrated author to an acquaintance, as they stood together under the porch of the Athenaeum. 'The Sepoys have taken to inflicting the most exquisite cruelties upon the Sikhs, and the Sikhs in return swear that they will stamp the Company's arms in red-hot pice [copper coins] over the body of every Sepoy who comes in their way. These are the sort of tidings that nowadays fill every heart in England with exultation and thankfulness'.

After the suppression of the Mutiny, a young man just arrived in India discovered that there were two men who were accounted the most welcome new additions to society in Calcutta. 'One was a jolly comical-looking chap, an excellent officer and a capital man for a small dinner-party. The other was most refined and intelligent, with a remarkably courteous and winning address. It was said that these two had hung more people than any other men in India'. One of them, however, 'was blamed by many for excess of leniency'. This man, Mr Hume, had distinguished himself 'by keeping down the number of executions in his district to seven, and by granting the culprits a fair trial. These he treated with fatherly tenderness, for he invented a patent drop for their benefit; so that men prayed—first, that they might be tried by Mr Hume, and next, that, if found guilty, they might be hanged by him'.

Mr Hume was something of an eccentric. Hanging—and humane hanging at that—was certainly too good for mutineers. It was more usual to blow them from guns. This method was, however, still thought to be humane. It also contained 'two valuable elements of capital punishment; it was painless to the criminal and terrible to the beholder'. The ritual was certainly hideous. With great ceremony, the victim was escorted on to the parade ground while the band played some lively air. Above, in the sky, the vultures waited as the victim's back was ranged against the muzzle of the gun and the straps tightened. Then the band would fall silent and the only sound would be the faint crackle of the port-fire, ready to be placed at the touch hole. At last, the air seemed to split. A head would come dancing across the ground, and an obscene shower of blood and entrails would cover both gunners and observers. Once, at Barrackpore, two Englishwomen clad all in white and riding white Arab horses spurred their mounts at the moment of explosion, and then rode away covered in scarlet, their horses dark with blood.

127

The Mutiny was a war carried on with sometimes bestial ferocity on both sides. Crazy with fear, the sepoys murdered English women and children, and the British retaliated with lynchings and village-burnings which made no discrimination between the guilty and the innocent. By 20 June, J. W. Kaye—the historian of the Mutiny—records: 'Soldiers and civilians alike were holding Bloody Assize, or slaying natives without any assize at all, regardless of sex or age. . . . Volunteer hanging parties went into the districts and amateur executioners were not wanting to the occasion. One gentleman boasted of the numbers he had finished off quite "in an artistic manner", with mango trees for gibbets and elephants for drops, the victims of this wild justice being strung up, as though for pastime, in the form of figures of eight'. Violence and cruelty bred further violence and cruelty.

Even the smile disappeared from Anglo-Indian portraits. A Calcutta journal reported favourably on the 'portrait of Captain Hazlewood which may be seen in Thacker and Spink's Gallery. The friends of the gallant officer will at once recognise the likeness, and feel confident that no undue lenity on his part will be shown to the murderers of women and children, for he has a stern expression of countenance as if he had just given an order to hang them and their favourers'.

It was little wonder that, in a climate of hysteria richly adorned with stories of atrocities, the British soldiers who were pouring into Calcutta and Bombay should have regarded the entire population as the enemy. They were very annoyed when their officers refused to allow them to kill all the Indians they saw. At one stage it became necessary to double the guard on Fort William to prevent the soldiers from setting off into the streets of Calcutta at night to polish off a few natives. The soldiers' ignorance of any language other than their own sometimes led to farcical tragedy, particularly when they *thought* they heard a word they knew. One soldier, his head full of the shocking tales which were current about the mutiny and massacre at Cawnpore, reported: 'I seed two Moors [Indians] talking in a cart. Presently I heard one of 'em say "Cawnpore". I knowed what that meant; so I fetched Tom Walker, and he heard 'em say "Cawnpore", and he knowed what that meant. So we polished 'em both off'.

Across the country was cut a swathe of burned villages and
battered towns. The great city of Delhi suffered terribly after its
recapture. 'All the city people found within the walls when our
troops entered were bayoneted on the spot; and the number was
considerable, as you may suppose when I tell you that in some
houses forty or fifty persons were hiding'. The mutineers had
purposely left vast quantities of liquor behind, and the British
troops went berserk. 'The troops', wrote Saunders, the Commissioner of Delhi, 'were completely disorganised and demoralised
by the immense amount of plunder that fell into their hands and
the quantity of liquor which they managed to discover'. They
spared neither people nor buildings. Troops occupied the mosques.
The Red Fort was taken over and some of the most exquisite of
its buildings were destroyed (apologists argued that, in any case,
they were of 'little architectural interest'!) In a Bombay newspaper, one writer advocated the entire destruction of the city,
and suggested that a vast pyramid should be raised from the
ruins. Mutineers and their supporters would provide the labour,
and when they died, as the writer believed they would (from over-
work), their bodies could be thrown into a tube in the centre of
the pyramid. When the work was finished and surmounted by an
immense statue of Retribution, a plaque was to be appended,
reading:

BENEATH THIS PYRAMID
LIE BURIED
A PALACE, ITS KING, ITS PRINCES
AND THE
MONSTERS OF THE BENGAL NATIVE ARMY THEY
INCITED TO MUTINY, TO MURDER, AND OTHER
CRIMES UNUTTERABLE.
STRANGER!
IF YOU WOULD KNOW WHERE
DELHI WAS,
BEHOLD ITS DEBRIS IN THE PYRAMID
YOU STAND ON
ANNO DOMINI MDCCCLVII

Fortunately, wiser counsels prevailed, and most of the destruction was limited to a number of buildings which intervened in the fire-path of the guns of the fort.

When the correspondent of *The Times* arrived in Delhi in May 1858, he found the Commissioner installed in a 'fine mansion with turrets and clock-towers, something like a French chateau of the last century'. On closer inspection, it showed signs of cannon-fire, but the interior was untouched by war. 'I found myself at once back in civilised life, amid luxuries long unknown. . . . The comfort and luxury of the house itself were a positive gratification to the senses. Large lofty rooms—soft carpets, sofas, easy chairs, books, pictures, rest and repose, within. Outside, kuskus-tatties and punkah-wallahs. The family were at their first breakfast when we went in. I found there were two breakfasts, one at eight, the other at three o'clock.' For visitors, an evening's amusement consisted of driving into the city to see the emperor. 'In a dingy, dark passage, leading from the open court or terrace in which we stood to a darker room beyond, there sat, crouched on his haunches, a diminutive, attenuated old man, dressed in an ordinary and rather dirty muslin tunic, his small lean feet bare, his head covered by a small thin cambric skull-cap'. When Russell was there, the ex-king was sick; 'with bent body he seemed nearly prostrate over a brass basin, into which he was retching violently'. Was this 'dim-wandering-eyed, dreamy old man, with feeble hanging nether lip and toothless gums'—was he, indeed, wondered Russell, the one 'who had conceived that vast plan of restoring a great empire, who had fomented the most gigantic mutiny in the history of the world, and who, from the walls of his ancient palace, had hurled defiance and shot ridicule upon the race that held every throne in India in the hollow of their palms?'

In an attempt to answer such questions, the British had put the king on trial a couple of months earlier. The trial had failed to clear the matter up. He was, of course, found guilty, but there was no question of executing him, for he had been guaranteed his life. But the trial gave a halo of martyrdom to the last of the Mughals.

By October 1858 the British had decided to send the king and his immediate family into exile at Rangoon, in Burma. The party consisted of the king himself and two of his wives, with two of his sons and a number of female relatives. With them went four women of the harem and five male and eleven female servants. In charge was Lieutenant Ommanney, who found the slow journey much to his liking, even though he had to get up at 1.30 a.m. in order to get the party organised for the road. This he found 'rather hard', especially as he did not manage to return to his tent for breakfast until 9 a.m. 'But', he assured the Commissioner of Delhi, 'I don't care a straw for any amount of work and am very jolly. I am Honorary Member of the Lancer Mess, breakfast, dinner, and tiffin, good stags at dinner twice a week, a pack of Hounds accompany the column on the march, and we have a run when we succeed in getting a jackal, there is a Hook[ah] Club and in short it is as comfortably and perfectly managed as any'.

As Ommanney with his escort of Lancers, their pack of hounds, and their royal charge, moved slowly across northern India, the obsequies of the Honourable East India Company were being pronounced. On 1 November 1858, at Calcutta, Madras, Bombay and a number of other places throughout India (including Delhi), a high-sounding proclamation bearing the name of Queen Victoria was read with suitable ceremony:

> Whereas, for divers weighty reasons, we have resolved, by and with the advice and consent of the Lords Spiritual and Temporal, and Commons, in Parliament assembled, to take upon ourselves the government of the territories in India, heretofore administered in trust for us by the Honourable East India Company . . .

The sonorous words of the proclamation rolled on, and translations were made into no less than seventeen languages.

The proclamation contained something for everyone. For the princes, security of tenure; 'we desire no extension of our territorial possessions'. For the heathen, a certain condescension; 'firmly relying Ourselves on the truth of Christianity . . . We disclaim alike the right and desire to impose Our convictions'. And for all, the proposition that, with the aid of a beneficent

God, a new and happy era was about to dawn; 'when, by the blessing of Providence, internal tranquility shall be restored, it is Our earnest desire to stimulate the peaceful industry of India, to promote works of public utility and improvement, and to administer the government for the benefit of all Our subjects resident therein. In their prosperity will be Our strength, in their contentment Our security, and in their gratitude Our best reward . . .'

And the Queen's peace over all.

13 *Mirror of indigo*

In the new India, the largest body of Europeans apart from those in the civil service and the army consisted of planters. Europeans had never been greatly interested in Indian agriculture as a whole, but the government held the opium monopoly, and indigo cultivation offered scope to European enterprise. At the end of the eighteenth century, planters had been invited to come to India from the West Indies, and very soon a thriving industry was established, mainly in and around Bengal.

The planters had soon proved themselves a tough and violent crowd, beating up the peasants and not infrequently murdering them, assembling armies of their own retainers and making war on their rivals. Because their estates were so inaccessible from the main centres of government, they had always been difficult to control. Though some of the planters were, in fact, men of humanity and even of taste, who built themselves great mansions in the prevailing Classical form, all lived in a patriarchal style—usually in more senses than one. There was often a sizeable Eurasian population on an indigo estate. The planters kept in close contact with other Europeans of the non-official community, particularly in Calcutta, where their interests dominated the English-language press. It was they who sponsored the abuse of Lord Canning and demands for vengeance on the mutineers, and they who constantly campaigned against officialdom, especially in the shape of the magistrates who tried to interfere when the planters 'disciplined' their workers. Planters had been active in the volunteer units raised at the time of the Mutiny, and they took back to their estates afterwards a racial animosity which seemed to surpass any they had felt before.

Very soon—encouraged, perhaps, by the disturbance of the Mutiny years—peasants began to refuse to cultivate indigo. The source of the trouble was the contract system. Few planters actually cultivated the indigo crop themselves. The usual method was to advance money to the peasant, who then grew the crop and sold it back to the planter when it was ripe. His buying price

K

was often too low, and the peasant preferred to grow a more profitable crop, such as rice. Some peasants took the advance and then neglected the indigo, so the planter sent his own men to supervise cultivation. If a peasant refused to plant at all, the planter, even though no contract had been signed, would send his men to sow the land forcibly, while bullies with clubs and spears drove the peasant off his own holding. When a courageous magistrate took action—and it needed courage, for the planter was quite prepared to threaten the magistrate with violence, too— the whole planting community howled to the governor of the province, and its newspapers hurled abuse at the magistrate concerned.

Under attack, the government did what all governments do in such circumstances. They appointed a commission of inquiry. The missionaries, in particular, provided evidence of the planters' oppression and brutality. The planters, in turn, accused the missionaries of inciting the peasants to refuse to grow indigo. While the commission was in the course of its inquiry, the government passed a temporary law which made breach of contract a *criminal* offence. This, of course, resulted in even greater hardship for the peasants, as the planters took every advantage of the law. Contracts were forged without a moment's hesitation. 'It makes one's blood creep,' wrote the viceroy, 'to think of what may have been done under cover of this gigantic system of fraud, bearing in mind the cases of blind men, lepers, bed-ridden men and children' who had been jailed for so-called violation of contract.

In the midst of a situation which one civilian thought might be the beginning of a full-scale agricultural uprising, a missionary placed a bomb on the fire. He had discovered a play written in Bengali, entitled *Nil Durpan* (The Mirror of Indigo), which criticised the whole business of indigo planting from the peasant's point of view. He mentioned it to J. P. Grant, the lieutenant-governor of Bengal. As it had now been recognised that one of the reasons for British unpreparedness at the time of the Mutiny was lack of information on native opinion, Grant asked the Rev Dr Long to translate the play. When the translation had been made, copies were—without Grant's knowledge—distributed to a large number of officials. When the planters heard of it, they complained strongly to Grant. He refused to apologise, except for the fact of its unauthorised distribution under a government frank. The planters' response was to take out a libel action against the translator.

The trial was a travesty. The Rev. Dr Long was given no chance of defence. The judge interpreted passages from the play in the most perverted manner. In the course of the dialogue, one character asked: 'Did not the magistrate say he will come here this day?' and another replied: 'No, sir. He has four days more to come. On Saturday they have a champagne-party and ladies' dance. Mrs Wood can never dance with anyone but our Sahib [the magistrate]. I saw that when I was a bearer. Mrs Wood is very kind'. This stimulated the judge to rousing condemnation. Would the jury believe, he demanded, 'that those women were in the habit of prostituting themselves in order to gain the decision of magistrates who were bound by oath to administer the law with strict impartiality? Would they believe that those magistrates were in the habit of violating the solemn obligation of their duty and conscience to gratify licentious desire?' This terrible slander, he argued, was aimed not only at the wives of planters; it was 'for the jury to consider whether it was not intended as a reproach on the whole middle class of the women of England'.

The judge's peroration was reported with great glee in the English papers. 'Would the reverend gentleman [Dr Long] point out how far he thought this *filthy* statement was calculated to bring about improvements in social morals. When he [the judge] read those *filthy* passages he blushed to think that a clergyman of the established Church of England could have lent himself to the propagation of so malicious and unfounded a slander. That statement would go forth to the mothers and daughters of the middle class in England to make them think that is the fate of their daughters here. Not a gentleman in any station but would tear the *filthy* production; but, above all, every civilian, soldier, and merchant, and he hoped every clergyman, would agree that it should never reach the firesides of England'. Poor Dr Long was sentenced to a month's imprisonment—in a very unpleasant cell —and a heavy fine. Pleased with themselves, the planters went home and bullied a few more peasants, an occupation they continued to enjoy throughout the good queen's reign.

Though indigo production declined as chemical substitutes took over, a flood of Englishmen arrived in India after 1860, many of whom became planters of the new crops, tea and coffee. All had been influenced by the wave of anti-Indian feeling which had swept over Britain at the time of the Mutiny, and in the closed society of lonely plantations they maintained their racial hatreds undisturbed, moderately secure in the knowledge that justice would never catch up with them—or if it did, that it would be mild. For the murder of his coachman, one Englishman was fined thirty rupees, a couple of pounds at the then rate of exchange. Even as late as 1901, two English planters, 'in order to obtain a confession of theft from a native Syce or groom, tied him up to a tree and flogged him to such an extent that he died in the evening of the same day. They then carried off his body to a distance of two miles and buried it, in the hope of escaping discovery'. When the affair came to light, other planters subscribed £1,000 for their defence and they were sentenced to only three years' simple imprisonment.

As the price of indigo declined, so too did the great mansions. Life became a little less extravagant, a little less like a pretence of Home. Pleasures became more rustic, but they still had their appeal.

In the 1880s, and after, the first task of a young man who found himself in Calcutta en route for a plantation in such a place as Tirhut, for example, would be to partake of an official luncheon with the proprietors or their agents. He would then spend a day or two at the Great Eastern hotel—a favourite resort of planters on leave—waiting for the order to join his 'concern'. The new assistant would be helped on his way by the railway, and at the station nearest his destination he would find awaiting him a bullock cart for his baggage, and a pony or horse for himself. These, and relays of fresh mounts, would have been arranged by the manager of the plantation. The mounts were never particularly good ones since the ordinary indigo planter, though 'the very soul of generosity', had more respect for his horse-flesh than to bestow it on a stranger, especially on roads which had been repaired with 'two feet and a half of loose earth and large clods just before a long season of heavy rains' and were usually in a state that 'may be imagined but cannot be adequately described'. All in all, it was wise for the new arrival to treat his mounts with suspicion. He himself might not have experienced up-country roads before, but they probably had, 'and they know a trick or two, and he must not be surprised at somewhat violent and exciting starts—full speed reckoning as the very lowest order of velocity, graduating from that upwards, to the sensation of being shot out of a rocket'. A really recalcitrant animal of the kind that sat down and firmly refused to move might be given the well-tried stimulus of having a fire of straw, sticks and dry grass lit under him. Generally speaking, however, the plantation hacks were not quite as bad as that. The alternative to a horse was a light cart made from an old indigo chest and four pieces of bamboo. It had the advantage of being practically indestructible, as long as the wheels stayed on.

Arrived at the plantation, the assistant would spend a day or two becoming acquainted with the manager at his house, and would then move into his own bungalow, a simple but often pleasant place. The kitchen was, as usual, some little way off from the house. It was probably still the traditional kitchen of Anglo-India. 'Is not hare (hair) soup served up regularly until the cook's ambrosial locks are perforce seized and shorn by the stern order of the sahib, who—with all his love of game soup and pie, to say nothing of curry—holds, in this case, with the fastidious man in the backwoods restaurant, who preferred his flies and molasses in separate plates, and likes his "hair", if it must come to table, placed in a prominent place, say, on a separate dish of the largest size, and sent thereon, with best compliments, back to the chef in the cook-room'.

The assistant's bungalow was small, but quite large enough for a bachelor. The doors would rarely be an exact match, nor would they be opposite each other. This was rather an advantage than otherwise, as aligned doors exposed the assistant to any 'Aryan brother who has a complaint of a peculiarly noxious or distressing character, such as wanting to borrow money on personal security or anything of that sort'. The hopeful borrower, unless his efforts were foiled by erratic architecture, 'simply reconnoitres until he finds a place in the garden . . . [from which] he can distinctly see through the house, so that, move which way the assistant will, the "grievancer's" eye is upon him'. Nothing could escape that basilisk stare. 'It's no use; he KNOWS you MUST look at him; he never stirs, he never speaks; he sits there, mute, asking for nothing, seeking nothing. Oh, no! Wishing for nothing. Only you will have to, and MUST, eventually, LOOK AT HIM; and herein lies his triumph!' The moment the 'grievancer' succeeded in catching the assistant's eye, there flashed upon his face, 'as from a lighthouse on the coast, suddenly such an expression of abject misery and woe, want and injured innocence, as no words but mute appeals can do justice to, dying away again as suddenly the instant your eye is removed from him'. This kind of harassment, of course, could wear down even the kindest-hearted of mortals, 'and it has even been known to attract a boot-jack, half a brick, or similar heavy bodies with great velocity to within an ace of the "watcher's" head, accompanied with much low and violent rumbling, as of bad language and ill-temper of a furiously aggressive but suppressed kind'.

Such distractions apart, the assistant found little in the way of entertainment on the plantation. There would be a visit from another assistant, once a month perhaps, or one from the manager who might invite the assistant to return with him and spend the night at his house, where 'if the manager is a family man, he may hear a few tunes on the piano, and a few of the Old Country songs which will remind him of those at Home'. Otherwise there was little until the cold season came round and the assistant could take off for Calcutta for a few days, 'where his numerous wants will inevitably lead him to China Bazaar, there to be assailed, by native brokers, hawkers, and middlemen clinging to his gharry with cries of "tin-box", "orginette", "meershum pipe", "portmantoo", "esleepinsuit", "ready med close", "photogripes taken" etc'.

The ordinary day meant rising at 5 a.m. and departing on a tour of inspection after a light breakfast of a cup of tea, a slice of toast, and a couple of eggs. Back home at 11 a.m., the young man would bathe, write a few letters, have lunch, and do the office work. Finally, an evening meal, a little recreation, and bed. It was a monotonous life, although frequently enlivened by a run with the hounds. 'Hounds' was, perhaps, rather an ample word, as the dogs were usually of assorted breeds or no breed at all, 'from the squab little bow-legged, half-bred, cur doggie to the no-less half-bred, lanky, big-jointed cross between a Rampore and a pariah dog, or a greyhound and a kangaroo dog'. There was no fox, only a jackal, which could be run best in the evening.

Such excitements were not for every day. In the normal course of events, the assistant spent much of his time in his bungalow, which could be made quite snug now that everything came from Home 'at such cheap rates'. A few choice and artistic oleographs on the walls—landscapes, perhaps, or some of Landseer's fashionable animals—might be offset by photographs of celebrated beauties. An assistant might keep birds, or fish. He could take up carpentry, or study 'the reading and writing of the language if inclined'. If evening still hung heavy on his hands, he might decide to exercise his talents for music. He could practise the violin to his heart's content, without fear of offending anyone. 'The native of India', in fact, was 'positively *fond* of discordant sounds; and he [the assistant] will probably, on slipping out into his verandah in the darkness of the stilly night, after performing every direst kind of excruciating discord on his instrument for the time being . . . find, as one assistant did, his chowkidar [watchman] behind the door, wrapped in profoundest extacies at the dulcet sounds he had been producing'.

Anyone who could play an instrument was appreciated at the festivities that the cold season brought. Racing, hunting, and hockey meets were held at the various plantations, and men rode more than a hundred miles to stay for a few days and enjoy the fun. Everybody who could attend, did. And what a sight it was, even if only because of the hats. The Bengal planter was famous for the strange variety of his headgear. 'Some resemble copper boilers in shape, with broad brims, and innumerable air-holes; others have a peak in front, and an apron behind, just (as far as shape is concerned) as if a child's pinafore had been tied upon a dragoon's helmet to cover the back of the neck; others rise in the most outrageous manner—cauldron-fashion—

139

as if the unfortunate individual's head had been introduced by mistake into a wooden washing-basin and had become fixed there'.

There was less variety in the names, for most of the planting families—and it was very much a family affair—were of Scottish origin. In fact, it was said that if anyone, at a Christmas week gathering, were to shout 'Mac!' from the verandah of the Tirhut Club, every face would simultaneously turn towards him.

Among the occasional events which lightened the planters' life were parades of the volunteer cavalry, the Bihar Light Horse, to which many of them belonged. Their uniform consisted of 'blue blouse, breeches, and Blucher boots, white pugree and regulation helmet with silver spike and chain, black and brown belt, Martini-Henry carbine and light sword'. They formed a brave sight, and they were efficient, too. But even thirty years after the Mutiny, fear still lingered. The government would not build forts. There was nothing to give the slightest protection in case of trouble. 'Have we again lapsed into that false and deadly feeling of security and *laissez faire* which preceded the mutiny and its horrors? . . . Are we to disregard all due precaution and to be in jeopardy even to the eleventh hour, because the sky is clear, and all seems tranquil around us? As the darkest night precedes the dawn, so also does the deepest calm forbode the storm. We are not pessimists—all we would urge is that we are a small handful of British folk in a foreign land, amongst the teeming populations of which, with friendship there is mixed up hate, with fairness fanaticism, and with justice intolerance'.

In the lonely up-country stations, even the queen's peace seemed fragile.

14 *An imperial assemblage*

The only feeling of insecurity Robert, Lord Lytton—poet and viceroy of India—might have felt one brilliant day in January 1877 was that the dais on which he was standing before the assembled troops and princes might collapse. It had nearly done so only a few days before, even though it was made of cast iron, the gold of the high Victorians, 'cold, new, flaunting and bare, without a rag of sentiment or beauty'. Despite its decorations, it had a decidedly tawdry look. They had heaped 'ornament on ornament, colour on colour, on the . . . dais, till the whole is like the top of a Twelfth cake. They have stuck pieces of needlework into stone panels, and tin shields and battleaxes all over the place. The size . . . gives it a vast appearance, like a gigantic circus, and the decorations are in keeping'. The metalwork had been gilded. On top of the bandstand-like structure rested the imperial crown on a red cushion, and from it fell drapes of red cloth embroidered with gold. At each angle there was a trophy of 'three satin bannerets, festooned outwards, displaying the cross of St George and the Union Jack. Below the cornice, the canopy was continued in alternate stripes of red and white satin, embroidered with golden *fleurs de lis*.' The rose, the shamrock, the thistle, and the lotus of India were all featured in the ensemble, as were the Irish Harp, the Scottish Lion Rampant, and the Three Lions of England. There were silver shields, monogrammed in gold, and the imperial crown and the royal arms were everywhere, embossed in gold, or worked in satin appliqué. Val Prinsep, the artist who had been commissioned to immortalise the scene on canvas, thought the whole thing was 'an Ossa of bad taste on the Pelion of shrieking colour'.

Colour shrieked just as loudly in the surrounding pavilions where the spectators waited for the show to begin. There were Indian princes in every conceivable combination of coloured silks and jewels. Mingling with them, 'so as to avoid questions of precedence which have excited bitterness and heartburnings in India from the remotest antiquity', were British governors and lieutenant-governors in uniform, each with his banner held over him. To the north, lines of troops were drawn up, their standards flying, their arms glittering in the sun. To the south, the princes' retainers stood with the elephants, who shuffled and trumpeted, their exotic trappings aflame with colour. Their masters, in the pavilions, were rather a curious collection. There was one wearing petticoats and an enormous yellow headdress. Another sported a creation of diamonds, with wings and a topknot. A third was clad in gilded armour.

When Prinsep had earlier visited the princes in their tents—he was supposed to paint the most important among them—he had found them even odder. 'One venerable gentleman . . . had a man grinding "God save the Queen" on a hand organ, when we entered his tent. [Another] had a band of bagpipes, and gave us "God bless the Prince of Wales", played by pipers as black as soot, but with pink leggings on their knees to make them like their Highland originals'.

On the great day, however, these unorthodox music-makers had been banished from the field. Today it was trumpeters and brass bands. The viceroy, wearing the long blue mantle of the Grand Master of the Order of the Star of India, took his seat on the throne. Major Barnes, the largest man in the army, was dressed in a herald's tabard for the ceremony of reading the proclamation. He pronounced the words loudly and clearly, but they came only in gusts to the more distant hearers—'Victoria Regina . . . imperial crown . . . letters patent . . . addition to the style and titles . . . INDIAE IMPERATRIX . . . EMPRESS OF INDIA'. Afterwards, the proclamation was read again in Urdu, then the trumpets sounded, the guns were fired, and the massed infantry sounded off a *feu de joie*. 'This was splendidly executed and with excellent effect, for it made the rajahs jump, and raised quite a stampede among the elephants, who "skedaddled" in all directions, and killed a few natives'.

Queen Victoria was now Empress of India, or in Urdu, Kaisar-i-Hind—the equivalent chosen because some scholarly advisor had pointed out that the emperors of Rome had been known as Kaisar-i-Roum. The imperial idea had come from Benjamin Disraeli, Earl of Beaconsfield, and when Lytton arrived in India he had reported (without foundation) that the suggestion had been received with enthusiasm. At Westminster, the idea met with criticism and even ridicule, but the queen herself favoured it.

Lytton saw the assumption of this grandiloquent title as an excuse for identifying the native princes with the imperial power. His poet's imagination turned them into feudal rulers, and to give the picture the correct mediaeval touch he sent a civilian— one Robert Taylor, who had an interest in heraldry—off round the country to invent for each prince an escutcheon, complete with supporters and a motto. To the jaundiced eye, it was more like providing the trimmings for a nineteenth-century Lancashire cotton magnate with a new peerage.

The banners on which the princes' new arms had been blazoned were of heavy Chinese satin. 'Their only fault, which I had not anticipated', Lytton reported to the new empress, 'is that the brass poles, which are elaborately worked, make them so heavy that it requires the united efforts of two stalwart High-landers to carry one of them; and, consequently, the native chiefs who have received them will, in future processions, be obliged, I anticipate, to hoist them on the backs of elephants'. The princes did no such thing. A later viceroy recorded that, since Lytton's time, 'they have reposed in the Durbar rooms or Treasuries, where I have sometimes come across them during my tours, dusty, faded and torn'. At the time, however, the princes were probably pleased with their new toys. The tone of their loyal addresses was certainly effulgent enough.

Proclamation day also brought amnesties for prisoners, which, according to the official history of the assemblage, ensued in 'a general falling-off in petty crimes and offences against discipline, which, to say the least, was unexpected and extraordinary'. Food and clothing were distributed to the poor, many of whom were in the midst of desperate famine. Loyal addresses poured in from all directions. 'O Mother, O Beloved, O residing in the Palace of London', said one, 'the descendants of the great Emperor of Delhi are burnt in the fire of your might. Surely today angels will sing your Majesty's glory in the heavenly regions'.

Anglo-India, however, was dissatisfied. There had been no

balls, and the ladies were furious after having brought 'trunks full of new dresses'. The only parties seemed to be full of Indians. People began to 'talk of the "Black Raj", where everything is sacrificed to the native'. The tents, too, were always so crowded. In one, the poles swayed in the most ominous manner. 'Had that weight of canvas fallen upon us and the lamps, we must have all been burnt alive. Then what promotion there would have been!' At the grand reception, the entrances to the viceregal tent were very small, 'and the lucky individual, English or Hindoo, who was nearest the door, was often shot into the presence by the pressure of the crowd behind in a way calculated to ruffle the most dignified comportment'. Young British officers at the reception make their dislikes apparent by exchanging loud remarks on the princes, and saying how much they would like to cut their ears off for the sake of their jewels—forgetting, or ignoring, the fact that quite a number of the princes understood English.

Even before the social events surrounding the proclamation, Lord Lytton had made himself unpopular. He had been responsible for causing a stir—as well as the expenditure of money—among the wives and daughters of the higher echelons of Anglo-Indian society. Previous viceroys had permitted a certain informality in feminine dress at the comparatively casual receptions known as 'drawing rooms'. Not so Lord Lytton. He had insisted that ladies who wished to attend state receptions at Government House must wear long trains, as was the custom at European courts. 'The innovation was generally condemned as costly, needless, and vexatious; but it pleased Lord Lytton to invest his office with all the ceremonial splendour that beseemed the vicegerent of so great a sovereign as the Empress of Hindustan'.

The commercial community—quick, as always, to respond to a slight and hate a viceroy—also found fault with the flamboyant poet. Poets, they granted, were all very well, and viceroys could not be avoided, but any interference with the divine right of a white skin was something else altogether. When Lytton heard of the thirty-rupee fine which was the only punishment imposed on the planter who had killed his coachman, he suspended the magistrate responsible, whose name was Leeds. One wit committed the event to verse:

An imperial assemblage

Robert Lord Lytton
Had little so sit on,
Being slender of body and limb,
Till he heard of the deeds,
Of the lenient Leeds,
And proceeded to sit upon him.

Lytton did not think the matter of much importance. To him, it was an administrative failure, 'a twopenny halfpenny case', as he wrote to the editor of *The Times*. But his official letter, criticising both the provincial government and the High Court which had refused to amend the sentence imposed by Leeds, was published, and the Anglo-Indian press was quick to take offence. There was much and bitter controversy over the affair.

But each controversy of Anglo-India was soon displaced by another, just as one viceroy was displaced by another. That was, perhaps, the trouble. They came for a few years, these great nobles, and what did they ever know of the country? 'He who is the axis of India, the centre round which the Empire rotates, is absolutely and necessarily withdrawn from all knowledge of India. He lisps no syllable of any Indian tongue; no race or caste, or mode of Indian life is known to him; all our delightful provinces of the sun that lie off the railway are to him an undiscovered country'. Not that it really mattered in the end. For, though India might revolve around the viceroy, the real world of the Anglo-Indians did not.

15 *The making of a memsahib*

While he was on leave, George Browne went to a tennis party at a Wiltshire rectory, where he met a girl named Helen. He had intended to go on from England to Switzerland before returning to Bengal but, instead, he got engaged to be married. It was arranged that Helen would follow him out to India, and they would be married in Calcutta.

Helen knew nothing about India except what was in the history books and what George himself, rather confusingly, had told her. She was a vicar's daughter and, in daydreams, fancied herself 'seated under a bread-fruit tree in her Indian garden, dressed in white muslin, teaching a circle of little "blacks" to read the Scriptures'. But there was little time for daydreams when she had to prepare her trousseau and all the other things she would need in India. She received a great deal of advice from ladies experienced in the ways of India, including the recommendation to take as little as possible with her. 'It is impossible to keep good dresses in India, the climate is simple *ruination* to them . . . Besides, the *durzies*, the native dressmakers, will copy *anything*, and do it *wonderfully* well, at about a fifth of the price one pays at home'. She was also advised to take as much as possible with her. 'I should say make a special point of having everything in reasonable abundance. The European shops ask frightful prices, the natives are always unsatisfactory'. She was warned, too, that India was at least two years behind Europe as far as fashion was concerned, and that unless she wished to offend people she should take care that her dresses were not too up-to-date.

The trouble was, as she was to discover later, that the advice came from people who had spent their Indian years in widely separated places, some in the dry north-west, others in the moist south. But on one thing all were agreed—Helen must wear flannel next to the skin. It helped to avoid chills which, according to the general consensus, were in India almost inevitably followed by fevers, diarrhoea, dysentery, and even cholera. As far as stockings were concerned, she was told that the open pattern 'commonly worn at Home in summer' was to be avoided at all costs, as it greatly facilitated 'the attacks of mosquitoes when on the plains, and of fleas when on the hills'. Muslin dresses were to be preferred to silk, as the latter were 'unendurable in hot weather, and even if worn are speedily soiled by excessive perspiration'. It all sounded not only uncomfortable but unromantic. At least the journey outwards was no longer quite the ordeal it had been even in the first years after the overland route had been opened up. M. de Lesseps had done what every British engineer had said could not be done, and had constructed a canal across the isthmus of Suez. Through the canal to India went the vessels of the P & O. Passengers went ashore at Gibraltar and Naples, and visited Pompeii under 'the guidance of a black-browed Neapolitan, representing Messrs Cook'. Port Said, with its gambling houses and brothels, was passed by. The canal proved dull but full of surprising smells, and the steamer then penetrated into the Red Sea where, at the height of the hot season, even strong men had been known to die in their berths of apoplexy brought on by the temperature. The P & O line, of course, did everything possible to relieve the heat with punkahs and ices and salt-water baths.

Arriving at her destination, which happened to be Calcutta, Helen found things much the same as her predecessors had done at the beginning of the Victorian era. The carriages were a little more modern. There were telegraph wires in the streets. Clothes, though a little out of date, were by no means antiquated. The church, in which the marriage of this new addition to Anglo-Indian society was to be celebrated, was a little unexpected, with its white stucco pillars, its cane chairs, and its punkahs, motionless now because of the cold weather.

Helen's honeymoon was to last for only five days, and was spent in a dak bungalow. She and George travelled by train, that great transformer of life—or of travelling life, at any rate—in the world of Anglo-India. There were now thousands of miles of track, and the traveller could go from Bombay to Calcutta or many other places in a state of reasonable comfort. Only if he travelled first class, of course, as the newlyweds did. George had once ventured into the second class, which proved to be no more than a large van with benches backed by a single wooden bar. There, at a temperature of 80°F, he had discovered that Indians did not make 'agreeable *compagnons de voyage* in close quarters. In the first place, they lubricate the body with oil, sometimes cocoanut, but often castor or margosa oil, the two latter kinds having a most foetid and, to a European, a most disgusting and nauseating smell'. They had other unseemly habits too, such as chewing betel, 'which causes a copious red expectoration, which is freely distributed on all sides, and dyes their teeth of every shade from crimson to jet black'. Worst of all was their habit of belching 'on all occasions, without the least attempt at restraint. Nothing is more surprising to an Englishman, accustomed to look on such an act as a gross breach of good manners; but the natives argue, that after a substantial meal, this is an appropriate method of venting their satisfaction—as it were by way of grace'. Fortunately, there was no chance of this kind of thing in the first class, which was deliberately made as expensive as possible simply to keep Indians out.

The dak bungalow had suffered no improvement through the decades. It remained as bare and inhospitable, and its menu varied not at all. Breakfast—*chota hazri*, or 'little breakfast', in Anglo-Indian jargon—consisted of 'tea in a chipped brown tea-pot, and big thick cups to drink it out of, one edged with blue and the other with green, and buttered toast upon a plate which did not match anything'. Beyond the desert of breakfast, there lay tiffin, and then dinner by lamplight. 'The courses consisted of variations upon an original leg of mutton which occurred at one of their earlier repasts, served upon large cracked plates with metal reservoirs of hot water under them, and embellished by tinned peas of a suspicious pallor'. There was also, inevitably, a fowl, which tasted to Mrs Browne like one of those 'indestructible picture books' printed on cloth. Sensible and experienced travellers normally carried with them what they chose to call a *pot au feu,* or 'pepper pot'. Helen came across this piece of advice in a compendium called the *Anglo-Indian's Vade Mecum,* which had been among her wedding presents. 'First get a medium sized iron pot, lined with enamel', she was advised. 'It ought to have a lid fastened by a hinge, and fitting tightly when closed. To prevent a tendency to burst when the pot is at the boil, there should be a little valve on the top of the lid, free to rise to the pressure of steam from below. So much for the pot; next for its contents. The evening before starting on a journey, put in a fowl, one or two pounds of mutton chops, some potatoes and onions—in fact any meat and any vegetables; add a due proportion of water, salt, pepper, and spices, and then allow all to boil slowly, or stew, for as long as is necessary. Now add a little Worcestershire or Harvey sauce, for piquancy, and the whole is ready. Take the pot with you, and on arriving at the halting station, heat it up again, and *set it on the table*. After dinner, let your servant kill and dress another fowl, add it, or some chops, steaks, a hare, jungle fowl, or anything else of the same kind that may be obtainable, a few hard-boiled eggs, vegetables, salt and pepper, and boil again; next day repeat the process *da capo*, and your pepper pot will last the whole journey, giving a savoury meal whenever required'. Helen was determined that there should be no such terrifying stews, or fowls, in the new Browne household.

But first they had to have a household. Before his marriage, George had lived in a *chummery*, a house divided among a number of bachelors who shared the cost of both house and food. There was no place for a wife there. The Brownes might have chosen to live in an hotel, but though some of these were good they were also expensive. The cheaper kind were usually owned by natives and were normally 'lacking in order, quiet, cleanliness and comfort—drawbacks which, though of comparatively slight moment to the passing traveller, are sufficiently serious to the permanent resident'. The Brownes might have taken a house with another couple, but Helen really wanted a house of her own, with a garden and a tennis court, and, if at all possible, a cocoa-nut palm. She also desired a verandah, with pillars. 'Pillars', it must be remarked, 'seemed so common an architectural incident in Calcutta that she thought they must be cheap'. George was more interested in drains, in which Calcutta remained deficient.

An empty Anglo-Indian house always had a melancholy air. If the previous tenants had been gone for only three weeks or

L   *149* so, still the garden ran wild, the walls had cracked, and there was a smell of desolation and decay. Some houses might have a 'luxuriant tangle of beaumontia and bougainvilleas, and trailing columbine' as well as a cocoanut palm and most other kinds of palm as well, but it usually turned out that many sahibs had died there—three in the last family alone, and of cholera.

At last the Brownes would find a house in a locality where a number of Europeans had already survived several years' residence. There might be room for a tennis court, and even for a formal garden. There would be palms, and a high wall sprouting with shrubs. Despite the pink outside walls and the light green interior, Helen might find that the house had some peculiarities. The rafters curved downwards, perhaps, and the floor sloped in several directions. 'Irregular holes appeared at intervals over the wall for the accommodation of punkah-ropes, each tenant having fancied a different seat outside for his punkah-wallah'. The bathrooms were at the rear of the house, 'arranged on the simple principle of upsetting the bathtub on the floor and letting the water run out of a hole in the wall inside the partition'. One of the rooms, which had once been lived in by Indians, had iron bars on the windows.

The task of furnishing a house in Calcutta could be gone about in one of several ways. The first, which was obviously only for the great, entailed going to a European cabinet-maker and ordering up the latest fashions of six months earlier. As well as being six months behind London, this cost six times as much as it would have done there. Alternatively, there were shops which stocked readymade English furniture, also rather expensive. On the whole, young people setting up house usually relied on auctions or the bazaar, 'where all things are of honourable antiquity'. There they would purchase 'pathetic three-legged memorials of old Calcutta, springless oval-backed sofas that once upheld the ponderous dignity of the East India Company' and similar items of Anglo-Indian history. These, with a few pieces of basketwork furniture, were almost enough. But no respectable household could do without one or two *almirahs*, vast cupboards designed to receive 'all your personal property, from a dressing-gown to a box of sardines'. It was not possible to live decently and respectably in India without an *almirah*. A few plated forks and some bazaar china completed the domestic appointments. There was no need for decorative extravagance. No-one respected an Anglo-Indian for it, and the monsoon and the servants soon tarnished its initial bloom. That kind of pretension was, in fact, frowned upon. The really acceptable index of wealth and status was 'the locality of your residence and the size of your compound'.

George brought two servants with him. The bearer, who had been with him for four years, looked after his clothes, rubbed him down every evening before dinner, and kept his money for him. Anglo-Indians very rarely carried money. Even the collecting plate in church was filled with notes of hand which had to be presented at the donors' houses in the following week. George's other servant was the butler who, in spite of having been dismissed every day for a week (during a particularly trying hot-weather season), had continued to turn up behind his master's chair each morning. When George went home to England, he had told the butler that he never wanted to see his face again. But 'it was the first one I saw when the ship reached the P & O jetty. And there was a smile on it. What could I do? And that very night he shot me in the shirtfront with a soda-water bottle'.

The household needed many more servants than these. In the domestic hierarchy, after the bearer and the butler came the cook. Choosing a cook demanded great care. It was by no means unknown for a cook to use his toes as a toast-rack, or his master's socks as a sauce-strainer. Without actually giving a man a trial, it was very difficult to arrive at an estimate of his worth. The reference system still flourished, and the battered written certificates were as misleading as ever, having been bought in the bazaar or inherited from a relative. It was useless to try and follow up a reference, even a genuine one, since the master or mistress who had written it was usually either dead or departed for Home.

George's bearer helpfully relieved Helen of the problem of finding servants by collecting a full complement. Doubtless he was 'in honoured receipt of at least half their first month's wages for securing their situations for them'. Among his finds was a scullion, whose function was to do everything he was told to do by the cook, the bearer, or the butler. Scullions were, on the whole, rather dubious characters—according, at least, to Mrs Flora Annie Steel, joint author of *The Complete Indian House-keeper and Cook*, which was to become Helen's domestic encyclo-paedia. 'In most houses', she said, 'the scullion is an unknown quantity, a gruesome ghoul of spurious cleanliness, bearing, as his badge of office, a greasy swab of rag tied to a bit of bamboo'. There were eight immutable laws of sculliondom:

'1 Plates are plates, and include cups and saucers, teapots, side-dishes, and milk jugs.
2 Spoons are spoons, and include knives, forks, toastracks, &c.
3 Water is water, so long as it is fluid.
4 Cloths are cloths, so long as they hold together. After that they are used as swabs.
5 The floor is a floor, and nature made it as a table.
6 Variety is pleasing; therefore always intersperse your stone-ware plates with china teacups.
7 At the same time, union is strength; so pile everything together, use one water and one cloth, and do not move from your station till everything is dried and spread carefully in the dust.
8 Only one side of a plate is used by the *sahib logue*; it is therefore purely unreasonable for them to cavil at the other side being dirty'.

Perhaps the most important but least considered servant was the sweeper. He did much more than sweep the floors. Indeed, he was the guardian of good health, for it was his task to empty the latrines and see that they were clean. He was always of the lowest caste, or of no caste at all, and was generally despised by the other servants. Less important was the water-carrier who, if in full-time employment, was responsible for bringing the water, seeing that it was boiled for use in the kitchen, and filling up the water pots in the bathroom. There was also a part-time servant who waged war on the family's clothes. If there was no well in the compound, this washerman took the bundle of clothes away for washing; he was not above washing them in water which had already been used for the clothes of smallpox or cholera victims. His laundry technique, though brutal, was ineffectual. 'Cold water, bad soap, and much beating on stones remove the dirt with less certainty than the buttons'. The only other indoor servant was Helen's maid, and the outdoor staff consisted of gardener and groom. The gardener's first duty was to produce flowers, and he managed this even when the household did not have a garden. It was said that a departing master once gave his gardener a reference which read: 'This [gardener] has been with me fifteen years. I have had no garden, I have never lacked flowers, and he has never had a conviction'. Like most legends of Anglo-India, this story was based on fact.

The new servants' references examined (and disbelieved), their wages established—and the cost of this small establishment seemed very large to Helen—the staff were put to their duties. An Anglo-Indian household on the traditional pattern had been established, and the time soon came for its first dinner party. What to serve?

There was plenty of advice available. Older Calcutta residents still served the turkey and ham that had featured on Calcutta menus for longer than anyone could remember. At the dinner tables of others, no less out of date, saddle of mutton and boiled fowl were invariably preceded by 'almond soup', which could include practically any ingredients as long as blanched almonds and buffalo milk were among them. The more progressive hostess might serve what the author of Helen's encyclopaedia tartly described as 'a badly cooked dinner in the style of a third class French restaurant'. Helen's other cookery book, hopefully subtitled *A Treatise on Reformed Cookery for Anglo-Indian Brides*, unfortunately turned out to have been designed for brides in Madras. It was full of recipes for what Helen's little experience of marketing told her must be a strictly local cuisine. One suggested menu for a 'little home dinner' included a dish of *Podolongcai au jus*, which proved to be something called 'snake vegetable' in a brown gravy!

The Brownes' dinner party produced no crisis in the kitchen, and the cook did not have hysterics. The table looked pleasant,

153

with flowers the gardener had produced (from some other garden). Protocol was carefully observed, and none of the ladies found herself preceded by her junior in the Anglo-Indian hierarchy. Fortunately, this presented no real problems, as a thoughtful government published everyone's post and pay and place in the order of precedence. At the end of the evening, according to custom, the gentlemen were sped on their way with cigars and whisky laid out on a table in the verandah.

All Anglo-Indian dinners were much the same, though hostesses higher up in the social scale would serve champagne, paté de foie gras, and exotic puddings.

The next excitement after Helen's dinner party was a Viceregal Drawing Room. The first problem to be surmounted concerned the kind of conveyance they should use to get themselves to Government House. The Brownes' only carriage was a *tum-tum,* which was the local name for a dog-cart. They decided they would have to use a hired carriage, or *ticca.* 'The ticca is an uncompromisingly shuttered wooden box with a door in each side and a seat across each end. Its springs are primitive, its angles severe. When no man has hired the ticca, the driver slumbers along the roof and the syce [groom] by the wayside. When the ticca is in action, the driver sits on the top, loosely connected with a bundle of hay which forms the casual, infrequent *déjeuner* of the horses. The syce stands behind, and if the back shutters are open he is frequently malodorous. There may be some worldly distinction between the syce and the driver, but it is imperceptible to the foreign eye'. A ticca would certainly indicate the Brownes' proper place among the lower reaches of Anglo-Indian society when it rattled up with the broughams, the landaus, and the victorias to Government House.

The ladies wore trains—Lord Lytton had seen to that—and there was a smell of camphor in the air which betrayed the fact that the dresses had recently been unpacked from their hot-weather boxes. Their Excellencies stood on a dais some little distance from the throne. Two stately lines of the Viceregal Bodyguard lined the approach, and ADCs moved swiftly around. On the viceregal right were the ladies of the Private Entrée. 'These ladies were the wives of gentlemen whose interests were the special care of Government. It was advisable, therefore, that their trains should not be stepped on, nor their tempers disarranged; and they had been received an hour earlier, with more circumstance, possibly to slower music, different portals being thrown open for the approach of their landaus—they all approached in landaus'. Helen's visiting card was passed from one ADC to another until it reached the Military Secretary, who read it out. Helen curtsied and passed on to join her husband who had been waiting outside the reception room. Everyone then retired to the ballroom, where they talked and bowed interminably until it was time to go home again in their broughams, landaus, victorias—and ticcas.

In the cold weather, Calcutta was almost pleasant, though some of the older men found it positively frigid and insisted on great fires. Most of the houses unfortunately, did not have fireplaces. When the hot weather came round, the viceregal caravan moved off to the rarefied heights of Simla. Families who were due for leave departed for Home on the steamers of the P & O, whose departures and passenger lists were chronicled in the newspapers. Everyone who could do so left for the hills. But some remained behind, and among these were the Brownes. Calcutta in the hot weather was like nothing Helen had ever known. The shops put up grass screens and employed coolies to keep the grass moist. The brain fever bird, so aptly named, kept up its incessant cry in the thickest parts of the trees— where no one could see it and shoot it. Cholera, a seasonal visitation, arrived at its appointed time. Life moved slowly. An early morning ride preceded a day's seclusion in bungalow or office, though time spent in the office was short since by noon no one was about and no one worked. From twelve until two it was best to lie down. Outside, 'the white sunlight lies upon the roads so palpable a heat that it might be peeled off: the bare, blinding walls, surcharged with heat, refuse to soak in more, and reject upon the air the fervour beating down upon them. In the dusty hollows of the roadside the pariah dogs lie sweltering in dry heat; beneath the trees sit the crows, their beaks agape; the buffaloes are wallowing in the shrunken mud-holes—but not a human being is abroad of his own will'. After the siesta came lunch, a little work, then a bathe and a breath of torrid air before dinner at eight and bed at half past ten.

The thermantidote, that unique invention of Anglo-India, helped to make the temperature a little more bearable. One Mr Johnson had become a particular benefactor by inventing an automatic watering device which at least reduced the number of servants needed. As well as being more effective than a punkah, the thermantidote had two great advantages. It was more difficult for its operator to fall asleep, and, since the machine usually filled a doorway, when the operator did doze off, the perspiring householder was discouraged from bursting out upon the offender to 'slay him on the spot, since to do this you must go round deliberately by another door'. Many people still hired punkah pullers in the hot weather, though contemporary opinion claimed that their only advantage was to keep off mosquitoes at meal times.

One of the milder ailments of the hot weather was prickly heat, 'a sort of rash which breaks out on you, and, as its name infers, prickly in its nature; I can only compare it to lying in a state of nudity on a horse-hair sofa, rather worn, and with the prickles of horse-hair very much exposed, and with other horse-hair sofas above you, and all round, tucking you in. Sitting on thorns would be agreeable by comparison, the infliction in that case being local; now, not a square inch of your body but is tingling and smarting with shooting pains, till you begin to imagine that in your youth you *must* have swallowed a packet of needles, which now oppressed by heat are endeavouring to make their escape from your interior, where they find themselves smothered in this hot weather'. There was no cure and very little alleviation. Mrs Steel recommended sandalwood dust, but without much enthusiasm; however, she added consolingly, 'those who suffer most from prickly heat are, as a rule, free from more serious ailments'.

The only surcease came with the rains, though they had a habit of being late, whatever the new meteorological devices might say. The garden became a jungle, almost overnight, flowers which had died in May put out shoots, and the grass could actually be *seen* growing. Less happily, the furniture began to perspire, mats to rot, the roof to leak, and cockroaches to appear in hordes. Boots and shoes grew a green mould overnight, and snakes had to be slaughtered on the verandahs.

The weather became a little cooler, however, and Anglo-Indian society revived, gave dinners, and even enjoyed the air at the Eden Gardens. There was a bandstand, of course. There could have been no promenade without it. There were also 'tall palms and red poinsettias, a fine winding artificial lake with a beautiful arched artificial bridge, realistic artificial rocks cropping out of the grass, and a genuine Burmese pagoda of white chunam, specially constructed for the gardens, in the middle of it all. The pagoda runs up into a spire, or a lightning conductor, or something of that nature; and on the top of this a frolicsome British tar once placed an empty soda-water bottle upside down . . . The native municipal commissioners regard this with some pride as a finial ornamant; certainly nobody has ever taken it down'. After the promenade the carriages would roll away to the echoes of 'God save the Queen'.

When next the cold weather came round, George had leave and there was enough money to go to the hills—not to Simla, 'which is heaven's outer portal, full of knights and angels', but to a place more suited to their means and their status. Going to the hills demanded a great deal of preparation. A house had to be rented. All of them had romantic names like Moss Grange and Ivy Glen, or Eagles' Nest and Sunny Bank, but were silent as to their exact location. The best thing to do was go and see for one's self. Helen's mentor, Mrs Steel, was firm on the question of location. She could not recommend a house on a ridge. 'Cholera (please do not start!) often dwells in the clouds . . . and may just rest on the ridge, to say nothing of its being enveloped in damp clouds, and at the mercy of the violence of the storm'. Mrs Steel also wrote feelingly about houses which had their back wall against the side of a hill, having herself 'had a providential escape from being buried alive in a landslip, by which, though life was saved, valuable property was lost'. Houses in valleys were too shut in and did not receive sufficient fresh air, and houses by the wayside lacked privacy.

Once a house had been chosen, whether by visit, recommenda-

157

tion, or chance, decisions had to be made on what to take. Hill houses were very sparsely furnished, and lamps, crockery and linen were the very least that had to be taken. As always, Helen found Mrs Steel invaluable. 'The following is a list showing the way in which the property of a family, consisting of a lady, three or four children, and an English nurse, might be packed and loaded:

1st camel load: Two large trunks and two smaller ones with clothing.

2nd camel load: One large trunk containing children's clothing, plate chest, three bags, and one bonnet-box.

3rd camel load: Three boxes of books, one box containing folding chairs, light tin box with clothing.

4th camel load: Four cases of stores, four cane chairs, saddle-stand, mackintosh sheets.

5th camel load: One chest of drawers, two iron cots, tea table, pans for washing up.

6th camel load: Second chest of drawers, screen, lamps, lanterns, hanging wardrobes.

7th camel load: Two boxes containing house linen, two casks containing ornaments, ice-pails, door mats.

8th camel load: Three casks of crockery, another cask containing ornaments, filter, pardah [purdah] bamboos, tennis poles.

9th camel load: Hot case, milk safe, baby's tub and stand, sewing-machine, fender and irons, water cans, pitchers.

10th camel load: Three boxes containing saddlery, kitchen utensils, carpets.

11th camel load: Two boxes containing drawing room sundries, servants' coats, iron bath, cheval glass, plate basket.

'Or the above articles could be loaded on four country carts, each with three or four bullocks for the up hill journey . . . A piano, where carts can be used, requires a cart to itself, and should be swung to avoid being injured by jolting. If the road is only a camel road, the piano must be carried by coolies, of whom fourteen or sixteen will be needed . . . When a march is made by stages, and one's own cows accompany, these latter should start, after being milked, the night before the family'.

Since the Brownes were childless, they were able to take rather less than Mrs Steel had felt bound to include in her list. They travelled by train for part of the way, and were soon in Dehra Doon, 'where all the hedges drop pink rose-petals, and the bulbul sings love songs in Persian, and the sahib lives in a little white house in a garden which is almost home'.

As far as the little white house was concerned, Mrs Steel had prepared them for it. The house *was* dirty. But 'do not be alarmed', said Mrs Steel drily. 'It is English people's dirt, not entirely natives' '. The older inhabitants of the town—and there were some who had retired there, instead of going Home to the colds and draughts of an England which had forgotten them, as they had forgotten it—said that little had changed, except the prices, for as long as they could remember. There were, of course, some new-fangled modes of travel. There was the jenny-rickshaw, for example, a kind of two-wheeled carriage (rather like a bath-chair with a hood) which was said to be the invention of an Englishman called Public-Spirited Smith. Some people gave the credit for inventing it to the Japanese, however, while others maintained that an American missionary named Goble had been responsible.

But to the Brownes, the pleasantest things about Dehra Doon were the cool night winds and the real fire which burned in the grate.

Though, on that first splendid visit to the hills, there were no Browne children, Helen's first baby arrived soon afterwards. A young mother had much the same problems in imperial India as she had done in the days when the Company ruled. A few wealthy households had English nurses, but for the majority there was no choice. It was an Indian nurse and, if necessary, an Indian wet-nurse—or no nurse at all. Some mothers, including missionary ladies, were horrified at the thought of a native wet-nurse. Mrs Steel was very stern with them on this subject. 'It must surely rouse surprise and regret', she exclaimed, 'that even those who profess to love the souls of men and women should find the bodies in which these souls are housed more repulsive than those of a cow or donkey or a goat'. Medically, there could be no rational objection to an Indian wet-nurse. 'What remains, therefore, but race prejudice to account for the fatuity of fearing lest the milk of a native woman should contaminate an English child's character, when that of the beasts which perish is held to have no such power?'

Nevertheless, a careful eye still had to be kept on the nurse and other servants. The opium pill was still a nurse's answer for a restless child, and an uninterested mother—of whom there were quite a few—would soon see her child in the local cemetery. More careful mothers were still inclined to fret over the moral problems involved when a child was brought up surrounded by Indian servants. They believed that a child would accept the standards of the heathen as his own. 'Let India's champions say what they will—it is still less easy to keep the eager, all-observant little minds fearlessly upright and untainted in an atmosphere of petty thefts and lies, such as natives look upon as mere common sense and good policy'. They worried about other dangers, too. 'The staple foods of childhood have far less nutritive value in India than in England, and the constant moving comes harder every year upon their sensitive nervous systems, to say nothing of the difficulty of obtaining pure and suitable food at Indian rest-houses and railway stations'.

Helen Browne, like other young mothers, knew that she would have to take her children to England before they reached the age of seven—this being the age after which, it was generally agreed, the *mores* of India would inescapably handicap them 'in the race of life'. The choice was between husband and children. 'Early or late the cruel wrench must come—the crueller, the longer deferred. One after one the babies grow into companionable children; one after one England claims them, till the mother's heart and house are left unto her desolate'.

If at all possible, it was best for a mother to go Home with her child, to see him settled with those who were to look after him. Where there was no family in England, it might be necessary to employ one of the professionals who specialised in looking after the children of exiles, though this solution was by no means to be recommended. It was unlikely that a husband would be able to accompany his wife on such a trip, and on board ship her talk would be all of 'the busy husband she had left, the station life, the attached servants, the favourite horse, the garden, and the bungalow. Her husband would soon follow her, in a year, or two years, and they would return together; but they would return to a silent home—the children would be left behind'. Returned to India, Helen would continue life as if nothing had changed. 'Heartlessness? Frivolity? In a few cases, possibly, but in most the sheer pluck of the race that has a prejudice in favour of making the best of things as they are, and never whimpering over the inevitable'.

Helen Browne has become a memsahib, 'graduated, qualified, sophisticated . . . She has lost her pretty colour—that always goes first, and has gained a shadowy ring under each eye—that always comes afterwards . . . Her world is the personal world of Anglo-India, and outside of it I believe she does not think at all. She is growing dull to India, too, which is about as sad a thing as any. She sees no more the supple savagery of the Pathan in the market-place, the bowed reverence of the Mussulman praying in the sunset, the early morning mists lifting among the domes and palms of the city. She has acquired for the Aryan inhabitant a certain strong irritation, and she believes him to be nasty in all his ways . . . She is a memsahib like another'.

16 *The day's work*

After the mutiny, a new generation of administrators arrived in India. They were known to the old hands as 'competition wallahs' for the sound reason that, instead of having been nominated by some interested party among the directorate of the East India Company, they had sat a competitive examination. This did not bring family traditions of service in India to an end; sons still followed their fathers—if they could pass the examination. But it introduced a new type of mind to the service, better in some ways, perhaps, more adequately educated, and a little more inclined to see more than one side of a question. The 'competition wallahs', however, were no less sure of their purpose in India or of their right to be there.

The examination itself was fairly stiff. The candidate was offered a wide range of subjects—mathematics, English, Greek, Latin, European languages, science, and others—from which he could choose to sit as many as he liked. Many young men went to a crammer, since it was rare to have the kind of mind possessed by William Hunter, who sat the examination in 1861. 'Whenever I read up a subject I become so interested in it that I go into the minutest points rather as if I intended to write a book than to stand a general examination. Never do I attack a subject without writing what would make a bulky pamphlet'.

A long and dusty hall in London's old Burlington House was the scene of the examination. Each of the 207 candidates had a little desk and chair upholstered in red leather. Around the depressing green walls hung stern portraits, which stared fixedly over the candidates' heads.

What kind of men were the young hopefuls? Some were the 'sons of clergymen who have staked a long and expensive education on the chance of success: younger sons of country gentlemen who have fallen into decay and just succeeded in giving their lads two or three years at Oxford, and then a 15-guinea-a-month cram with some private coach'. But there were also quite a few wealthy 'swells' who came up to town for the examination and stayed at such fashionable hotels as Morley's. Among them were men who had failed the previous year and were making a second and last attempt to succeed. The questions were altogether too hard for some of them, even at first sight. 'After eyeing their papers with a blank, dreary gaze, they slowly take out a cigar case, examine its contents, smell its Russian delicacy, extract a cigar, put on their hats and march out. "Cabby, drive to Morley's". And this is repeated twice daily; meanwhile they eat like prize fighters to support the waste of the body and of the mind'. Others would sit with the examination paper in front of them, 'looking suicidal for half an hour', then they too would disappear.

Young William Hunter, of course, did not leave until he had completed his papers to his satisfaction. He found the questions 'rational, well considered, and easily enough answered', as long as you had 'read extensively, and above all, thought carefully over what you have read'. Hunter himself had no intention of failing, for, as he wrote to his fiancée after he arrived in India, 'I aspire to a circle far above the circle of fashion. I mean the circle of Power'. Hunter was not a swell, but one of the new middle class on which India was soon to depend—and not only India, but the great expanding empire of the high Victorian age. When he set off for India, he left his fiancée a two-volume life of Edmund Burke and the gold chain of his watch, which he suggested she might use 'with a locket of my hair as a bracelet or a necklace'.

Hunter found Calcutta very pleasing, physically at least, but he was not much taken with the ways of Anglo-India. He did not approve of people who ate and drank too much and then blamed the effects on the climate. He also found that the social necessity of paying calls interrupted his work on learning languages. After putting in an appearance at Government House, he made the same comments as those who had gone before him, and those who were to go after, for there was very little change in the protocol of viceroys and their receptions. The mosquitoes were as energetic as ever, and the ladies as overwhelming. Hunter lamented to his future wife that, frequently, a woman 'takes away her husband's chance of greatness' by demanding, after

her day of idleness, that he 'amuse her by conversation or backgammon all evening', instead of permitting him to study. Duly
warned, his fiancée came out to India, where they were married
and posted to an up-country station.

Hunter looked about him and saw an India that made him
proud to be English. 'Here we Englishmen stand on the face of
the broad earth, a scanty pale-faced band in the midst of three
hundred millions of unfriendly vassals. On their side is a con-
genial climate and all the advantages which home and birthplace
can give; on ours long years of exile, a burning sun which dries
up the Saxon energies, home sickenings, thankless labour, disease
and often-times death far from wife, child, friend or kinsman'.
How had this all come about, he demanded rhetorically. 'How is
it that these pale-cheeked exiles give security to a race of another
hue, other tongues, other religions, which rulers of their own
people have ever failed to give?' The answer was evident. 'There
are unseen moral causes which I need not point out . . .'.

Not all the competition wallahs married as early in their careers
as Hunter, nor were they as articulate. As a man of ideas, an
intellectual, Hunter was in a minority. But all went through the
same procedures, and what they did with their experience was
up to them. Most of them were first sent out to the great time-
less countryside of India, the district. Changes might have taken
place in the face and character of the cities during Victoria's reign;
the appearance of Bombay and Madras might have been completely altered by great new buildings; and even Calcutta, least
altered of all, might have acquired a few of the appurtenances
of modern life. Under pressure from the Sanitary Commission,
drains—of a kind—had been introduced, and the possession of a
water closet became a symbol of rank and wealth. Tramways,
electric light and telephones might have added luxury to life.
But only in the cities. The countryside, except in a few places
close to the railway lines, remained essentially the same as it
had always been, and the competition wallah found himself at
one with his predecessors—alone, ignorant, and responsible.

The principle of pushing its employees in at the deep end in
the hope that they would soon learn to swim remained an integral
part of Indian Civil Service policy. A young man was sent

straight off into the district, given a few weeks to appreciate the difficulties, and then expected to deal with some of them. He would have to try cases which were apparently simple but, in fact, enmeshed in contradictions and dubious evidence. He would have to make a variety of inspections, of everything from ferries to police stations, and, most important of all, of the land records. With some such experience behind him—a year, perhaps, of decisions right and wrong—the civilian would move on to higher things, to similar responsibilities in a larger area with a greater need for action.

Work in the services was, however, becoming more specialised. Where there had been no fixed line between different types of appointment, one was soon to have to be drawn. Did the civilian wish to go into the political service? This might mean the North-west Frontier, or a native state. It could be interesting, boring, or even dangerous. It could also be a subject for satire. 'The Government of India keeps its Political Agents scattered over the native states in small jungle stations. It furnishes them with maharajas, nawabs, rajas, and chuprassies [orderlies], according to their rank, and it usually throws in a house, a gaol, a doctor, a volume of Aitchison's Treaties, an escort of native Cavalry, a Star of India, an assistant, the powers of a first-class magistrate, a flag-staff, six camels, three tents, and a salute of eleven or thirteen guns'.

In some states the political agent, or Resident, might have nothing more to do than pay an occasional ceremonial visit to the prince. He might occupy himself by trying to persuade the ruler to build a school, or a hospital, and he might even succeed —especially if a visit of inspection by the viceroy or, at the very least, by a governor might result.

In the larger states, however, a political agent's life could be hedged with real dangers. In the state of Baroda, the maharaja conspired to murder the Resident with, it was alleged, poison in a glass of fruit juice, and had to be deposed lest other princes were encouraged to follow his example.

For men who delighted in exotic display, there was nothing to beat a career as political agent. In the Rajputana, for example, one Resident found the 'whole feeling of the country . . .

M

mediaeval. The Rajput noblesse caracoles along with sword and shield, the small people crowd round with rags and rusty arms . . . I am afraid we do not altogether improve the nobles by keeping them from fighting'.

Failing the political service, a man might choose between the judicial and administrative branches. A judge's work in India was very different from that at Home. There were no juries in cases involving Indians. The judge would have the advice of native assessors, men of standing in the community, but he was not obliged to accept it. As a job, it was difficult but not un-rewarding, since promotion was comparatively quick in the judicial service. As time passed, the young civilian's life changed only in the degree of responsibility he bore. A description of life in the district in the 1860s could stand, with only minor changes, for the remainder of the queen's reign and beyond. 'Here is Tom, in his thirty-first year, in charge of a population as numerous as that of England in the reign of Elizabeth. His Burghley is a joint magistrate of eight-and-twenty, and his Walsingham an assistant magistrate who took his degree at Christ Church within the last fifteen months. These, with two or three superintendents of police, and last, but by no means least, a judge, who in rank and amount of salary stands to Tom in the position which the Lord Chancellor holds to the Prime Minister, are the only English officials in a province one hundred and twenty miles by seventy'. Tom is all-powerful in his district, or very nearly so. Above him there is a senior official, and beyond, the secretariat and the governor, but they are a very long way off.

Tom's day is full. In the hot weather, 'he rises at daybreak, and goes straight from his bed to the saddle. Then off he gallops across fields bright with dew to visit the scene of the late dacoit robbery; or to see with his own eyes whether the crops of the zemindar [landlord] who is so unpunctual with his assessment have really failed; or to watch with fond parental care the progress of his pet embankment'. After this, he might have a run with the hounds, as motley a collection as the indigo planters' packs. 'On their return, the whole party adjourn to the subscription swimming-bath, where they find their servants ready with clothes, razors, and brushes'. Afterwards, 'seated under a punkah in his verandah, he works through the contents of one despatch-box, or "bokkus", as the natives call it, after another; signing orders, and passing them on to the neighbouring collectors; dashing through drafts, to be filled up by his subordinates; writing reports, minutes, digests, letters of explanation, of remonstrance, of warning, of commendation'. Noon is the time for tiffin, then Tom goes down to the court house for a session of decisions on land and revenue. If there are few cases, time may permit a game or two of rackets before Tom sets out for a ride with his wife or billiards with the superintendent of police. By ten o'clock he has dined and gone to bed.

In the cold weather, like his predecessors before him, Tom travels about the further reaches of his district, enjoying the pleasures of camp life. After a morning of inspections, it is invigorating to bring down a bird or two for the pot, and pleasant, 'as you reach the rendezvous in the gloaming, rather tired and very dusty, to find your tents pitched, and your soup and curry within a few minutes of perfection, and your [servant] with a bottle of lemonade . . . and the head man of the village ready with his report of a deadly affray that would have taken place if you had come in a day later'.

During the latter part of the nineteenth century, the practice of detaching military officers for civil duties declined, but did not cease. In the 1860s, many young officers found themselves in charge of reorganising the police. One who did so ended up much wiser in the ways of persuading 'criminals' to confess. The police would fill the nose and ears of a suspect with cayenne pepper, or suspend him head downwards in a well. Women and children were merely hung up by their hair or their thumbs. Many of these practices, though not all, were swiftly stopped. Nor did bribery and extortion disappear when new men were appointed.

The usual serious crimes in an Indian district were murder and robbery. There was nothing straightforward about even a simple robbery. One young superintendent of police received a note from a senior British official complaining of a burglary and saying that his wife's jewels had been taken. When the superintendent arrived at the bungalow, the memsahib was in bed. Her

servant, however, told him that the jewels were kept, with some
silver spoons, in a box under the bed in which the master and
mistress slept. She herself slept in the bathroom leading off the
bedroom, in the company of two pet dogs. 'I thoroughly examined the premises, and set spies in the bazaar with curious results.
In the first place, I found that the dogs had not barked, but
passed a quiet night. It was true that the iron gauze outside
the pantry window had been cut away, but no marks of violence
or footsteps were visible outside, while in the bushes near, one
of the police discovered a stout pair of scissors freshly broken,
the points of which fitted into the marks on both box and
window. On searching the house of the chief goldsmith in the
bazaar the jewels were found in his strongbox: I pointed out
to him the serious position in which he was placed by this discovery, and he then stated that the jewels were sold to him
by the lady's ayah, who, in her turn, on being threatened with
the law, confessed that she had sold them by her lady's own
orders. The result was an unpleasant one to communicate to the
lady's husband'.

There could be danger for police officers as well as for Residents. Some of the areas were loosely administered and populated
by tribesmen. While one police officer was peacefully engaged
in playing his violin in his own tent, a bullet struck him, although
the assault was apparently not intended as a criticism of his
musical ability. His wound was in the thigh and bled badly, but
his escort managed to get him to a dugout canoe and away from
the scene of the attack. The wound soon healed—which the
victim ascribed 'to the simple abstinent life which I had led for
so many weeks previous to the accident. No bread, no beer, no
butter, no flesh save an occasional chicken, a dish of rice, and
sometimes fish, with constant exercise in the open air was
evidently uninflammatory diet'. Recovered, he went off and did
his best to kill himself in pursuit of the culprit. Yet he found
many of the people he had to deal with 'the simplest, the most
kindly folk'. They were 'truthful, and capable of strong attach-
ments; having also a great appreciation of straight and even-
handed justice. I found them ground down by ignorant,
narrow-minded chiefs; harassed by litigious, lying Bengali usurers

. . . They needed schools, they needed religious teaching, they needed simple, upright dealing, and protection for their lives, and their belongings. These needs I set myself to supply'.

Among the considerable difficulties which had to be overcome was the resistance of the more conservative elements among the tribal chiefs. One chief had even suborned the superintendent's subordinates and was able to read all his personal letters and reports. Carefully resealed, these were then returned to the police sergeant for delivery. The superintendent settled this matter by placing a large packet in the next postal bag, heavily and ostentatiously sealed, and marked 'urgent'. The bag was not given to the postal runner until a time which would make it impossible for him to reach the police post before sundown. It seemed likely that, when the package was taken to the chief, it would remain in his hut until the next morning. Journeying through the night, the superintendent himself arrived at the police post just before dawn. When the sergeant, who was himself a tribesman, was brought out and threatened with a loaded revolver, he admitted that the postbag was in the chief's possession. The small party, taking the sergeant with it, made its way to the village and surprised the chief with the letters open all about him. 'It was a strange scene, lit up by the first rays of the morning sun. The platform, with the astonished chief, surrounded by my five policemen with fixed bayonets, myself barelegged, with pointed revolver, clad in country home-spun, all wet and dripping, muddy and torn, after our night's travel and swim across the river. Below us a surging crowd of muttering villagers, among whom some spears began to show'. But opposition failed to develop when it was made clear that the chief would unhesitatingly be shot if any attempt was made to prevent his arrest.

Back at the police station, the superintendent transformed himself into magistrate and opened the trial. The defence was simple. It was not the chief who had opened the letters but his principal adviser. The chief's brother confirmed this. The adviser was immediately arrested and within quarter of an hour was on his way down river to jail. Then a deal was arranged. The police agreed to accept the adviser as scapegoat if, in, return, the chief would resign his authority to his brother 'and seek the rest and repose he so much needed in a religious life'. At the jail, the adviser was told of the arrangement and invited to confess all, which, in return for a guarantee of protection, he did. So the chain of evidence was complete, to be held in reserve for any sign of trouble from the new chief. The superintendent himself had to pay a price for thus establishing authority, with 'a bad attack of fever and ague, brought on by the fatigue of the night march, the cold swim across the river, with the subsequent excitement, which prevented my drying my wet clothes'. After twenty years' service, which included a full-scale military expedition against the tribesmen, the superintendent's rewards were ill health, the honorary rank of lieutenant-colonel, and a pension of £190 a year. But he also had the consolation that, twenty-five years after his going, his name was still widely known in the wild hills—severely mangled by the tribal language—and his exploits had taken on the lineaments of myth.

The wild places and the lonely places were still the main centres of Anglo-Indian work. Elsewhere there was a vast spectrum of activity, from the world of the European businessmen to that of the engineers who built the railways. The immense extent of railway construction attracted time-expired soldiers to work as gang foremen and in the other middle layers of authority. The railways also became the cynosure of the Eurasian population, already entrenched in the posts and telegraphs.

At the head of all—and believed by some not to do any work at all—was what one satirist called 'the Great Ornamental'. The viceroy and governor-general was by no means just ornamental, however, and well the satirist knew it, for in going on to describe the viceroy's office (that 'censorium of the empire'), he was compelled to admit that 'every pigeon-hole contains a potential revolution; every office-box cradles the embryo of a war or dearth'. Some viceroys' pigeon-holes were fuller than others. More than one viceroy suffered physically from his period of service, however short it might be in comparison with the tour of duty expected from ordinary men. One viceroy even died in India at the hand of an assassin; his memory was enshrined in a number of memorial halls. The opening of one of these, at

Allahabad, was distinguished by the presence of Lord Lytton, and an enormous crowd—enormous, that is, for Anglo-India—gathered for the occasion. An amateur chorus 'of all the best and the most cultivated gentlemen and lady singers of that part of India . . . accompanied by an admirably touched organ' sang an ode to Lord Mayo, the murdered viceroy, set to a tune from Rossini's *Moses in Egypt*:

> On thee, great Shade! we call—
> Unseen, though still at hand—
> To consecrate this Hall
> In Thine adopted land:
> Long may that honoured name
> Bestow its favouring fame,
> > Mayo!

> While Jumna's water pours
> Her tribute to the sea,
> Still may these votive towers
> Proclaim our love for thee;
> Thy noble life laid low
> By treason's felon blow,
> > Mayo!

> For thou wert of the few
> Who conquer Destiny;
> Brave, merciful and true,
> All that a chief should be.
> Hail to the mighty dead
> Whose life for us was sped,
> > Mayo!

Usually viceroys achieved the memorial hall but not the assassin. Some of them, however, did inspire homicidal thoughts among members of the civil service and the army. Such a one was Lord Curzon who, though not by temperament really a Victorian at all, was by an accident of history to preside over the obsequies of the queen's India. Curzon's day ran far into the night. He read state papers 'from 10 a.m. with the exception of an hour or two for meals, or a public function or a private drive, until 2 a.m. the following morning or sometimes later'.

He protested strongly at the way his subordinates worked, for he found the bureaucratic methods of the government of India positively ludicrous. 'Your despatch of August the 5th arrived', he wrote to the secretary of state for India in London in 1899. 'It goes to the Foreign Department. Thereupon clerk No. 1 paraphrases and comments upon it over 41 folio pages of print of his own composition, dealing solely with the Khyber suggestions in it. Then comes clerk No. 2 with 21 more pages upon clerk No. 1. Then we get to the region of Assistant Secretaries, Deputy Secretaries, and Secretaries. All these gentlemen state their worthless views at equal length. Finally we get to the top of the scale, and we find the Viceroy and the Military Member, with a proper regard for their dignity, expanding themselves over a proportionate space of print. Then these papers wander about from Department to Department, and amid the various Members of Council. Each has his say, and the result is a sort of literary Bedlam. I am grappling with this vile system in my own Department, but it has seated itself like the Old Man of the Sea upon the shoulders of the Indian Government, and every man accepts, while deploring, the burden'.

Curzon inquired into everything and interfered in everything, from the drains of Calcutta to the hushing up (by officials) of a case of rape in Rangoon. His inquisitions, his sarcastic style when giving a reprimand, alienated the services from him. But the machine went on. One day's work still followed the pattern of yesterday's work, and it seemed as if tomorrow's work would be much the same, too. Most of the men who operated the machine would have agreed with Curzon when he said at a banquet given in his honour in Bombay: 'If I thought it were all for nothing, and that you and I, Englishmen and Scotchmen and Irishmen in this country, were simply writing inscriptions on the sand to be washed out by the next tide; if I felt that we were not working here for the good of India in obedience to a higher law and a nobler aim, then I would see the link that holds England and India together severed without a sigh. But it is because I believe in the future of this country and the capacity of our own race to guide it to goals that it has never hitherto attained, that I keep courage and press forward'.

17 *Picnics and adultery*

A writer in the satirical journal *Vanity Fair* once summed up the world of Anglo-India as 'duty and red tape, picnics and adultery'. There was a general impression that Anglo-Indian society was immoral. Most of the criticism was aimed at the women. In the Victorian ethos, men had their pleasures—but women 'fell'. One moralist went so far as to suggest that Anglo-Indian women were not only frivolous, but that they did their utmost 'to divert the energies of the men from work . . . to pleasure and frivolity likewise'.

Men scarcely needed to be diverted. In the wild and lonely places, the sahib had his Indian mistress or patronised the better class of courtesan from the nearest town. If his tastes were more specialised, he found no difficulty in satisfying them. The bazaars knew all about the sahib's weaknesses, and there was no shortage of pimps. In the army, homosexual liaisons were comparatively easy to arrange, although they often led to blackmail and, not infrequently, to dismissal from the service. The heterosexual requirements of the common soldier were reasonably and hygienically catered for, by registering prostitutes at the military stations. Unfortunately, Her Majesty heard of this. The practice was stopped, and the natural consequence was that there was an appreciable increase in venereal infection.

There was a steady business in pornographic books and pictures, which only the better-off could afford, and in the larger towns could be found one or two well organised and furnished brothels offering a wide choice of European and Asian women. Calcutta had all the appurtenances of Europe, including a home for 'fallen' white women who had made their tragic journey down the scale from high-class establishments to the 'boarding houses' for visiting sailors. But the main reservoir of talent was, as always, among the amateurs. According to popular belief, most of the hardest-worked amateurs were to be found on the Olympus of Anglo-India, the viceregal hill station of Simla.

Simla changed very considerably after 1860. When Lord

173

Lawrence was appointed viceroy in 1864 his doctors made it a condition that he should spend the hot-weather months in the hills. The government in London agreed and, though other rulers of India had spent some time in Simla, it was because of Lawrence that it became irrevocably the summer seat of the imperial government. 'No doubt such a change as I propose is a serious one and requires much consideration', he wrote to the secretary of state in London. 'I do not, however, think that a better arrangement is to be made. The work now is, probably, treble, possibly quadruple, what it was twenty years ago, and it is for the most part of a very difficult nature. Neither could your Governor-General and his Council really do it in the hot weather in Calcutta. At the best, as you say, they would work at half speed . . . This place of all hill stations seems to me the best for the Supreme Government'. Lawrence did not particularly enjoy Simla once he got there. He was not much of a man for gaiety. Lady Lawrence, too, found it 'one long round of large dinner parties, balls, and festivities of all kinds'. Even though she attempted to introduce some more rational entertainment in the form of 'Shakespeare readings, and tableaux', it all remained very trying.

The house Lawrence occupied was, for some reason, called 'Peterhoff'. Lord Lytton with his poetical turn of phrase, later described it as 'a sort of pigsty'. Lady Dufferin, the wife of another viceroy, found it too much like a cottage, very suitable for private life but not for official life, as the rooms were very small. 'Altogether', she wrote in her diary, 'it is the funniest place'! At the back of the house you have about a yard to spare before you tumble down a precipice, and in front there is just room for one tennis court before you go over another'. The ADCs were billeted in various bungalows, equally precariously sited, and had to 'go through perilous adventures to come to dinner'. Earlier viceroys had put up with the disadvantages of the house because of the cost of building a new one, but Dufferin, feeling that imperial prestige (as well as the comfort of the queen's representative) was at stake, managed to persuade the home government that the expense was justified. Lady Dufferin, no doubt, had something to do with her husband's persuasiveness. When a ball was held at 'Peterhoff', the conservatory had to be converted into a sitting-room. The nights were cold, however, and the frequenters of the dark places behind the potted palms 'were unable to enjoy it as much as I had hoped'.

The new building was known, more appropriately, as Viceregal Lodge, and the Dufferins occupied it in July 1888. After 'Peterhoff'—in fact, by any standards—it was luxurious. There was even electric light, and Lady Dufferin found that 'the lighting up and putting out of the lamps is so simple that it is quite a pleasure to go round one's room touching a button here and there, and to experiment with various amounts of light'. The architectural style was reputed to be 'English Renaissance', but a later secretary of state described it as 'exactly like a Scotch hydro—the same sort of appearance, the same sort of architecture, the same sort of equipment of tennis lawns and sticky courts, and so forth'. Lady Dufferin was as impressed by the 'offices' as she was by the lighting system. She also found the laundry of interest, and wondered how the washermen would like it. 'What they are accustomed to is to squat on the brink of a cold stream, and there to flog and batter our wretched garments against the hard stones until they think them clean. Now they will be condemned to warm water and soap, to mangles and ironing and drying rooms, and they will probably think it all very unnecessary, and will perhaps faint with the heat'.

With so much more space at their disposal, viceroys could now expand their social activities. Very soon after its first occupation, Viceregal Lodge became the scene of 'brilliant' entertainments. These owed much to the organising ability of the viceroy's military secretary, who, from 1881 until 1894, was Lord William Beresford. But the men who made or broke viceregal receptions and dances were undoubtedly the aides-de-camp.

An ADC had 'four distinct aspects or phases—(1) the full summer sunshine and bloom of scarlet and gold for Queen's birthdays and high ceremonials; (2) the dark frock-coats and belts in which to canter behind his Lord in; (3) the evening tail-coat, turned down with light blue and adorned with the Imperial arms on gold buttons; (4) and, finally, the quiet disguises of private life'.

In his first phase, the ADC was so gorgeous that 'the splendour of vice-Imperialism seems to beat upon him most fiercely'. Frock-coated and belted, he seemed to eager young ladies the key to the delights of Viceregal Lodge. 'He passes into church or elsewhere behind his Lord, like an aërolite from some distant universe, trailing cloudy visions of that young lady's Paradise of bright lights and music, champagne, mayonnaise, and "just-one-more-turn", which is situated behind the flagstaff on the hill'. In his evening garb of 'tail-coat, with gold buttons, velvet cuffs, and light blue silk lining', he might have a certain weakness for flirtations in the verandah. But off duty and in plain clothes the ADC was quite 'of the earth'. He had even been known to 'lay the long odds at whist, and to qualify, very nearly, for a co-respondentship'.

Behind the mask of brilliant entertainments and romantic ADCs lay the real face of government. In spite of its butterfly reputation, Simla did house the administration of the empire, and that administration was not carried out from the ballroom and the supper table. Throughout the season, the whole decision-making apparatus of India was concentrated on this ridge of the Himalayas, cut off from the plains by fifty-eight miles of indifferent road. From the end of this road, at Kalka, a railway had been constructed in the 1880s to Ambala in the Punjab. The journey from Simla to Kalka was made in a carriage, a special one for people of importance, a hired tonga for everybody else. The tonga, a two-wheeled vehicle pulled by one horse, covered the journey in stages. If there were no landslips or other delays, the route could be covered in eight hours. On more than one occasion, the government of India was totally cut off from the India it governed when the road was blocked by fallen rocks and the telegraph lines brought down by torrential rain.

It was, all things considered, an odd place for the government to roost for nearly seven months of the year. In fact, Simla was very odd altogether. It straggled across several spurs of mountain about 7,000 feet above sea level. None of its roads was really wide enough for a carriage, so only the viceroy, the commander-in-chief, and the lieutenant-governor of the Punjab were allowed to use one. Most other people used the rickshaw or the horse. The architecture of the town was terrible. Lady Curzon, on her first visit, decided that 'the Public Works and other buildings have made it monstrous. All the public buildings are crosses between chalets and readymade iron houses, and their fluted roofs cover the hillsides'. There was something essentially un-Indian yet not-quite-British about it all, even though the Anglo-Indians had tried their best to cut the real India out of Simla and replace it with something that was more like Home. It had finished up a rather exotic Home. The scattered houses trembled on hilltops and clung precariously over deep valleys. They were usually one-storeyed bungalows built of wood and surrounded with flowers. Everywhere the roofs were covered with the ugliest building material ever invented—corrugated iron. The larger buildings ranged in style from railway Gothic of the most overpowering kind to publican's Tudor, and the army headquarters has been accurately described as looking as though ' a number of trams had been piled untidily on top of each other and bolted together with flying steel rods'. The whole town gave the impression of having been transported from Surrey in a badly packed parcel and accidentally dropped in Tibet.

The new arrival first saw Simla from the Mall. The tonga office was there, crowded with the jaded faces of those who were just arriving from the hot and weary plains, and with the fresh glowing faces of people about to leave Simla and return to duty. Just below the Mall was the famous Peliti's Grand Hotel, where the comfortable sitting room invited the visitor 'to read and dream in the great chairs, and the well-ordered café is of never-failing interest, for here in the groups of laughing, faultlessly dressed English men and women he finds the true Anglo-Indian'. Among them would be found most of the characters enshrined in Rudyard Kipling's *Plain Tales from the Hills*—which was not altogether approved of when it was published. People who were not staying in their own houses would live in one of the hotels, or, if they were unattached men, at the Club, a fine establishment with accommodation for about seventy members and all the fittings requisite to a club. There was a dining room, with portraits of the late commander-in-chief and other worthies, a band to supply music on Saturdays (which were guest nights),

177

and a pretty cottage-like annexe officially known as The Chalet but generally known as The Hen-House, in which members could entertain ladies.

Not everyone in Simla was a visitor. There were a number of people who had made it their permanent home when they retired from one of the services. Allan Octavian Hume was one resident who had been in the civil service; he had ended his official career as secretary of a government department. In Simla he lived in a house called Rothney Castle, on which he had lavished a great deal of money in the hopes, it was rumoured, that he might sell the house to the government of India as a residence for the viceroy, in place of the miserable 'Peterhoff'. He had added enormous reception rooms suitable for large dinner parties and balls, a superb conservatory, and an immense entrance hall festooned with a valuable collection of animal horns. He had brought out a European gardener to see to the grounds, and the results were so magnificent that many people were prepared to venture the difficult approach road in order to admire them. At one time, Hume had collected birds. 'Possessed of ample private means, he had in his employ an army of collectors, some of them Europeans working on liberal salaries even beyond the limits of India proper, while many private collectors, falling under the influence of Mr Hume's genius, gave him strenuous assistance in all parts of the Indian Empire'. But then Mr Hume discovered Theosophy. As one of the tenets of this new belief opposed the taking of life, Mr Hume sent off telegrams to the collectors instructing them to shoot no more birds. The collection, now very large, was offered to the British Museum, from which it was ultimately transferred to the Natural History Museum in South Kensington.

It was, perhaps, fitting that Theosophy should find powerful adherents in Simla. The town at least lay on the way to those mysterious Himalayan fastnesses, so vaguely defined, which housed the *mahatmas* who had revealed much arcane knowledge to the founder of the movement, Helena Petrovna Blavatsky. For some reason, very strong efforts were made to attract adherents in Simla, especially from among the ranks of high government officials. It was, in fact, rumoured that Madame Blavatsky was a Russian agent and that she had been kept under constant surveillance by the police since she arrived in India. Allan Octavian Hume was indifferent to these slanders, and Madame became a frequent guest at Rothney Castle. There she would receive communications from her 'guide', Kut Humi, in the form of letters written on palm leaves. One such letter, which floated down from the ceiling at nine o'clock on a July evening in 1879, was handed, by Madame herself, to a sceptic. 'I read it. Addressed to Madame, the purport of it was that she need not trouble herself with attempts to make proselytes of the incredulous. Enough that those who believed and practised should gain the higher plains of knowledge and power. What mattered it to them that the rest of human kind wallowed in ignorance. The adepts could smile at them in contempt from their superior height! The text of the letter might indeed have been that to preach to the ignorant would be to "cast pearls before swine". Reading through the letter it struck me that Kut Humi must have had considerable intercourse with America, as more than one of the phrases appeared to savour of the Yankee dialect'.

Madame Blavatsky could produce more than palm-leaf airmail. At the dinner table, with a carefully selected body of believers and potential believers, she could be prevailed upon to give an example of the power 'which the true Theosophist acquires by asceticism, faith and self-denial'. First she would protest, 'like a young lady asked for a song: "It is very trying to me; it exhausts much; no, no, I cannot, I cannot"; but further pressed, at last exclaimed, "Well then, I must, but it is hard, it is hard! Mrs Hume! (turning to her hostess) what is there that you would like? You shall say. Have you lost anything that you would find?"

'*Mrs Hume*—"Yes. A year or more ago I lost a brooch. Find that and it will be indeed wonderful".

'*Madame*—"It is hard but IT SHALL BE DONE!! Khitmatgar [butler]! Bring me one lantern!" The lantern brought, Madame rose, led the way through the opened doors leading to the garden; there halting, she pointed to a bush and commanded, "Dig there!!" A spade produced, earth was removed and lo! there was the brooch. The guests wonderstruck and, some of

179

them at least, convinced, returned to the table where a succinct account of the miracle was drawn up and signed by all present'.

On another occasion, Madame, finding that there were not enough cups at a picnic, discovered by her incredible powers of divination that another cup of exactly the same design had been buried under a bush.

These activities caused a considerable stir in certain sections of Simla society, a stir which even survived a number of exposures of Madame's conjuring tricks. Mr Hume himself had the best of both worlds by describing her as the most marvellous liar he had ever met, but excusing her on the grounds that her lies and her tricks were designed with the honest object of converting people to 'a higher faith'.

Eventually Madame Blavatsky disappeared from Simla and Mr Hume took up another hobby. This time it was more far-reaching. He founded the Indian National Congress, the organisation which was later to become the instrument of India's fight for freedom from the British.

Most Anglo-Indians regarded Hume's foundation of the Indian National Congress as just another of the eccentricities with which Simla abounded. Some of these were forgivable; others were not. It was virtually impossible, for example, to accept the propriety of Mr Charles de Russett becoming a *sadhu*, a holy man, especially as he had been educated in the best Christian tradition at Bishop Cotton's School in Simla itself. It was no good advertisement for that excellent establishment—intended for the education of children whose parents could not afford to send them to school in England—for one of its alumni to be seen about Jakko Hill, surrounded by monkeys, and clad only in a piece of yellow cloth. After spending a couple of years' novitiate with another *sadhu*, de Russett had wandered around Simla for a time wearing a leopard-skin headdress, but he soon retired into seclusion where, according to one man who met him in the 1890s, 'no doubt he commands the highest respect from the natives, and lives idle, happy, and contented, without any anxiety about the morrow!'

An eccentric of another kind was to be given a measure of immortality in the works of Rudyard Kipling. This was a dealer in curiosities who had arrived in Simla in 1871, after having apparently been an advisor to the raja of Dholpur. He called himself Jacob, though everyone doubted that this was his real name, and the doubts were fed by several conflicting stories which were circulated about his origins. His little shop was described by the novelist, Marion Crawford, in 1879: 'At first glance it appeared as if the walls and ceiling were lined with gold and precious stones; and in reality it was almost the truth. The apartment was small—for India at least—and every available space, nook and cranny, were filled with gold and jewelled ornaments, shining weapons, or uncouth but resplendent idols'. There were ghost daggers from Tibet, prayer wheels, gilt Buddhas rapt and serene, portable altars of fine red lacquer glistening with gold and pieces of coloured glass. There were Persian water jugs of elegant design, and incense burners heavily inlaid with turquoise and lapis lazuli. Great banners showing the terrible faces of the Budhist hells hung from the walls or cluttered the floors in rolls. Jewellery, raw turquoises from Tibet, rubies and zircons from Burma, finely veined jade from China, all awaited the sahibs and memsahibs, the native princes, and the rich merchants of the bazaar. But Mr Jacob seemed to give the impression that he did not care about selling his stock, especially to fools who would not appreciate its rarities. His prices were high, and needed the support of a good sales technique. Jacob received potential customers in a room where 'lamps of the octagonal Oriental shape hung from the ceiling, and fed by aromatic oils, shed their soothing light on all around. The floor was covered with a soft, rich pile, and low divans were heaped with cushions of deep-tinted silk and gold. On the floor in a corner . . . lay open two or three superbly illuminated Arabic manuscripts, and from a chafing dish of silver near by a thin thread of snow-white smoke sent up its faint perfume through the still air'.

Without much difficulty, Kipling converted this mysterious dealer into Lurgan Sahib, the trainer of secret agents in *Kim*. Jacob was believed in Simla to be either a Russian spy—they were very popular in late Victorian India—or a British secret agent. Certainly, he was a remarkable linguist, an adept conjuror and, it was generally agreed, a hypnotist of a high order. Simla felt very much duller when he left, after having been ruined by

N

the costs of a case he had successfully brought against the ruler of Hyderabad in 1891, for breach of an agreement whereby Jacob was to purchase 'the Imperial Diamond' for the prince for over 4,500,000 rupees (about £300,000 at the then rate of exchange).

Madame Blavatsky and her black (or grey) magic, the European *sadhu* practising yoga and other heathen arts, and the strange activities of Mr Jacob in his house of wonders—all these were supplemented, in native eyes, by the mysterious rites the sahibs carried out in their *jadoogur*, or magic house. In English —the Freemasons' Lodge.

Freemasonry was very solidly established in Anglo-India. There was a lodge in practically every station of consequence, and everywhere it was thought by the Indians to be a house of magic. In western India, it was often known as the *shaitankhana*, the house of the devil. In south India, the Tamil name meant 'cut-head temple', because it was believed that part of the rite of initiation including the cutting off and restoring of the initiate's head. In Simla, there had been a lodge since 1838, and towards the end of the century there were four. The only magic practised in public was the annual ball the masons gave to the viceroy, which was one of the most brilliant functions of the Simla season. Lady Dufferin noted in her diary for 10 September 1888 that it was 'very pretty entertainment'. When the viceregal party arrived at the Town Hall, they 'were met at the door by a number of gentlemen in aprons, sashes, white cloaks, and black cloaks, red tunics, stars, crosses, medallions, orders and emblems of all sorts and kinds. Some of them carried long silver sticks with a dove on the top of each, and these marched before us, and we went in procession down the room between lines formed by the rest of the brethren'. The party stayed until twelve, 'and then marched away in procession, the Masons singing a song and sending us off with three cheers'.

Yet Simla was a worldly rather than an other-worldly place. Even the church had a distinctly secular aura. Sunday, of course, was a day of demonstration at which obeisance was paid to the god who watched over Anglo-India. But the service was more of a ritual than anything else. The viceroy would appear in his carriage, to join the ladies in their great hats and their menfolk inside Christ Church for a short sermon by the archdeacon.

The archdeacon of Simla was supposed to occupy an eminence in the church hierarchy above even bishops of the plains. Transported to the plains, he himself remained a mere archdeacon (usually the archdeacon of Calcutta), but the viceregal atmosphere of Simla lent him a special air of authority. He was believed by some to be the guardian of public morality. 'A word, a kiss, some matrimonial charm dissolved—these electric disturbances of society must be averted. The Archdeacon is the lightning conductor; where he is, the leaven of naughtiness passes to the ground, and society is not shocked'. He was assumed to be a man of the world, and his relations with the ladies of Simla were regarded as 'more than avuncular and less than cousinly; they are tender without being romantic, and confiding without being burdensome. He has the private entrée at . . . breakfast; he sees loose and flowing robes that are only for esoteric disciples; he has the private entrée at five o'clock tea and hears plans for the evening campaign openly discussed. He is quite behind the scenes. He hears the earliest whispers of engagements and flirtations. He can give a stone to the Press Commissioner in the gossip handicap, and win in a canter. You cannot tell him anything he does not know already'. But even Archdeacon Baly, the original of this portrait, could hardly have known as much about the intrigues of Anglo-India as Horace Goad.

Horace Goad had the reputation of being the smartest police officer in north-west India. From 1877 until his retirement in 1895, there was little that did not reach his ears about what went on in Simla. No secret was safe from the servants in an Anglo-Indian household. When a clandestine meeting took place behind Jakko Hill, the rickshaw pullers only looked as if they were asleep. There was constant espionage, not necessarily with any hope of gain, but often merely for the sake of gossip. On the whole, it was innocent enough, although the native princes filled Simla with their agents during the season and kept the British under constant surveillance, hoping to discover some special knowledge which might later be used to their advantage. In due time, Horace Goad heard most of the scandal. He spoke a number of dialects with great fluency and, as Kipling said when he modelled a character on him, was supposed 'to have the gift of invisibility and executive control over many Devils'. Goad was also capable of disguising himself so well that he was thought to have occult powers. Indeed, native children were often silenced by the threat of being handed over to him. He committed suicide in Ambala in 1896, and no one was at all surprised that a government office in Simla should burn down the same evening. It was assumed to be Goad's funeral pyre, and ever afterwards it was insisted in the bazaar that his spirit had been seen in the flames.

What was there for Goad Sahib to know about Simla? Were the women really promiscuous? The divorce courts supply some evidence, but only in cases where people more intimately concerned than Horace Goad lighted on the truth. Newspapers in both India and Britain were full of criticisms of Simla. It was such a luxurious place that it was sometimes called 'the Capua of India'. Articles frequently appeared under such headlines as 'Revels on Olympus', but the detail was always rather thin and there was more innuendo than fact. One defender of Anglo-Indian virtue claimed that newspaper correspondents, forced to follow the imperial government up to its summer residence, found themselves short of copy and had to fill up space somehow. Government business, he suggested, was conducted with such discretion that there was seldom any hard news. 'Hence there is little for the newspaper correspondents to write about except the gaieties of the place; and so the balls and picnics, the croquet and badminton parties, the flirtations and rumoured engagements, are given an importance which they do not actually possess'. Besides, he argued, 'wherever youth and beauty meet, there will, no doubt, be a certain amount of flirtation, even though the youth may be rather shaky from long years of hard work in the hot plains of India . . . and though the beauty be often pallid and passé; but anything beyond that hardly exists at Simla at all, and has the scantiest opportunity for developing itself'. Furthermore, 'the young officers and civilians who go up to Simla for their leave are usually far-seeing young men who have an eye to good appointments, and, whatever their real character may be, are not likely to spoil their chances of success by attracting attention to themselves as very gay Lotharios'. But this kind of defence, however comprehensive, was never really accepted. Undeniably, though the majority of women in Simla were as chaste as any heroine of Victorian verse, quite a number were not.

There were many temptations of the kind which breed quickly on boredom. Though there was plenty to do in Simla as well as dance and picnic, though there were 'good works' in the charitable societies which proliferated as a kind of surrogate for Victorian India's guilts, and art exhibitions full of amateur renderings of 'Sunset over Jakko Hill', yet society was so luxurious and cosseted that charity and art could fill only a small part of the time. The rest was thick with pitfalls. Among the very worst were 'amateur theatricals and the military men on leave'. When both came together at the Dramatic Club there was plenty of material for scandal. Too much scandal and the military man on leave might find himself back with his regiment in the plains, while the lady's husband would arrive up at Simla for a few days to enquire into the truth of a deliberately indiscreet letter he had received from a well-wisher. Many husbands found nothing more than gossip and were able to return to the cholera and the heat with doubts at least temporarily assuaged. Their optimism might not, however, match that of a distinguished fellow civil servant, who celebrated his return to the plains in the following terms:

Farewell to Peliti, whose menus delicious,
    Have helped our digestion the long season through,
Farewell to the scandals so false and malicious,
    And all the more piquant, for not being true.
Au revoir to the ladies, farewell to them never,
    Who are most of them pretty, and all of them good,
Whose saintly example and gentle endeavour
    Would surely reform me, if anything could.

Nor might they gain much comfort from Lord Curzon's Olympian *fiat*, that Simla was no longer to be 'a holiday resort of an Epicurean Viceroy and a pampered government'. It was hardly the viceroy or the government of India that worried them.

18   *The last frontier*

Though the world of Anglo-India had a kind of sameness, an identity of background, beliefs and training, India itself did not. Bengal, the Punjab, Bombay and Madras had little in common except for those who ruled. But at least they were a part of India. Burma was not. Yet it was ruled from Calcutta, just as if it had been. Madras might remain 'the benighted province'—a district of strange names 'all *ungas* or *rungas* or *pillays* or *polliums*'— but at least it was possible to get there by train. Burma, un-doubtedly a part of Anglo-India, even if a part separate and unique, was not only on the other side of the Bay of Bengal but also a new province—the last frontier, in fact, of British India.

The British had actually swallowed Burma in three gulps. In 1826, after a war in which twenty-four times as many men died of disease as of wounds, the East India Company acquired the Burmese provinces of Assam, Arakan, and Tenasserim. For the next quarter of a century, relations between British India and Burma were either fragile or non-existent. They were inclined to founder on the rocks of Burmese royal protocol. Should the British representative at the Burmese court sit on a chair in the king's presence? Should he insist on wearing shoes inside the royal palace? Must he really bow towards the royal apartments as he passed? In the end, it was decided that he could not remain in the Burmese capital at all.

Preoccupied elsewhere—with the disastrous first war with Afghanistan and the face-saving conquests of the Sikh wars— the British ignored Burma as far as possible. But, confidence restored after the defeat of the Sikhs, in 1852 they chose to answer what were taken as deliberate insults to British subjects in Rangoon with war. The result was the annexation of Lower Burma, which deprived the Burmese of all access to the sea except by way of British territory.

A revolution in 1853 brought to the Burmese throne a king who was shrewd enough to recognise the necessity of keeping on reasonable, if not cordial, terms with the British. But after his death in 1878 a series of intrigues resulted in the accession of a weak ruler, Thibaw. The murder of most of the other potential candidates for the throne followed soon after. The British were prevented from taking action at the time by the demands of the second Afghan war, in which they were currently engaged, but as the years passed it became obvious that Upper Burma would not be allowed to remain sovereign for long. As chaos and anarchy grew in the kingdom, the French—new to the business of empire-building in Asia—began to intrigue at the court of Mandalay, and their activities threatened the British in their most sensitive spot, their domination of much of Burma's economic life. The French were anxious to obtain trade concessions from Thibaw, which would undoubtedly have damaged Britain's commercial interests. The climax came when Thibaw, believing the promises of French agents and urged on by French merchants and bankers, decided to put the squeeze on the major British trading organisation in his kingdom. This, the Bombay Burmah Trading Corporation, held the concession for extracting teak from the forests north of Toungoo, part of which were in Upper Burma. The corporation was accused of extracting more teak than it had paid for, of bribing Burmese officials, and of failing to pay Burmese foresters the amounts due to them. Without delay and without the formality of examining the evidence the corporation was found guilty of defrauding the king of the equivalent of £73,333 and the foresters of £33,333. The corporation was ordered to pay twice the first sum to the king, and the second to the foresters. In default, its timber and property would be seized. This decision was published in August 1885.

Arbitration was appealed for, and the appeal was rejected. Since the war department in Calcutta had had a plan ready for some years for the invasion of Upper Burma, the viceroy felt able to issue an ultimatum. This he did on 30 October. The expiry date was 10 November. It caught Thibaw unawares. In reply he refused to reopen the case, but conceded that a British envoy would be acceptable at Mandalay, 'as in former times'. This would not do for the viceroy. As a contemporary soldiers' song put it:

Thibaw, the Burma King,
Did a very foolish thing,
When he set his hostile forces in array;
For he little thought that we,
From far across the sea,
Could send our armies up to Mandalay.

On 14 November, British troops moved up the Irrawaddy river by steamer, and in nineteen days Thibaw was a prisoner in his own palace. The campaign cost the British twenty dead and a few wounded. In the following January, Upper Burma was annexed. In February, it became a province of the Indian empire.

The same month saw the viceroy, Lord Dufferin, and his wife boarding a river steamer at Prome, the end of the railway from Rangoon. Lady Dufferin found the steamer splendid. Her boudoir was full of smart furniture—'such plush tables, stuffed armchairs, gold-headed scent-bottles!' Unfortunately, it was also very chilly and the viceroy caught a cold which had to be treated with hot sal volatile, a mustard poultice, and a day in bed. This was a pity, as the vessel only travelled by night and there was much to see. The Irrawaddy river was very fine, and the scenery was interesting 'without being very striking . . . white sandy shores, rocky banks, fair-sized hills, and always plenty of trees'.

Soon a steamer hove into view bearing the victorious British commander, General Prendergast, and the last British Resident at the court of Burma. The viceroy was told that the source of all the trouble had been Queen Supayalat, whom the English officers called 'Selina Sophia' and the soldiers, with more felicitous inaccuracy, 'Soup-plate'.

When the viceregal yacht arrived at Mandalay, it appeared very dull compared with local examples of the shipbuilder's art. In particular, there was a 'wonderful old barge' made up of 'two boats joined together, with a seven-roofed pinnacle over the centre, two large gilt ornaments at the stern, and two great gold and silver gods at the prow'. At the landing place there were troops and sailors, gaily-dressed Burmese, and two thrones with embroidered peacocks on the backs and a white canopy, a symbol of royalty, above. A thirty-one gun salute was sounded, and

addresses were presented by the European inhabitants as well
as by some Burmese merchants, which gave the viceregal party
their first opportunity of hearing Burmese spoken! 'It is read in
a very sing-song manner, and with a very long drawl on an occasional word, which has a funny effect'.

The journey to the palace was made over a bed of roses, strewn
before the party by Burmese women. When the viceroy entered
the Hall of Audience, 'there were four men playing drums, and
I think it was one of the most comic things I ever saw. The
drums were hanging up and had white muslin petticoats round
them, and the men who played them danced about and made
grimaces, and threatened them with their fists as if they were
living things and as if they were having a good joke together'.
But these heathen frivolities were banished on the following
Sunday when a church service was held in the audience hall,
with the army chaplain standing in front of the throne, and the
soldiers assembled in lines between the great teak columns
decorated with gilding and flashing pieces of mirror.

Distressingly enough, there was by no means as much loot
as everyone had hoped. Thibaw's ladies had been 'much too
sharp for our soldiers, and managed to walk off with everything.
There is positively only one jewel, and that is French—it is a
necklace of small diamonds and rubies, and an ornament for the
hair in the shape of a peacock, to match; one very big, but bad
emerald, and three large good ones; that is absolutely all. There
are a number of Geneva watches, and some small French ornaments, but nothing even worth buying as souvenirs, for these
odds and ends are European things'. Nevertheless, the Indian
empire had been enlarged by a piece of territory larger than
Britain.

Lady Dufferin found Rangoon pleasanter than Mandalay. It
had been British for so long that it almost seemed like home—
or, at least, like Anglo-India. There was a great ball in a magnificent room which had forty large doors in its walls. But where
the ball shone was 'in its really scientific arrangements for
flirtation. There it was unsurpassed; and a General, whom I took
round the "dark places", kept saying: "Well, I have been forty
years in India, and I never saw anything like this!"' The gen-

eral's 'this' was a covered way made of latticework, which had been arranged in niches enclosed by plants and red and white curtains. Each niche was just big enough for two, and the lighting was suitably dim. 'I made a sort of state promenade down these alleys, giving a shock to each couple as I passed, and discovering the Military Secretary in the last one. I hear I also greatly discomposed a lofty official, who confided to a friend that he never would have gone there had he known Her Excellency would pass through'.

Rangoon had greatly benefited from British rule, for the bazaars were full of the products of Manchester. How pleasing it was for Lady Dufferin to see how well the Manchester manufacturers had studied their customers' tastes. 'I have some lovely cotton pocket-handkerchiefs, with a Burmese peacock spreading its tail over the whole centre, which are nevertheless produced by Lancashire looms'.

The viceroy and Lady Dufferin departed. The soldiers and the administrators remained. But the newly acquired territories, refusing the blessings of the queen's peace, dissolved very quickly into disorder. The Burmese army, after recovering from the shock of defeat, broke up into guerrilla groups and harassed large British forces for five years. Full pacification was not achieved for even longer. The administration of Burma called for the same qualities as the Punjab had demanded before the Mutiny—youth, quick thinking, and above all freedom from rules and regulations. Naturally enough, it attracted men who found the hand of government in India heavy and remote. Burma, like the Punjab in its early days, was ruled from the saddle. But it was ruled with surprisingly little anguish, without puritanism, without doubt, and almost entirely without that consciousness of the presence of God which had given the Punjab administration its special character. The reasons for this were not difficult to find. The Burmese were very different from Indians. They were gay by nature, and, though Burma was a poor country, everyone seemed to live with a sense of style and colour which was quite different from India. Burmese society, lacking the formalities of caste, was highly egalitarian. As Lady Dufferin learned from the British Chief Commissioner, 'Burmese women are great personages, and play a great part in their households. They choose their own husbands and divorce them when they like, retaining their own property and all that they have earned'. In Burma, in fact, women had more rights than their counterparts in Britain. Because education was controlled by Buddhist monks, there was a high level of literacy in the country, which also extended to women. For these reasons, and because few Englishwomen went out to Burma, there resulted a relationship between British and Burmese which was unknown between British and Indian.

Liaisons of some permanence between Englishmen and Indian women had been common in the eighteenth century. The custom had only decreased when there was a growing influx of Englishwomen into India. Though some Englishmen still married Indian women of the upper classes, most of the liaisons were of the type which produced the witticism: 'Necessity is the mother of invention and the father of the Eurasian'. In Burma this was not the case. The Englishman, lonely in the wilder parts of the country, often married a Burmese girl and set up house in a formal manner, without being in the least a subject of criticism to his fellows. A house would suddenly take on the feeling of home, and the servants would be kept in order. The table would be well stocked, and gay with flowers. An officer who had been in action against the guerrillas would find it a pleasant place to return to. Men discussed their problems with their wives, and learned more about the country than they would ever have done in lonely isolation.

There was, of course, some disapproval—among missionaries, and among those who ruled Burma from Rangoon. One of their fears was that there would be corruption, that a Burmese wife or housekeeper would accept money in exchange for influencing the sahib. Sometimes this did happen, but not very often. Occasionally, too, there was trouble. More than one young Englishman was murdered because, instead of making a decent arrangement with the unmarried daughter of a Burmese, he chose to pay his attentions to a Burman's wife. Under pressure from the moralists of Rangoon, the government of India forbade intimate relationships between the races. These instructions were commonly

191

ignored, however, even though some young men found themselves transferred to less happy posts as a result.

For the remainder of the queen's reign, Burma in many ways remained cut off from the tiny, stifling world of Anglo-India, a cheerful, violent arcady on the marches of the empire.

19 *The 'damned-nigger party'*

At the time of the indigo disturbances in the early 1860s, the division between the administrators and the non-official community was precise. Few of the civil servants sided with the planters and their friends, and the majority were vocally on the side of the peasant. For nearly twenty years afterwards, the tradition that the civil service was there to protect Indians remained. But as time passed and the older men were replaced by the competition wallahs, the tradition began to include a proviso —i.e. for 'Indian' should be read 'peasant'. By the 1880s, officials and non-officials alike were united in their dislike of 'educated' Indians. The dislike was soon to turn to hatred.

Did the British fear that westernised Indians might insist on taking advantage of the promises in the queen's proclamation, to the effect that no discrimination would be exercised against Indians in recruitment for the civil service? Did they think Indians might, perhaps, come to dominate the service? Certainly, everything was done to make it difficult for Indians to compete with Englishmen. Wilfred Scawen Blunt, a contemporary and not always well-informed critic, thought such attitudes were a matter of breeding. 'A young fellow, say the son of an Ulster farmer', he wrote, 'is pitchforked by a successful examination into high authority in Bengal. He has no traditions or breeding for the social position he is called to occupy, and is far more likely to hobnob with the commercial English of his district than to adapt himself to the ceremonial of politeness so necessary in Oriental intercourse'. Blunt was, perhaps, though a radical, also something of a snob.

It was certainly true, however, that a different type of Englishman was now to be found in many branches of the administration. This was the case, not so much in the civil service, which still attracted men of some quality and education, but in the newer branches such as the police. Having originally been filled by army officers, posts in the police were afterwards taken over by the kind of men portrayed by Trollope—'the amiable detrimental, the younger son, or the sporting public schoolboy, too lazy or too stupid for the Army, but prepared to go anywhere or do anything which did not involve prolonged drudgery'.

In time, even the civilians began to join an alliance of sentiment which, for the first time, united what had once been the two warring nations of Anglo-India. Together they formed what an ex-viceroy, Lord Northbrook, described in 1883 as the 'damned nigger party'.

The characteristic of a party member was an arrogant attitude to the natives. This was particularly displayed on the railways. Indians had found this new mode of travel much to their liking and the result was that, for the first time, English men and women found themselves in really close contact with a large number of Indians. Every critic of Anglo-India was able to bring back at least one tale about the arrogant, and sometimes brutal, behaviour of the English on trains. Most of these tales were true. Blunt himself recorded what had happened when he was being seen off at a station by some distinguished Indians, including a local princeling who had been honoured with the Order of the Star of India. An English traveller took exception to the Indians crowding the platform near his compartment and threatened them with a stick. When Blunt intervened, the traveller responded with 'indignation at my venturing to call him to account. It was his affair, not mine. Who was I that I should interpose myself between an Englishman and his natural right?' The railway officials refused to do anything, and it was only under pressure that the police finally made some protest to the Englishman, a respectable-looking, middle-aged doctor. On this occasion, formal complaints were lodged and, with the interference of the viceroy, an apology was finally extracted from the doctor, though it was not a very gracious one. However, as the viceroy's secretary put it: 'The mere fact of a European addressing a formal apology to a native gentleman is worth something'. Most victims received no apology, nor even any reply to their complaints, even in the not unusual event of their having been beaten and thrown out of compartments for which they had purchased tickets, when some European chose to join the train at a wayside station.

In hotels, native guests, whatever their rank or standing, were not permitted. This was usually a matter of business rather than of race prejudice on the part of the proprietors. They knew very well that English guests would either insist on any Indian in the hotel being removed, or would leave themselves. There might even have been violence. Was it not still possible to find notices displayed in public places, saying 'Gentlemen are earnestly requested not to strike the servants'?

The attitude to 'educated' natives was salted with an extra dislike. The Anglo-Indian image of the 'good' Indian was usually the image of a child, wayward, sometimes immoral, but in need only of a little fatherly correction to keep him on the right path. In response to this treatment, he was expected to be loyal and not to question the master's rights or decisions. The educated Indian, however, *did* question. To the European, this was not only intolerable, but manifestly against the law of nature. It took no heed of that 'cherished conviction which was shared by every Englishman in India, from the highest to the lowest, by the planter's assistant in his lowly bungalow and by the editor in the full light of the Presidency town—from those to the Chief Commissioner in charge of an important province and to the Viceroy on his throne—the conviction in every man that he belongs to a race whom God has destined to govern and subdue'. That being so, 'however well educated and clever a native may be, and however brave he may have proved himself, I believe that no rank which we can bestow upon him would cause him to be considered as an equal by the British officer'.

The trouble, from the Anglo-Indian's point of view, was that too many people in Britain were having liberal feelings about India. Members of Parliament travelled out to the country and took home ideas for reform. Of course, as every Anglo-Indian knew, they never understood anything about the real India—'Mr Cox, the member of parliament—perhaps you may remember him'. 'A little red-haired fellow, was he? who wrote a book about India on the back of his two-monthly return ticket?' Unfortunately, they were still inclined to be influential at Home. There was very little that the Anglo-Indian could do about this kind of tourist except laugh at him. The travelling MP usually arrived with a letter of introduction from the last place he had visited. 'He will immediately proceed to make himself quite at home in your bungalow with the easy manners of the Briton abroad'. Announcing his plans, 'he will ask you to take him, as a preliminary canter, to the gaol and lunatic asylum; and he will make many interesting suggestions to the civil surgeon as to the management of these institutions, comparing them unfavourably with those he has visited in other stations'. In the evening, when he 'ought to be bathing', he will write an article for some well-known journal like the *Nineteenth Century* with the title 'Is India worth keeping?'

This type of criticism formed a kind of private joke amongst Anglo-Indians, laughter amongst friends. But the serious side of the itinerant MP was not to be ignored. 'Mosquitoes are troublesome and cholera is disconcerting, but they are bearable beside the man who invariably knows the answers to his own questions before he asks them'. It was really too bad that 'this ridiculous old Shrovetide cock, whose ignorance and information leave two broad streaks of laughter in his wake, is turned loose upon the reading public! Upon my word, I believe the reading public would do better to go and sit at the feet of Baboo Sillabub Thunder Gosht, B.A.'— from whom he probably got all his misinformation in the first place.

It was in the latter part of the nineteenth century that the inoffensive word 'babu' began to take on an offensive connotation. Originally a term of respect, it had come to mean a native clerk who wrote English. But with the expansion of English education after the Mutiny it was applied to practically any educated Indian and, in particular, to the Bengali. 'The pliable, plastic, receptive Baboo of Bengal eagerly avails himself of this system [of English education] partly from a servile wish to please the *Sahib logue*, and partly from a desire to obtain a Government appointment'. What made a babu? 'When I was at Lhasa the Dalai Lama told me that a virtuous cow-hippopotamus by metempsychosis might, under unfavourable circumstances, become an undergraduate of Calcutta University, and that, when patent-leather shoes and English supervened, the thing was a Baboo'. The babu had become something to be laughed at, especially for his comic English. His misuse of the language of Shakespeare was a proof of the foolishness of his pretence to equal, or come anywhere near, a real Englishman. His references to 'Simpson and Delilah' and 'Mr Monty Cristo' were typical of the breed, and how well Mr Anstey had crystallised the babu in the character who, confronted with the decision whether to accept a duel or receive a kicking, wept 'to find himself between a deep sea and the devil of a kicking' then 'accepted the challenge, feeling like Imperial Caesar, when he found himself compelled to climb up a rubicon after having burnt his boots'.

All the laughter was not quite loud enough to drown the fear. State education seemed to be producing a kind of Frankenstein monster. Government schools merely inspired young Indians to try for better scholarships to better schools and then to better universities. All would expect government jobs. Would they be satisfied when they got them? 'What are you to do with this great clever class, forced up under a foreign system, without discipline, without contentment, and without a god?' It seemed all too possible that the time might soon come when the babus might 'wax fat with new religions, music, painting, Comedie Anglaise, scientific discoveries; they may kick with those developed legs of theirs, until we shall have to think that they are something more than a joke, more than a mere *lusus naturae,* more than a caricature moulded . . . in a moment of wanton playfulness'. What was now laughable, 'the patent-leather shoes, the silk umbrellas, the ten thousand horse-power English words and phrases, and the loose shadows of English thought', could turn to sedition, with another Mutiny, perhaps, as the consequence. Anglo-India felt that it was best not to give the babus a loophole through which they might penetrate into the structure of power. In any case, it was argued, they were totally unrepresentative of the real India, the India of the peasants. Babus, 'whom we have educated to write semi-seditious articles in the native Press', represented 'nothing but the social anomaly of their own position'.

The general attitude of dislike, reinforced by the prejudices of Englishwomen—who were the most vocal in their abuse of 'those horrid natives'—had by 1880 produced a sullen mood among

Anglo-Indians. Within three years a new viceroy, Lord Ripon, had succeeded in changing this into one of violence and hysteria. The issue was a comparatively minor one, a matter of criminal jurisdiction. Should Indian magistrates be permitted to try Europeans? In the principal cities, they had the right to do so, but everyone believed that if an Indian magistrate tried to act harshly against a European the attempt would soon be squashed. In the countryside, however, there were few Europeans and the pressure of Anglo-Indian opinion could hardly be expected to carry as much weight as in the cities. Because of this, Indian magistrates in the countryside had not been given the power to try Europeans. This was a clear case of racial distinction, and it was underlined by the fact that, when an Indian magistrate who had had overall powers in a city moved to a post in the countryside, he lost them. Lord Ripon, a Liberal, was offended by the situation. He had already antagonised Anglo-India by introducing reforms into local government so as to expand Indian participation. Now he decided to correct the legal anomaly. The result was the Ilbert Bill, named after the Law Member of the viceroy's council, Sir Courtenay Ilbert. The viceroy did not anticipate opposition to the bill, since most of the legal safeguards enjoyed by Europeans remained intact. The principle of *habeas corpus* was left unchanged; anyone charged with a capital offence was to be sent for trial to a High Court; and the right of appeal to a High Court against *any* conviction was confirmed. No one warned the viceroy that there might be trouble. Officials who were consulted on the matter, with one exception considered the bill as no more than an administrative measure and foresaw no difficulties. As officials, they themselves were of course unlikely to be faced with criminal prosecution, but it was surprising, in view of their now close contact with the non-official community, that they gave no hint of the possibility of an impassioned reaction from that source. A day or two after the bill was announced in February 1883, however, the Calcutta correspondent of the London *Times* reported that the government had 'suddenly sprung a mine on the European community'.

Anglo-Indians, who had not been consulted over what they chose to regard as a matter of great importance to their lives, believed that there was a government conspiracy to raise up the Indian at the expense of the European. It was merely an error that not even members of the Calcutta bar had been consulted, but Anglo-Indians did not care. The viceroy had already shown himself a traitor to British interests in India, and the Ilbert Bill was the last straw. The first to react were members of the bar, who met to organise opposition. An arrangement was arrived at with the influential newspaper, *The Englishman*. British businessmen who had interests in the countryside, in tea gardens and indigo plantations, immediately contributed support and money for a campaign against the bill. Letters were sent to Europeans resident outside Calcutta, and there was an immediate response from the planters who, more than anyone else, feared the coming of Indian magistrates who might try to put a stop to them 'beating their own niggers'. At meetings of planters, it was made quite clear that the first Indian magistrate who presumed to try a European would be summarily dealt with.

Support came in not only from planters, merchants and lawyers, but also from many officials who were disturbed at the Liberal trend of Ripon's policies. The lieutenant-governor of Bengal openly opposed the bill. The Chief Justice and ten British judges of the Calcutta court supported the agitation. Elsewhere there were suggestions for amendments. *The Englishman* printed inflammatory comments and, when a certain amount of natural irritation was shown by the native-owned press, declared: 'We are on the eve of a crisis which will try the power of the British Government in a way in which it has not been tried since the Mutiny of 1857'. It was surprising that Indians showed little more than irritation in the face of so much abuse, the general tenor of which was summed up in the opening lines of a letter signed 'Britannicus', which appeared at the height of the agitation. 'The only people who have any right to India are the British', it said. 'The SO-CALLED Indians have no right whatever'.

At a large protest meeting held in Calcutta Town Hall, angry speeches were made denouncing the bill. A leading lawyer warned his fellow-countrymen to beware of 'the wily natives who creep in where you cannot walk, because you cannot walk unless you walk upright'. The wily natives, he said, had the ear of the viceroy and had poisoned it with lies. He called upon his audience to swear by all that was sacred to them not to surrender their rights.

A Eurasian and Anglo-Indian Association was formed that night to fight the bill, and a memorial was sent to the viceroy. 'Natives of India', it maintained, were not 'the peers or equals of Englishmen', and the trial of an Englishman by someone who was not his peer was, without doubt, 'a trespass on the principle which . . . [was] the foundation of English constitutional law'.

The meeting was almost hysterical in its denunciation of the bill, but the deep feelings expressed were not totally irrational. Genuine fear did exist, and not only among those activated by spite and bloody-mindedness. Apparently progressive people— and there were some—also found the bill repugnant. Mrs Annette Beveridge, who had gone out to India at the invitation of Indians, to help Indian women, wrote in a letter to *The Englishman* that the bill would subject 'civilised women [she meant English-women] to the jurisdiction of men who have done little or nothing to redeem the women of their own races, and whose social ideas are still on the outer verge of civilisation'. Her concern was 'not pride of race . . . it is the pride of womanhood'. The general impression was created that, if women were brought before an Indian magistrate in the countryside, they would find themselves either in jail or in the magistrate's harem. 'Would you', wrote the editor of the *Friend of India*, in the hope of arousing sympathy in Britain, 'would you like to live in a country where at any moment your wife would be liable to be sentenced on a false charge, the magistrate being a copper-coloured Pagan?' The watchword became 'protect innocent womanhood', and a 'ladies' petition' was organised and sent to the viceroy in an attempt to appeal to his sense of English chivalry!

The opposition did not confine itself to memoranda and memorials. It organised itself for positive action. All the English press, with one exception, supported the agitation, and carried attacks not only on the viceroy but upon Indians in general. *The Englishman* was the most virulent of all, and was delighted to print such scurrilous material as the following advertisement:

WANTED Sweepers, Punkah Coolies, and Bhisties [water carriers] for the residents of Saidpur. None but educated Bengali Baboos who have passed the [university] Entrance Examination need apply. Ex-Deputy Magistrates (Bengali) preferred.

By the summer of 1883 opposition had spread. The English press was appealing to members of the volunteer forces to resign, and there was strong feeling among army officers. Three attempted rapes of Englishwomen by Indians were immediately associated with the bill, and European opinion was roused almost to madness. A Calcutta magistrate sentenced a washerman, whom he alleged had insulted his (the magistrate's) mistress, to six months' hard labour, and publicly boasted of his harshness. The suggestion was even made at a public meeting, and received seriously, that, as the government in London appeared indifferent to Anglo-Indian interests, India should secede from Britain. Unfortunately, the people of Britain were indifferent, too, though *The Times* was strongly on the side of the European community in India. The Anglo-Indian Association had employed an agent named Atkins to try to rouse the British working classes, but he did not have much success. He was received by the secretary of state, however, and wrote to India to say—quite without foundation—that the government disclaimed all responsibility for the bill. This only inspired the Anglo-Indian community to continue its agitation.

Throughout the hot weather, Ripon had been in the hills. When he returned to Calcutta in December 1883 he was booed in the streets. There was even a conspiracy to overpower the guards at Government House, kidnap the viceroy, and place him forcibly on board a ship for England. *The Englishman* welcomed Ripon's return by describing him as 'the Mammon of unrighteousness whose temple has been set up on the banks of the Hughli'. The viceroy's advisors were now strongly opposed to the bill. There were reports from the criminal intelligence department that many planters were planning to come to Calcutta for a monster demonstration and that there might be violence. As there were only seventy European police in Calcutta and to use Indian police would inflame the situation, there seemed no alternative to calling the army out. But to use European troops against Europeans would be unthinkable. Under such a combination of pressures, Ripon gave in. Negotiations were opened with the leaders of the Anglo-Indian community, and what was called a 'compromise' was arrived at. It was, in fact, nothing of the sort. The Anglo-Indians, a tiny minority in the mass of India, had defeated the viceroy. It was hardly an accident that in the last days of 1883, when the Europeans were celebrating their victory, the Indians of Calcutta were convening their first National Conference.

Ripon went home, and a viceroy with a proper sense of the fitness of the *status quo* arrived to replace him.

The 'damned nigger party' did not dissolve itself after this success. It retained its membership and gained more adherents as the nineteenth century drew to a close. The Europeans' contempt for the educated Indian, with his English-style organisations asking for English-style political reforms, set other Indians to searching for more positive forms of action. Appealing mainly to the religion of the masses, they tried with some success to incite them against the British. Violence, and the assassination of British officials, were the not infrequent result. On such occasions, the Anglo-Indian press became its old self again and advocated the most indiscriminate 'justice', on traditional Mutiny principles. Even without the stimulus of terrorism, justice remained partial. Indians did not even have the right of self-defence. On one occasion, when British soldiers attacked and wounded a village boy and were themselves threatened with retaliation by the villagers, the local European magistrate acquitted the soldiers, sentenced the villagers to long terms of imprisonment, and had the wounded boy whipped.

But Anglo-Indians did not really fear Indians. What the Anglo-Indian was frightened of was that a liberal-minded government in London might try to force the government of India to bring in reforms which would allow Indians to hold positions of authority. Reform, not revolution, menaced Anglo-India. When

Indians were cheeky, they could be slapped down. When they were violent, they could be shot. Until the end of the queen's reign, Anglo-Indians always comforted themselves with the thought that, as long as the government did not weaken, they were safe, for:

> Whatever happens, we have got
> The Maxim gun, which they have not.

20 *The great queen dies*

The news that the queen had died at Osborne on 22 January 1901 brought a feeling of loss to Anglo-Indians, as it did to millions of her subjects in other parts of her empire, regardless of race or colour. The queen and her empire had seemed so inextricably entwined that it was hard to believe they could be parted. Her presence, at once remote and comfortingly maternal, was represented by countless statues scattered over much of the world's surface, yet her association with India had seemed particularly intimate. Anglo-Indians, in their clubs, had to look around to assure themselves that the world had not come to an end.

It was more than a queen who had died. An era had passed away in that modest palace on the Isle of Wight, where two of the queen's Indian servants stood vigil over her body. It seemed only proper that Indians should perform this rite—for India had always held a special fascination for Victoria, just as she held a special place in the minds of a surprising number of the people of India. Their mourning, which had all the appearance of being genuine, was shown in many spontaneous gatherings on the night when news of her death became known.

Many speeches were made, and the funeral orations were full of the most impeccable sentiments. Lord Curzon, the viceroy, suggested that a vast memorial be erected to her name, inscribed 'in letters of gold upon marble or upon bronze, both in English and in the vernaculars, [with] the famous Proclamation of 1858, and such other messages as the Queen has, at various times, addressed to the Indian people'. Comparing the queen with one of the great Indian rulers of the past, he went on: 'The Emperor Asoka has spoken to posterity for 2,200 years through his inscriptions on rock and on stone. Why should not Queen Victoria do the same?'

A year later, when he unveiled a statue of the queen which would ultimately stand outside the memorial, Curzon summed up for himself and others what all believed the queen had meant to India. The British empire, he said, 'did not merely exist, or develop, or expand, by some hidden law of nature while she sat upon the throne. No, it breathed with her breath, and was instinct with her being. She was both the daughter and the mother of Empire, the daughter because her own life and character were profoundly affected by its evolution, the mother because she presided over the central hearth from which it sprang, and nursed and shaped its limbs for action. Every man who lived, or who died for the Empire, did it also and mainly for the Queen. If she knew nothing of his service, he was content; if she heard of it, he was flattered; if she rewarded it, he was overjoyed. So it came about that this single and simple girlish figure that gradually ripened, first into womanhood, then to maturity, and finally to a revered and venerable old age, will be known in history as one of the greatest empire-builders that the world has seen. For she laid the foundation-stones of her august dominion not only on the continents and oceans of the universe, but in the hearts of her devoted people; and in death as well as in life she continues her immortal reign'.

With these words ringing in its ears, and with its sense of assuredness still unimpaired, Anglo-India turned to face the as yet unrecognised challenge of the twentieth century.

A bouquet of flowers
from an Anglo-Indian garden of verse

Towards the end of 1886, in *Longman's Magazine*, the then arbiter of literary fashion in England, critic Andrew Lang, reviewed an anonymous collection of verses which had just been published under the title of *Departmental Ditties*. He remarked, somewhat condescendingly, that the book was 'a quaint and amusing example of the variety of literature known as Anglo-Indian verse . . . On the whole these are melancholy ditties. Jobs and posts and pensions, and the wives of their neighbours, appear to be much coveted by Her Majesty's Civil Servants in India'. The anonymous author was Rudyard Kipling, and his work was indeed in the Anglo-Indian tradition. But Kipling was a professional, whereas most Anglo-Indian poets were amateurs. Their subjects were sometimes martial—songs of war and heroism— but mostly they dealt with the problems and the humours of Anglo-India, and their verse was essentially parochial.

Bad verse—and most Anglo-Indian poetry barely reached the upper levels of mediocrity—is often revealing. The hates, the nostalgias, and (what was more surprising in an age of confidence) an almost pathological melancholy, were articulated by part-time poets whose full-time occupations included fighting wars and ruling subject peoples. The following selection from the vast mass of Anglo-Indian verse displays most of its conventions and, in particular, that unity of love and hate with which Anglo-Indians viewed a country which was, for some of them at least, both a land of exile and a land of regrets.

THE ARMY OF THE INDUS

[an ode composed at the beginning of the first Afghan war]

There have, as ancient poets tell, been mighty men ere now,
With lance in rest, and plate on breast, and iron helm on brow;
And many battles have been fought—great wars by land and sea—
In Greece and Rome and Portugal and France and Italy;
But the 'Army of the Indus', in the bright land of the Sun,
Will outshine all their lustre and eclipse them every one.

Old Homer tells of warlike men in that great siege of Troy,
Of Ajax and Achilles, and of Priam's darling boy . . .
I doubt not they were valiant men; but valiant men are we,
And of all the men that ever fought, Sir Harry Fane for me.

Old Rome was famed for deeds of arms and wondrous skill in war,
And seldom from her Eagle was sweet Victory afar . . .
But whatever were their heroes, and whatever they have done,
The 'Army of the Indus' shall eclipse them every one.

And in King Arthur's reign there was of Knights a fine array,
Sir Gawaine and Sir Percival—Sir Ector and Sir Kaye . . .
I doubt not they were gallant souls—great Knights of high degree,
But of all the Knights that e'er drew sword Sir Harry Fane for me.
&c &c

Anon. 1838
Quoted in the *Calcutta Review*
January–June 1849

THE FIELD OF FEROZSHAH

[First Sikh war. 1845]

Our wounded lay upon the ground,
  But little help was nigh;
No lint or bandage for the wound!
  They laid them down to die.
Their wounds unstaunch'd, with cold and thirst
Our heroes suffered then the worst
  Upon that fatal plain.
Many a man whose wounds were slight
Thro' the fell horrors of that night
  Will never fight again . . .

At length our gallant cavalry
  Scarce fifteen hundred men,
The flower of Britain's chivalry
  Prepare to charge again.
That gallant chieftain Colonel White,
  These heroes bravely led;
They sought the hottest of the fight,
  Their path was strewn with dead.
'Twas plainly marked for all to see
Where charged our British cavalry.

> By a young soldier [Sergeant Bingham]
> who fought in that glorious campaign
> (London 1848)

THE PLANTER'S DAUGHTER

On the banks of Ganges' water,
  When the wind blew fierce and hot,
Was the Planter's lovely daughter,
  Fairest of the lot:
For his bride a soldier sought her,
  But Pa and Ma said nay,
And the Planter's lovely daughter
  Might not disobey.

On the banks of Ganges' water,
  When the rainy season fell,
There I saw the Planter's daughter
  All call'd her the belle;
Now another lover sought her,
  A rich Civilian he;
On the banks of Ganges' water,
  None so sad as she.

On the banks of Ganges' water,
  When the pleasant winter came,
Still was seen the Planter's daughter,
  And her soldier flame;
But the Planter's lovely daughter
  From thoughts of him was free,
On the banks of Ganges' water,
  A Judge's bride was she.

'Regld. Fitz Fulke:
Indian Melodies—No. VI'
in *The Delhi Sketch Book*
April 1, 1852

TO MY DOCTOR

Give me but five months of Simla;
    Let me see it ere I die;
Fresher are its mountain breezes,
    Than this hateful burning sky.
Oh! my heart is sick and heavy,
    Agra gales are not for me;
Though the khuds be tempest riven,
    Place me there and set me free . . .

Pray, remove my indigestion,
    Liver pains and other ills;
Should you fail, I think you're bound to
    Sign my Papers for the Hills.
Like a Turkey in his coop, Sir,
    Must I hourly droop and pine;
Mourning o'er those *'cute Sangrados,*
    In the days of auld-lang-syne.

Mourning o'er the leave of absence
    Granted to the favour'd few;
Men who've just arriv'd from England,
    Men who never sickness knew.
Shedding tears of bitter anguish—
    Unavailing though they be—
O my fond, my cherish'd Doctor,
    Grant me leave on dear *M.C.* [medical certificate]

Anon. in *The Delhi Sketch Book*
July 1, 1852

MASSACRE AT CAWNPORE 1857

They ranged themselves to die, hand clasping hand—
That mournful brotherhood in death and woe—
While one with saddened voice, yet calm and slow,
Read holy words about yon better land,
Upon whose ever-blushing summer strand
Comes never shadow of a fiendish foe,
Nor hellish treachery like to that below
Is with malignant hatred coldly planned—
Then prayed. O Crucified, didst Thou not stoop
Down from above with Thy deep sympathy,
Soothing the suffering, bleeding, huddled group,
While the fierce vollies poured in hurriedly,
And with uplifted swords the yelling troop
Rushed to complete their deed of perfidy?

But all is over—the fierce agony
Of men who could not their beloveds save
From unheard tortures, and a common grave
Heaped high with quivering, crushed humanity—
The frantic woe of women forced to see
Their tiny infants, unto whom they clave
With love which could all fear and torment brave,
Dashed down upon the ground unpityingly:
And nought remains but the wet, bloody floor,
And little rings of soft, white baby-hair
Mingled with long, dark tresses, dimmed with gore,
In hopeless tangles scattered here and there,
And God's own blessed Book of holy lore,
Sole comforter amid that deep despair.

Mary E. Leslie
*Sorrows, Aspirations, and Legends from
India* (London 1858)

THE GRIFFIN'S LOVE SONG [and see opposite]

(Air: *'Come into the Garden, Maud'*)

Come into the pawnee, love,
  For the dark pagodas have flown,
Come into the pawnee love,
  I am here at the dhoby alone;
And the catamarans are wafted abroad,
  And the musk of the Tahsildar blown.

A beautiful petal has fallen
  From the spray of the purple peon;
The crystal mofussil is rippling
  In the smile of the jutka moon;
And the distant cheetahs are warbling
  A pensive cardamum tune.

Arise, O my tattie, my love!
  Awake, O my tiffin, my dear!
Come into the pawnee love,
  For thy faithful chuckrum is here.
The tappal sighs, 'She is late, she is late!'
  The banghy whispers, 'She's near!'

She is coming, my godown, my ghaut!
  She is coming, my dawk, my sweet!
My cutcherry leaps, and my tope
  In my bosom begins to beat—
O my love, my massoolah, my ghee,
  Thy poochie is at thy feet!

Anon.
The Chutney Lyrics (Madras 1871)

THE NEW ARRIVAL'S LOVE SONG [*translation*]

Come into the water, love,
   For the dark temples have flown,
Come into the water love,
   I am here at the washerman alone;
And the rafts are wafted abroad,
   And the musk of the tax-man blown.

A beautiful petal has fallen
   From the spray of the purple messenger;
The crystal ex-urbia is rippling
   In the smile of the taxi-cab moon;
And the distant cheetahs are warbling
   A pensive cardamom tune.

Arise, O my screen, my love!
   Awake, O my lunch, my dear!
Come into the water love,
   For thy faithful old coin is here.
The mail sighs, 'She is late, she is late!'
   The parcel post whispers, 'She's near!'

She is coming, my warehouse, my quay!
   She is coming, my letter post, my sweet!
My courthouse leaps, and my orchard
   In my bosom begins to beat—
O my love, my surf boat, my clarified butter,
   Thy joss-stick is at thy feet!

THE SONG OF DEATH

My fellow-exiles, fill your glasses,
  We'll sing one song before we die:
The tiger in the jungle-grasses
  Has sucked the peasant's life-blood dry:
Forth from his hole the cobra creeping
  Steals slow across the cottage floor
To where yon weary mother's sleeping—
  Methinks her babe will wake no more . . .

What doughty bands of fell diseases
  Come flying on the summer's breath!
See each its struggling victim seizes,
  And whirls him down the Dance of Death.
Through peopled towns the foul winds sighing,
  Where Cholera glides, that shape of dread,
Are filled with murmurs of the dying,
  Or voices weeping o'er the dead . . .

India, thy sun with fiery glances
  Has laid full many a Briton low;
Thy Juggernaut of Death advances,
  Girt with all spectral forms of woe.
Accept this earnest of our duty,
  Thy slaves, and not thy sons, are we;
Thou grave of England's strength and beauty,
  Hear how we sing to Death and thee!

W. Trego Webb
Indian Lyrics (Calcutta 1884)

THE SUCCESSFUL COMPETITOR

[Problems of being a Civilian]

Explain why this was entered, that omitted,
Why A was flogged, and B and C acquitted,
Note whence this shameful error of three pai,
And why Ram Chandra did not dot an 'i' . . .

'Tis not enough the solid hours to waste
Among conflicting precedents and paste;
'Tis not enough to watch the turning scale
And check each ser of gunny in the jail;
To penetrate the city's slums and sinks
Concocting bye-laws subtler than the stinks . . .

For the good Magistrate, our Rulers say,
Decides all night, investigates all day;
The crack Collector, man of equal might,
Reports all day, and corresponds all night.
Oh, could I raise my fascinated eyes
From salt, stamps, cesses, income-tax, excise,
Or quit the bench, and loose my courser's rein,
To scour observant o'er the teeming plain . . .
Then all were well; and I might touch the goal,
A square, round man, within a round square hole.

T. F. Bignold
*Leviora; or the Rhymes of a
Successful Competitor* (Calcutta
1888)

THE POLICE-WALLAH'S LITTLE DINNER

[*The guests*]
There's McCaul, the Collector, our biggest gun,
    A capital hand at whist,
And passable company, when he's done
    Prosing over 'the List'.

I'm sick to death of his grumbling, though,
    For ever about his luck;
And the story I rather think I know
    Of every pig he's stuck . . .

There's Tomkins, our Civil and Sessions Judge,
    A pompous ponderous Beak,
Who sneers at McCaul's decisions as fudge—
    We know it's professional pique . . .

There's little Sharp, the Surgeon, in charge
    Of the Central Suddur jail:
He's a habit of taking very large
    Potions of Bass's ale;

A good little fellow—a first-rate pill—
    Zealous beyond the ruck;
You couldn't consult a better, till
    Nine o' the night has struck . . .

There's the Padre, the Reverend Michael Whine,
    The sorrowfullest of men,
Who tells you he's crushed with his children nine,
    And what'll he do with ten?

A circle of worthy folk, indeed,
    Each of [them] in his sphere;
But it's heavyish work to have 'em to feed
    More than twice in the year . . .

First we had Mulligatawny soup,
    Which made us all perspire,
For the cook, that obstinate nincompoop,
    Had flavoured it hot as fire.

Next a tremendous fragmentary dish
    Of salmon was carried in—
The taste was rather of oil than fish,
    With a palpable touch of tin.

Then, when the salmon was swept away,
    We'd a duckey stew, with peas,
And the principal feature of that *entrée*
    Was its circumambient grease.

Then came the pride of my small farm-yard—
    A magnificent Michaelmas goose:
Heavens! his breast was a trifle hard;
    As for his leg, the deuce!

Last we'd a curry of ancient fowl:
    In terror a portion I took—
Hot?—I could scarce suppress a howl—
    Curse that fiend of a cook! . . .

Then there was sherry, and handing round
    Of ginger and other fruits;
Then, in a silence quite profound
    The lighting of big cheroots.

Then came cards, and soda-and-b.,
    On to the snowy board;
And four of us made a whist partie,
    And the little Doctor snored . . .

Then there was brandy-pawnee round,
    And the Parson ate some cake;
And the Doctor snored with a horrible sound,
    And choked himself awake.

Lastly we each the other bored
    With the usual district gup,
And then they departed. Oh, thank the Lord
    The party has broken up!

> 'Aliph Cheem' [Walter Yeldham]
> *Lays of Ind* (Calcutta 1875)

THE LAND OF REGRETS

. . . What lured him to life in the tropic?
    Did he venture for fame or for pelf?
Did he seek a career philanthropic?
    Or simply to better himself?
But whate'er the temptation that brought him,
    Whether piety, dulness, or debts,
He is thine for a price, thou hast bought him,
    O Land of Regrets! . . .

From the East came the breath of its odours
    And its heat melted soft in the haze,
While he dimly descried thy pagodas,
    O Cybele, ancient of days;
Heard the hum of thy mystic processions
    The echo of myriads who cry,
And the wail of their vain intercessions,
    Through the bare empty vault of the sky . . .

He was touched with the tales of our glory
    He was stirred by the clash and the jar
Of the nations who kill *con amore*
    The fury of races at war;
'Mid the crumbling of royalties rotting

Each cursed by a knave or a fool,
Where kings and fanatics are plotting
  He dreamt of a power and a rule;
Hath he come now, in season, to know thee;
  Hath he seen, what a stranger forgets,
All the graveyards of exiles below thee,
  O Land of Regrets?

Has he learned how thy honours are rated?
  Has he cast his accounts in thy school?
With the sweets of authority sated,
  Would he give up his throne to be cool,
Doth he curse Oriental romancing,
  And wish he had toiled all his day,
At the Bar, or the Banks, or financing,
  And got damned in a common-place way?

Thou has tracked him with duns and diseases,
  And he lies, as thy scorching winds blow,
Recollecting old England's sea breezes
  On his back in a lone bungalow;
At the slow coming darkness repining
  How he girds at the sun till it sets,
As he marks the long shadows declining
  O'er the Land of Regrets.

Let him cry, as thy blue devils seize him,
  O step-mother, careless as Fate,
He may strive from thy bonds to release him,
  Thou hast passed him his sentence—Too Late;
He has found what a blunder his youth is,
  His prime what a struggle, and yet
Has to learn of old age what the truth is
  In the Land of Regret.

                    Sir Alfred Lyall
                    Verses written in India (London 1889)

FOR ENGLAND HO!

The morning sun is shining o'er the harbour of Bombay,
And the gallant trooper *Crocodile* is getting under weigh;
Her snowy sides give shelter to a thousand men or so,
My regiment and another; and the word's 'For England Ho!'

We've worked our foreign service out, our full apportioned time;
Eleven lagging years we've spent in India's sunny clime—
Eleven years—a goodish hole to knock out of a life,
A change-effecting term on soil where cholera is rife.

Yes, change indeed! We left old England full six hundred strong;
And scarce three hundred faces to the ancient roll belong.
Three hundred comrades blotted out! The tribute that we pay
To death and sickness as the price of Oriental sway!

No part we've played in battle scenes, no glory have we won.
We've done our duty quietly, as nowadays 'tis done;
Ours certainly has been the uneventfullest of trades—
A round of drills, diversified with funeral parades . . .

Still, as I cheer I can't expel the sorrow from my mind,
I cannot drown the memory of those we leave behind.
I wave my cap to India, fast sinking in the blue,
But the shadows of my comrades seem to wave me their adieu.

Good-bye, my friends: although the bullet did not lay you low,
A thought, a tear upon your graves, at least your brothers owe;
Ye died for England, though ye died not 'mid the cannon's boom,
Nor any 'mention in despatches' glorified your tomb.

The breeze is fair, the sails are spread, the screw goes grinding
    round,
The hills beyond Bombay are dwindling to a little mound.
One last long look! Farewell, farewell, thou region of the sun!
Old England is before us, and our exile it is done!

'Aliph Cheem' [Walter Yeldham]
Lays of Ind (Calcutta 1875)

The World of Anglo-India

1. Calcutta was known as the 'city of palaces'. Its architecture, both public and private, was neo-classical in inspiration, a conscious reminder of the alien origins of British rule.

2. In the capital of British India there was little compromise with either the Indian climate or Indian architectural forms. But in the countryside, the houses of the rulers came to terms with both. The bungalow—the word comes from *bangla,* meaning 'from Bengal'—was a version of the common double-roofed house, its veranda dressed up with vaguely classical pillars. The church, however, had to have its steeple and classical portico.

3. For the indigo planter an elegant mansion in a park.

4. For his assistant, a simple building, crudely constructed and plainly furnished.

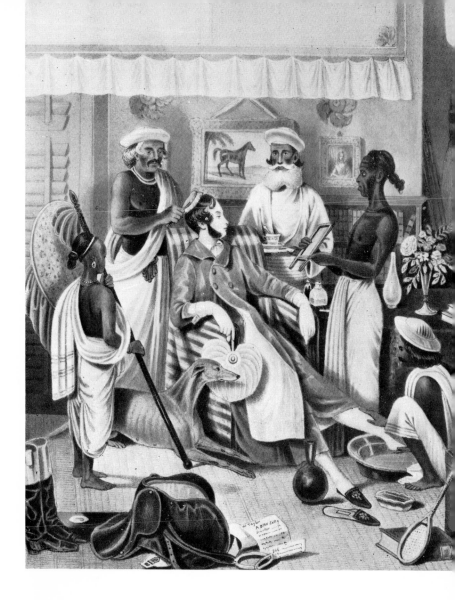

5. *Above.* An elegant young 'civilian' of the 1840s submits to being dressed and otherwise prepared by his personal servants to face the rigours of the day.

6. *Below*. At a small dinner party in the 1860s, a civilian and his wife entertain a naval and a military officer. Anglo-Indian society was by no means unsophisticated. The era of vulgar nabobs —the tough, and often rough, founders of the empire—was over by the time Queen Victoria came to the throne. Men and women of fashion did their best to live as well as, or even better than, their own class did at home. In the eighteenth century, dinner had been eaten at the hottest time of day, a gargantuan feast after which most of the guests were carried away, dead drunk, by their servants. By the 1830s, dinner was usually taken in the evening. By the middle of the century, a wide variety of imported canned goods had brought great changes into the Anglo-Indian diet, and a society which had grown both consciously refined and demonstrably puritan now disapproved of open drunkenness.

7. A viceregal dinner party was more formal and luxurious than one in a private house, though the standard of cooking was not necessarily better. Some of the viceroys brought their own European chefs with them, but even their creations suffered from the fact that, in Calcutta, the kitchens were housed in a separate building three hundred yards away across an open space from the dining room. The food was carried to the table in great iron boxes warmed by burning charcoal.

8. At the end of a year
in India, a young man
ceased to be a 'griffin',
or newcomer. The end of
griffinage was celebrated
at a party in the Mess or
the club. But by that time
(9) the griff was probably
inescapably in debt at
ruinous rates of interest
to native moneylenders.

10. Before the coming of industrial ice-making at the end of the nineteenth century, ice was a luxury. It was made in open pans during the cold weather and stored for warm-weather use. From 1833, ice was imported from North America, but it was only available at the port of arrival.

11. To supply a growing demand, native merchants set up shops dealing in goods imported from Europe. Simla bazaar c. 1900.

12. The foundation of Anglo-Indian life was a well-run household. Each servant had his task, with firm lines of demarcation. This picture shows the minimum staff for a modest establishment.

13. Cluttered
with furniture
and pattern, this
room might have
been in England
were it not for
the punkah
overhead.

No one, however, could have confused an Indian cook or the store-room of an Indian household with anywhere else. The cook shown opposite (14) was described as 'very cleanly'—a tribute to his mistress, for most cooks were not. It was always wise to keep strict control of the stores. The judge's wife above (15) supervised her kitchen with 'a detective's skill'.

The kitchen (*below*) was always at some distance from the house and very basically equipped (17). On the way to the dining room, food not only got cold but was open to attack from predatory birds (16).

As a sanctuary for the male, Anglo-India created the club and
(18) the coffee-shop. There, in the morning, the men of the station
would gather to drink coffee or tea and retail the scandal of the
day. There would be a billiard table for the energetic, and the
latest periodicals and newspapers from the provincial capital as
well as from 'Home'.

The amusements available to Anglo-Indians were even more limited than those enjoyed by their contemporaries in Britain. Sport played a great part in the lives of the men, and most stations were able to mount a hunt. The 'hounds' were a very mixed bunch of breeds and pedigrees, and were known as a 'bobbery' pack (19), Anglo-Indian jargon for 'an ill-matched lot'. Not surprisingly, they were very difficult to control, which added to the excitement of the chase, if not always to its success. Children had even larger areas of boredom than their parents, and had little to do but play with their servants and be taken for rides (20). In the evenings they would ride, sometimes in little carts, to join their parents at the bandstand (21) where the musicians of the regiment entertained the station with marches and waltzes until dusk and dinnertime.

Two aspects of the power structure of British India. At its head the viceroy—in this case, John Lawrence (1864–69)—and the members of the viceroy's executive council (22) who were responsible for such matters as finance and law. The council also contained two military men, the commander-in-chief and another senior officer whose duty was to be at the viceroy's side to offer advice while the C.-in-C. was in the field. The Indian Army retained its slightly exotic air until the very end of the empire. Here (23), General Sir John Hearsey wears the dramatic, flowing uniform of the 2nd Bengal Irregular Cavalry.

24. *Opposite above.*
Madras.

25. *Opposite below.*
Rangoon.

26. *Right.* Hazardous
surf at Madras.

27. *Below.* Calcutta.

The importance of the business community in the economic and
political life of British India was undeniable. The great ports were
its centres, and the business quarters were usually the most
Europeanised parts of the cities.

28. Official buildings in the principal cities were often of a peculiarly hybrid architecture. This, the Municipal Hall in Bombay, mixed Victorian Renaissance with oriental domes.

Some Indian Servants

Whatever the architectural style of his office, the civilian would usually ride or be driven to his work. His wife would then begin her day by consulting with the butler and the cook about the day's menus and the state of supplies, and would authorise expenditure. On the veranda, the *durzee,* or tailor, would be at work under the watchful eye of the *ayah,* or lady's maid. As the master departs (29), the dog-boy prepares to take his charges for their exercise. No Anglo-Indian household would have undermined the image of the English as a nation of animal-lovers by failing to have at least one dog.

A Punjab Court-Room

30. The civilian's place of work was not usually a fine building in one of the principal cities but a somewhat battered office or court-room, where the majesty of empire was supported on a creaking chair and the bar of justice was a ricketty table covered with a tattered cloth. In theory, the law was the same in both city and district, but in the latter it might often be tempered by the magistrate's intimacy with local conditions.

The planter occupied a very special place in Anglo-Indian society. His high standard of living was often a cause for envy: the caption to this illustration is 'A Farmer Prince' (31). But the members of the community were more crudely racialist than most Anglo-Indians. If they lived high, they also worked hard, supervising all activities from the morning muster of workers shown below (32) to the final processing of the crop, whether tea, coffee or indigo.

Before the construction of railways, travel over long distances was particularly trying. The government and private organisations ran a system of stage coaches. Illustrated here (33) is one of these coaches changing horses at a way-station along the Grand Trunk Road which ran from Calcutta to Delhi and beyond.

On the larger rivers, part of the journey could be made on a 'flat' drawn by a steamer (34). Some flats were uncovered, but others had cabins of varying standards of luxury.

If, by necessity or inclination, a man travelled alone, he might have to cross a river on a primitive raft (35), ride under a parasol on a camel (36), or be transported in a palanquin (37).

38. *Below.* A new cadet travels in state to join his regiment.

In the cold-weather season, it was the duty of the district official to tour the area he ruled, not only to see for himself the progress of such developments as irrigation works, but to bring justice to those who could not, or would not, make the journey to his headquarters. He would receive petitioners (39), like the widow whose husband has been carried off by a tiger and who begs the official to hunt it down and slaughter it.

Camp life on tour could be extremely comfortable. The civilian would often be accompanied by his wife and always by a large retinue of servants. Returning from a day's inspection in the 1870s, the Collector of Meerut found a chicken cooking on the spit and a bottle of oil laid out for the salad dressing (40).

Y^e Turn spitte

Y^e sallade oil

Usually the army and the civil service went about their separate tasks, meeting only in the social obligations of Anglo-India. In the Mutiny of 1857, however, they came together in action and in suffering.

Some of the sepoy regiments were disarmed before they could mutiny (41, *below*), but British troops still had to be brought in (42, *opposite*).

43. *Below*. Reinforcements marching to battle, with pack animals.

44. Brigadier-General John Nicholson, the 'Hero of Delhi'.

The rebels' capture of Delhi and its subsequent recapture by the British, after a long and bitter siege, were two of the most important events of the Mutiny. The psychological effect of the mutineers' occupation of the old imperial city of the Mughal emperors was enormous, for it seemed as if, by that single act, traditional India had risen against the British conquerors. When the British re-took it, many Indians who had wavered in their support of the rebels felt that their cause was on the wane. To the British, it meant that the initiative had been regained after a period of profound humiliation.

45. The imperial city of Delhi, from a music cover.

For the men, women and children besieged in the Residency at
Lucknow, news of the recapture of Delhi was an earnest that they
themselves would be saved. General Havelock's first relief of
Lucknow (46) came only five days after the fall of Delhi to the
British, but Havelock's force was too weak to break out again.
The comfort and hope he brought, however, enabled the besieged
to hold out for another two months until the release of men from
Delhi allowed Sir Colin Campbell to break through to Lucknow
and withdraw the defenders to safety.

47. One method of
execution used by the
British was to blow
mutineers from guns.

48. The ruins of the
Residency were
preserved as a shrine
where the Union Jack
always flew.

Along the main roads of British India, the government built and maintained travellers' rest-houses, known as *dak* bungalows. This one (49) was at Kishnagur in Lower Bengal.

Travellers' bungalows were infamous for their bad cooking and general indifference to the welfare of their guests. But Kishnagur had Peter (50), a Eurasian whose virtues were sung in prose and verse.

Travel for adults was ordeal enough, but when there was also a family to transport the difficulties multiplied. Still, the children, with their nurse and personal servants, could have a coach to themselves (51) with their baggage piled on top. The preparations necessary for a journey even in the 1870s were immense and detailed, as *dak* bungalows supplied even fewer comforts for children than they did for adults. Yet quite young children often travelled for very long distances with only servants to look after them.

The coming of the railways changed the whole nature of travel in India. The railways were swift and, generally speaking, comfortable—at least as long as the traveller was on the train. First-class carriages were fitted up in great luxury, but the facilities at wayside stations were often primitive. The architecture of small stations was simple (52, *opposite above*), but at the great termini such as Bombay (53) it could be palatial, if slightly peculiar.

54. *Above.* An Indian temple made a fine focus for a pleasure expedition, as well as for the background of a photograph, but Anglo-Indians were not really much interested in Indian art. It was not until 1898 that genuine attempts were made to preserve India's monuments.

Before 1858, the practice of taking to the hills in the hot weather was already established. As the railways spread, more and more Anglo-Indians rushed to the cool heights whenever possible. There were varying degrees of fashionableness. In the Himalayas, Mussoorie (55) attracted the middle levels of the Anglo-Indian hierarchy; in south India, Ootacamund drew the governor of Madras and his satellites to enjoy luxurious facilities which included a club-house that cost over £10,000 to build (56). But the viceroy's summer resort of Simla (57, *opposite below*) was an even more extravagantly equipped haven for the great.

According to a late Victorian satirist, hill stations were notorious for picnics and adultery. Adultery required some measure of privacy, but picnics were essentially gregarious—and, for the photographer, prim and formal (58). The cartoon, however, saw further than the lens (59). Even in arcady, there were often uninvited guests, the ubiquitous insects of the Indian countryside, to add an unromantic element.

For those who preferred exercise—the Englishman's prophylactic against pleasure, and evil thoughts—there was in the hills the opportunity for long walks (60), through grass that was almost like English grass, and in the company of a lady, even though she might prefer to ride.

India offered many opportunities for hunting. A tiger-hunt required little more than a well-equipped camp (61), a good rifle, and beaters. That characteristic Anglo-Indian sport, pig-sticking (62), needed a good pony and a strong wrist. But sometimes the hunted turned on the hunter (63, *above*), in this case the Prince of Wales, later King Edward VII.

The empire had its pomp and circumstance to impress the native princes and reassure the rulers. At Delhi in 1877, a great display was made (64) to announce the queen's assumption of the title of Empress of India. The viceroy, Lord Lytton (65), who loved drama, added style to the ceremony by wearing an ermine cloak and a gold-mounted topee.

66. Until medicine caught up with the diseases of India, death remained omnipresent—although most Victorians did not erect such grandiose tombs as their predecessors had done.

For the queen-empress herself there could be no tomb in India. But there was to be a monument. The Victoria Memorial Hall (67) in Calcutta has the queen's statue at its gate. Inside are collected the relics of her empire and of those who built it. Its architecture is suitably Eurasian and, through the morning mists, it gleams whitely—the sepulchre of an empire.

Notes on Sources

Page	Line	Source
1	TO HER MAJESTY'S EASTERN DOMINIONS	
1	11	Emily Eden *Up the Country*, ed. E. Thompson. Oxford 1937
2	10–27	J. H. Stocqueler *Handbook to India*. London 1844
2 to 3	28 1	G. Campbell *Modern India*. London 1852
3 to 5	9 10	Stocqueler, see p. 2 above
5	14	Anon. [J. W. Kaye] *Peregrine Pultuney, or Life in India*. London 1844
5 to 6	32 12	Stocqueler, see p. 2 above
6	18	Thomas Hood *I'm going to Bombay*
6 to 7	27 6	Stocqueler, see p. 2 above
7	13	Anon. [Fanny Parkes] *Wanderings of a Pilgrim in Search of the Picturesque*. London 1852
7 to 9	34 17	Stocqueler, see p. 2 above
9	19	L. von Orlich *Travels in India*. London 1845
2	THIS SPLENDID EMPIRE	
13	2	Richard Heber *Narrative of a Journey through the Upper Provinces of India*. London 1828
13	19	J. L. Morison *Lawrence of Lucknow*. London 1934
14	10	W. H. Sleeman *Rambles and Recollections of an Indian Official*, ed. V. Smith. London 1898
14 to 15	36 3	Victor Jacquemont *Letters from India*. London 1834
15	26	Morison, see p. 13 above
16	7	Sleeman, see p. 14 above
16 to 17	24 3	Lady Edwardes *Memorials of the Life and Letters of Major-General Sir Herbert B. Edwardes*. London 1886
17	27	Henry Lawrence *Essays*. London 1839
19	7	Mrs Postans *Western India in 1838*. London 1859
20	27	Heber, see p. 13 above
21	4	Emily Eden *Letters from India*. London 1872
21	21	J. W. Kaye *The Life and Correspondence of Charles Lord Metcalfe*. London 1854
21	28	*Private Letters of the Marquess of Dalhousie*, ed. J. G. A. Baird. Edinburgh 1911

Page	Line	Source

3   BOMBAY DUCKS

22	24	Mrs Postans, see p. 19 above
to 23	3	
23	5–13	Stocqueler, see p. 2 above
23	20	Mrs Postans, see p. 19 above
24	2–13	Anon. *Life in Bombay.* London 1852
24	15	Mrs Postans, see p. 19 above
to 25	18	
25	25–33	Viscountess Falkland *Chow-Chow.* London 1857
25	35	*Life in Bombay,* see p. 24 above
to 27	2	
27	7	Falkland, see p. 25 above
27	20	Stocqueler, see p. 2 above
to 28	17	
28	20	*Life in Bombay,* see p. 24 above
to 29	7	
29	18	Mrs Postans, see p. 19 above
29	35	*Life in Bombay,* see p. 24 above
to 30	1	
30	10–32	Stocqueler, see p. 2 above
30	35	Mrs Postans, see p. 19 above
to 31	4	
31	9	Stocqueler, see p. 2 above
31	37	*Life in Bombay,* see p. 24 above
to 32	1	
32	7	Falkland, see p. 25 above
32	11	*Life in Bombay,* see p. 24 above
32	16–35	Falkland, see p. 25 above
33	4–7	*Life in Bombay,* see p. 24 above
33	12–36	Falkland, see p. 25 above
34	21–34	Stocqueler, see p. 2 above
34	38	*Life in Bombay,* see p. 24 above

4   BENIGHTED PROVINCE

36	8	Stocqueler, see p. 2 above
36	20	J. C. Maitland *Letters from Madras by a Lady.* London 1843
36	27	Captain Bellew *Memoirs of a Griffin.* London 1843
36	32	Stocqueler, see p. 2 above
37	2–32	Bellew, see p. 36 above
37	36	Stocqueler, see p. 2 above
to 38	11	
38	17	Maitland, see p. 36 above
38	26	Bellew, see p. 36 above
38	32	Maitland, see p. 36 above
to 39	24	
39	27	Anon. *Indian Domestic Economy and Receipt Book.* Madras 1860
to 40	5	

Notes on Sources

Page	Line	Source
40	9–19	Maitland, see p. 36 above
40	32	Sir H. B. Edwardes and H. Merivale *Life of Sir Henry Lawrence*. London 1872
41	4–14	*Life in Bombay*, see p. 24 above
41	20	Maitland, see p. 36 above
to 44	27	

5 CITY OF PALACES

46	11	Bellew, see p. 36 above
46	21	Stocqueler, see p. 2 above
46	25	Bellew, see p. 36 above
47	2	Colesworthy Grant *Rural Life in Bengal*. London 1860
47	10	Bellew, see p. 36 above
48	12	W. H. Carey *The Good Old Days of the Honourable John Company*. Calcutta 1906
48	26	Bellew, see p. 36 above
49	3	Lord Roberts *Forty-one Years in India*. London 1898
49	22	W. H. Russell *My Indian Mutiny Diary*, ed. M. Edwardes. London 1957
50	7	Orlich, see p. 9 above
50	21–35	*Peregrine Pultuney*, see p. 5 above
51	2	Stocqueler, see p. 2 above
51	12	Sir George Campbell *Memoirs of my Indian Career*. London 1893
51 to 52	17 6	*Peregrine Pultuney*, see p. 5 above
52 to 53	10 9	Carey, see p. 48 above
53 to 54	13 19	Dalhousie, see p. 21 above
54	29	Eden, see p. 1 above
54 to 55	37 16	Orlich, see p. 9 above
56 to 57	1 36	*Peregrine Pultuney*, see p. 5 above
58	7	Stocqueler, see p. 2 above
58	16	Eden, see p. 1 above
58	30–36	W. Knighton *Tropical Sketches*. London 1855
59	1	Russell, see p. 49 above

6 UP THE COUNTRY

60	16	Russell, see p. 49 above
61	11–26	Stocqueler, see p. 2 above
61	29	Mrs Colin Mackenzie *Life in the Mission, the Camp, and the Zenana*. London 1854
62	2	Richard Burton *Goa and the Blue Mountains*. London 1857

Notes on Sources

Page	Line	Source
62	32	Roberts, see p. 49 above
to 63	1	
63	3	G. F. Atkinson *Curry and Rice (on Forty Plates)*. London 1859
63	20–26	Grant, see p. 47 above
64	9	Atkinson, see p. 63 above
66	14–38	'Punjabee' *Oakfield, or Fellowship in the East*. London 1853
67	10–23	Mackenzie, see p. 61 above
68	9	Atkinson, see p. 63 above
68	27	Stocqueler, see p. 2 above
69	19	Lady Edwardes, see p. 16 above
70	5	Maitland, see p. 36 above
70	14	Falkland, see p. 25 above
71	14	Atkinson, see p. 63 above
to 72	1	
72	6	Lady Edwardes, see p. 16 above
72	14–35	Atkinson, see p. 63 above
73	2	John Lang *Wanderings in India*. London 1859
74	5	Eden, see p. 1 above
74	18	Russell, see p. 49 above
74	25	Atkinson, see p. 63 above
75	19	Lang, see p. 73 above

7 NAVEL OF THE WORLD

Page	Line	Source
79	31	Eden, see p. 1 above
to 80	6	
82	6	Lang, see p. 73 above
82	36	Flora Annie Steel *On the Face of the Waters*. London 1897
to 83	18	
84	34	Dalhousie, see p. 21 above

8 UNTO THE HILLS

Page	Line	Source
86	9	*Life in Bombay*, see p. 24 above
86	16	Burton, see p. 62 above
87	4–13	Falkland, see p. 25 above
87	18	*Life in Bombay*, see p. 24 above
87	26	Falkland, see p. 25 above
to 88	13	
88	15	*Life in Bombay*, see p. 24 above
to 89	19	
89	24	Maitland, see p. 36 above
to 90	6	
90	9	Sir J. F. Price *History of Ootacamund*. Madras 1908
90	22	Burton, see p. 62 above
to 91	16	
91	29	Parkes, see p. 7 above
92	7	Eden, see p. 1 above

Notes on Sources

Page	Line	Source
93	12–22	Dalhousie, see p. 21 above
93	32	E. J. Buck *Simla Past and Present*. Calcutta 1904
94	1–26	Lang, see p. 73 above
95	1–12	Mackenzie, see p. 61 above
95	23	Lang, see p. 73 above

9 THE WILD AND LONELY PLACES

97	7	Lady Edwardes, see p. 16 above
to 100	8	
100	13–15	E. Thompson and G. T. Garratt *Rise and Fulfilment of British Rule in India*. London 1934
101	33	Morison, see p. 13 above
to 102	19	
102	25	Henry Beveridge *A Comprehensive History of India*. London n.d.
102	29	William Napier *The Conquest of Scinde*. London n.d.
102	32–36	William Napier *Life and Opinions of Sir Charles Napier*. London 1860
102	37	T. E. Colebrooke *Life of the Hon. Mountstuart*
to 103	1	*Elphinstone*. London 1884
103	12	Thompson and Garratt, see p. 100 above
105	17	*Narrative by Major-General John Campbell C.B. of his Operations in the Hill Tracts of Orissa for the Suppression of Human Sacrifice and Female Infanticide*. London 1861

10 AT THE EDGE OF THE ABYSS

108	38	Henry Lawrence to Lord Canning, 18 April 1857
to 109	3	
109	22	George Trevelyan *The Competition Wallah*. London 1895

11 UP AMONG THE PANDIES

112	1	Based on Hugh Gough *Old Memories*. Edinburgh
to 114	14	1897
115	33	Russell, see p. 49 above
to 116	3	
116	22	Anon. [Katherine Bartrum] *A Widow's Reminiscences*
to 123	36	*of Lucknow*. London 1858

12 BLOODY ASSIZE

124	15	J. W. Kaye *A History of the Sepoy War in India*.
to 125	5	London 1880
125	8–26	Michael Maclagan *Clemency Canning*. London 1962
125	36	R. Collier *The Sound of Fury*. London 1963
to 126	18	
126	26	Trevelyan, see p. 109 above
to 127	20	

Notes on Sources

Page	Line	Source
127	24	Colebrooke, see p. 102 above
128	6–14	Kaye, see p. 124 above
128	16	Dennis Kincaid *British Social Life in India.* London 1938
128	34	Trevelyan, see p. 109 above
129	3–11	M. Edwardes *The Necessary Hell.* London 1958
129	24	Anon. *Tom Cringle's Letters on Practical Subjects.* Bombay 1863
130	5–30	Russell, see p. 49 above
131	7–15	Lieutenant E. S. Ommanney to Chief Commissioner Delhi, 9 October 1858
131 to 132	23 8	G. B. Malleson *History of the Indian Mutiny.* London 1880

13 MIRROR OF INDIGO

134	22	S. Gopal *British Policy in India.* Cambridge 1965
135	9–36	Trevelyan, see p. 109 above
136	13	B. B. Misra *The Indian Middle Classes.* London 1961
136 to 139	25 26	Based upon W. M. Reid *The Culture and Manufacture of Indigo.* Calcutta 1887
139 to 140	33 3	Knighton, see p. 58 above
140	12–27	Reid, see p. 136 above

14 AN IMPERIAL ASSEMBLAGE

141	6–28	Val Prinsep *Imperial India.* London n.d.
141	32	J. Talboys Wheeler *The Imperial Assemblage at Delhi . . . 1877.* London n.d.
142	12–33	Prinsep, see p. 141 above
143	14	Lady Betty Balfour *The History of Lord Lytton's Indian Administration.* London 1899
143	22	Curzon of Kedleston *British Government in India.* London 1926
143	29	Wheeler, see p. 141 above
143	33	Balfour, see p. 143 above
144	1–12	Prinsep, see p. 141 above
144	26	L. J. Trotter *History of India under Queen Victoria.* London 1886
145	2	H. Keene *A Servant of John Company.* London 1897
145	18	G. R. Aberigh-Mackay *Twenty-One Days in India.* London 1910

15 THE MAKING OF A MEMSAHIB

146	10–27	S. J. Duncan *The Simple Adventures of a Memsahib.* London 1893
147	2–4	E. C. P. Hull *The European in India.* London 1871
147	14	Duncan, see p. 146 above
148	4–16	Hull, see p. 147 above

Notes on Sources

Page	Line	Source
148	23–31	Duncan, see p. 146 above
148 to 149	37 30	Hull, see p. 147 above
149 to 151	33 38	Duncan, see p. 146 above
152 to 153	6 5	Flora Annie Steel and G. Gardiner *The Complete Indian Housekeeper and Cook.* London 1888
153	10–12	Duncan, see p. 146 above
153	34	'Wyvern' *Culinary Jottings.* Madras 1891
154 to 155	17 6	Duncan, see p. 146 above
155	31	Phil Robinson *In my Indian Garden.* London 1884
156	12	Steel and Gardiner, see p. 152 above
156	18	Lieutenant Majendie *Up among the Pandies.* London 1859
156	31	Steel and Gardiner, see p. 152 above
157	7–16	Duncan, see p. 146 above
157 to 159	29 2	Steel and Gardiner, see p. 152 above
159	6	Duncan, see p. 146 above
159 to 160	10 7	Steel and Gardiner, see p. 152 above
160	15–33	M. Diver *The Englishwoman in India.* Edinburgh 1909
161	3–12	Aberigh-Mackay, see p. 145 above
161	13–24	Duncan, see p. 146 above

16 THE DAY'S WORK

Page	Line	Source
162 to 164	18 17	F. H. Skrine *Life of Sir W. W. Hunter.* London 1901
165	17–24	Aberigh-Mackay, see p. 145 above
165 to 166	38 4	Mortimer Durand *Life of Sir Alfred Comyn Lyall.* London 1906
166 to 167	15 21	Trevelyan, see p. 109 above
168 to 170	4 17	T. H. Lewin *A Fly on the Wheel, or How I Helped to Govern India.* London 1912
170	27–33	Aberigh-Mackay, see p. 145 above
171	3–28	Keene, see p. 145 above
171 to 172	35 38	M. Edwardes *High Noon of Empire: India under Curzon.* London 1965

17 PICNICS AND ADULTERY

Page	Line	Source
173	8	Diver, see p. 160 above
174	6–20	Buck, see p. 93 above
174 to 175	27 11	Lady Dufferin and Ava *Our Viceregal Life in India.* London 1899
175	13	Edwin Montagu *My Indian Diary.* London 1930

Notes on Sources

Page	Line	Source
175	19	Dufferin and Ava, see p. 174 above
175 to 176	32 14	Aberigh-Mackay, see p. 145 above
177	2–18	M. Edwardes, see p. 171 above
177	26–29	Kincaid, see p. 128 above
178 to 180	19 2	Buck, see p. 93 above
180	33	J. C. Oman *Mystics, Ascetics and Saints of India*. London 1894
181	5–31	F. Marion Crawford *Mr Isaacs: A Tale of Modern India*. London 1882
182	23	Dufferin and Ava, see p. 174 above
183	7–22	Aberigh-Mackay, see p. 145 above
184	1	Rudyard Kipling *Miss Youghal's Sais*, in *Plain Tales from the Hills*.
184 to 185	24 1	Buck, see p. 93 above
185	13	Diver, see p. 160 above
185	25	Lepel Griffin, in Buck, see p. 93 above
185	34	M. Edwardes, see p. 171 above

18 THE LAST FRONTIER

Page	Line	Source
186	7	Rudyard Kipling *William the Conqueror*, in *The Day's Work*
188	1	Contemporary soldiers' song, quoted in Sir Ian Hamilton *Listening for the Drums*. London 1946
188 to 191	15 3	Dufferin and Ava, see p. 174 above

19 THE 'DAMNED-NIGGER PARTY'

Page	Line	Source
193	20	W. S. Blunt *India under Ripon*. London 1909
193 to 194	34 3	J. C. Curry *The Indian Police*. London 1933
194	23	Blunt, see p. 193 above
195	7	Thompson and Garratt, see p. 100 above
195	17–35	Flora Annie Steel *The Hosts of the Lord*. London 1900
196	2–11	Aberigh-Mackay, see p. 145 above
196	14–17	Flora Annie Steel *For the Faith*, in *The Flower of Forgiveness*. London 1894
196	17–22	Aberigh-Mackay, see p. 145 above
196	28–33	*Fraser's Magazine*, August 1873
196	33–38	Aberigh-Mackay, see p. 145 above
197	7–10	'F. Anstey' *A Bayard from Bengal*. London 1900
197	16–18	W. W. Hunter *The Old Missionary*. London 1889
197	20–25	Aberigh-Mackay, see p. 145 above
197	25–35	Balfour, see p. 143 above
198	35	*The Times*, 4 February 1883

Notes on Sources

Page	Line	Source
199	26–28	M. Edwardes *British India*. London 1967
199	32–34	Kincaid, see p. 128 above
199 to 200	37 1	*The Englishman*, 1 March 1883
200	7–11	Memorial of 8 March 1883, in C. H. Phillips (ed.) *The Evolution of India and Pakistan, Select Documents*. London 1962
200	19–23	*The Englishman*, 6 March 1883
201	2–6	*The Englishman*, 29 March 1883
201	32–33	*The Englishman*, 14 December 1883

20   THE GREAT QUEEN DIES

204 to 205	24 19	*Speeches of Lord Curzon of Kedleston, Viceroy and Governor-General of India*. Calcutta 1902

Index

A

ABBOTT, James, 97
Addiscombe military college, 4
Adventurers, military, 19/20
Afghan war, first, 15, 17, 92, 100
AHMAD ULLAH, 'Maulvi of Faizabad',
    107
Aides-de-camp, 33, 87, 154/5, 174/6
Alexandria, 7
ALLARD, General, 19
Ambala, 176, 184
Amusements (evening promenades,
    picnics etc), 25, 92/3, 157, 184/5
ANDERSON, William, 98
Anglo-Indian Association, 200/2
ANSON, General, 110
Army, East India Company's:
    Irregular cavalry, 78/9
    Officers, 14, 16/7, 66, 89
    Other ranks, British, 17/9, 42/3
    Pensioners, 42
    Sepoys, 116/32 *passim*
    Strength, 4, 12, 110
Army, the Queen's:
    Officers, 78
    Strength, 110
Army, *see also* Political Officers
Atfé, 7
AUCKLAND, Lord, 1, 55, 63
Auckland Hotel, Calcutta, 49
AURANGZEB, 78
AVITABILE, General, 19

B

Babu English, 197
Babus, 196/7
BAHADUR SHAH II, 77, 84/5, 114, 130/1
BALY, Archdeacon, 183
Bangalore, 89
Bannu, 97
Barrackpore, 110/1
Barrackpore House, 53/4
BARTRUM, Bobbie, 116/23 *passim*
    Katherine, 116/23
    Robert, 116/8, 121/3

BAUGH, Lieutenant, 111
Bengal Club, Calcutta, 49/50
BERESFORD, Lord William, 175
Berhampore, mutinous outbreak at,
    110
BEVERIDGE, Mrs Annette, 200
Bihar Light Horse, 140
Bishop Cotton's School, Simla, 180
BLAVATSKY, Helena Petrovna, 178/80
BLUNT, Wilfred Scawen, 193/4
BOILEAU, Mrs, 118
Bombay, 22/35
    Hotels, 22
Bombay Duck, 22
Brothels, 173
Brown Bess musket, 109
Bummelo, 22
Bungalows, *see* Houses *and* Dak
    Bungalows
Burlington House, Old, 162/3
Burma, 107/8, 186/92
BURTON, Richard, 61/2, 90/1

C

Cairo, 8
Calcutta, 1, 8, 46/59, 122, 124/5, 138,
    147/57, 163/4, 198/202
    Hotels, 49, 136, 149
Camp, life in, 101/2, 167
CAMPBELL, Captain John, 104/5
CANNING, Lord, 124/5
Carriages, 25, 137, 154, 159, 176
Cartridges, greased, 109/10
Cawnpore, 107, 121, 128
Ceylon, 8
Chapatis, 106/7
Charter Act 1833, 12
Children, 19, 40/1, 159/60
China Bazaar, Calcutta, 138
'Chits', 28, 36
Cholera, 92, 155, 185
Christianity, 21, 74
Christians:
    'Curry and rice', 44
    Militant, 21, 67, 97, 106/8

Index

Chummery, 149
Churches and chaplains, 64, 74, 88, 94/5, 182/3, 189
Civil Service and Servants, East India Company's, 2/3, 20, 57
Pay and promotion, 14, 34
Uncovenanted, 79
Civil Service, Indian, 162/7, 193
Promotion, 164/7
Climate, 22/3, 25/6, 51, 155/7, 176
CLIVE, Robert, 10
Clothing, male, 5/6, 27, 139/40, 175/6
female, 6, 29/30, 146/7, 154
Clubs :
Calcutta, 49/50
Madras, 37/8
Simla, 177/8
Tirhut, 140
Coffee shop, 71
Competition wallahs, 162/4, 193
COOK, Messrs Thomas, 147
COURT, General, 19
CRAWFORD, F. Marion, 181
CURZON, Lady, 177
Lord, 171/2, 185, 204/5

D
Dak bungalows, 62/3, 147/8
Travel, 60
DALHOUSIE, Lord, 15, 84, 93
Dances and balls, 26, 32, 55, 87/9, 174/6, 189/90
Dancing girls, 41, 55
Dapoorie, 87
DARBY, Dr, 120/2
Death, 46/7, 55/6, 119/20
Debt, 89
Dehra Doon, 159
Delhi, 77/85
Imperial Assemblage 1877, 141/4
Mutiny at, 114, 129
Red Fort, 83/4, 129
Shalimar Gardens, 78
Delhi Gazette, 79
Delhi Sketch Book, 79, 93
Dinner parties, 25/6, 32, 71/2, 89, 174, 179/80
DISRAELI, Benjamin, 142
'Drawing Rooms', viceregal, 144, 154/5

Drunkenness, 19, 67
'Ducks', 22
Duels, 56
DUFFERIN, Lady, 174/5, 182, 188/91
Lord, 174, 188
Durbar 1877, 141/4

E
East India Company, 1/132 passim
see also Army and Civil Service
EDEN, Emily, 1, 21, 54, 58, 79, 92, 95
Fanny, 1
Eden Gardens, Calcutta, 157
Education, state, 197
EDWARDES, Herbert, 15/6, 57, 97/8
Enfield rifle, 109
Englishman, The, 199/201
Entertainments (theatricals etc), 16, 57/8, 73/4, 174, 185, 189
Eurasians, 13, 19/20, 59, 79/80, 101, 170, 191

F
FALKLAND, Lady, 29, 32, 87
Firozpur, battle of, 96
Food :
At sea, 8/9
European, in India, 27/8, 31, 62, 72, 75, 86, 89, 92, 106, 119, 137/8, 148/9, 153/4
Indian, British attitude to, 42
Fort William, Calcutta, 46/9, 58, 128
Freemasonry, 182
Friend of India, 124
Furniture and fittings, 23, 51/2, 65, 81, 90, 150/1, 158/9

G
Ganges river, 1
Gardens and garden parties, 54, 65, 82, 89, 150, 153, 178
GARDINER, Alexander, 20
Gibraltar, 7
GOAD, Horace, 183/4
Gossip and scandal, 57/8, 67, 71, 183
GOUGH, Lieutenant, 112/4, 123
Government House, Bombay, 32
Calcutta, 52/3, 55, 154/5, 163, 201
Governors-general and viceroys, 20, 161, 170/2

Governor-general's/viceregal yacht, 53/4, 188
Grand Trunk Road, 77
GRANT, J. P., 134
Great Eastern Hotel, Cairo, 8
  Calcutta, 136
Griffin, or griff, 23, 48

H
Haileybury college, 2
HALE, Mrs, 119
HARDINGE, Sir Henry, 96
HAZLEWOOD, Captain, 128
HEARSEY, General, 111
HEBER, Bishop, 13, 20
Hill stations:
  Life in, 26/7, 86/95, 159, 173/85
  Hotels, 88, 91, 177, 185
  Houses, 27, 87, 90/1, 157, 159, 177/8
Himalaya, ss, 123
Himalaya mountains, 77, 91, 102, 176
HINDU RAO, 81/2
Homosexuality, 100, 173
Hookahs, 59, 131
Horses and horse racing, 58, 136, 139
Hospitality, 22, 43, 71/2
Hotel de l'Europe, Alexandria, 7
  Cairo, 8
Hotel de l'Orient, Alexandria, 7
Hounds, 91, 138
Household management, 67/8, 151/4, 158/9
  see also Kitchens, *and* Servants
Houses:
  Bombay, 22/4
  Calcutta, 46, 149/50
  Delhi, 80/1
  Hill stations, 27, 87, 90/1, 157/9, 177/8
  Madras, 38
  Up country, 64/5, 137
HUME, Allan Octavian, 178/80
HUNTER, William, 162/4
Hunting, *see* Sport
HYDERABAD, nizam of, 182

I
Ice, 9, 57, 72/3
Ilbert Bill, 198/202
Imperial Diamond case, the, 182

India:
  British conquest, 10/12
  British purpose in, 21, 164
  European numbers in, 12
Indian Army, *see* Army
Indian Civil Service, *see* Civil Service
Indian National Congress, 180
Indians, relations with, 20, 41/4, 75/6, 81/3, 133/6, 143, 194/203
Insect collecting, 70
Insects, *see* Pests
Irrawaddy river, 188

J
JACOB, A. M., 181/2
JACQUEMONT, Victor, 14/15
JAMES, Mrs, *see* MONTEZ, Lola
Jampan, 95
Jennyrickshaw, 159
JHANSI, rani of, 107
Jumna river, 77

K
Kalka, 176
KENNEDY, Captain, 14/15
Khonds, the, 103/5
KIPLING, Rudyard, 177, 180/1
Kitchens and cooks, 68, 137, 151/2
KNIGHTON, William, 58
Kohinoor diamond, 100

L
LANDSEER, Sir Edwin, 139
Languages, Indian, British ignorance of, 14, 40
LAWRENCE, Henry, 13, 15, 96/7, 101, 109, 115/7, 120
  Honoria, 101/2
  John, 100/1, 174
LEEDS, Mr, 144/5
LESSEPS, Ferdinand de, 147
Letters to 'Home', 69
Literature, read by British in India, 29, 56/7, 69
  Urdu and Persian, 78
  written by British in India, 69, 206/20
LONG, Rev. Dr, 134/5
Lucknow, 106, 115/6
  Residency, 114/23

LUMSDEN, Harry, 97
LYTTON, Lord, 141/5, 154, 171

M
Machchi Bhawan, 116, 119
MACKENZIE, Mrs Colin, 61, 94/5
MACPHERSON, Lieutenant, 104/5
Madras, 8, 22, 36/45, 89
Mahableshwar, 26/7, 86
Malta, 7
Manchester, 190
Mandalay, 188/9
MANGAL PANDY, 111
Marriage market, 6, 33
Martini-Henry carbine, 140
MAYO, Lord, 170/1
Meerut, outbreak at, 112/4
Members of Parliament, travelling,
    195/6
Meriah sacrifice, 103/5
METCALFE, Sir Charles, 21, 81
    Sir Thomas, 81
Metcalfe House, Delhi, 81/2
Missionaries, 12, 21, 44/5, 74
MONTEZ, Lola, 92/3
MOOLRAJ, dewan, 98
Mooltan, memorial at, 98/100
Morley's Hotel, London, 163
Moses in Egypt, 171
Mughal princes, 83
'Mulls', 22
Mussoorie, 91
Mutineers, punishments devised for,
    126/9
Mutiny 1806, 107
    1824, 107
    1852, 108
    1857, 106/32

N
NANA SAHIB, 75/6, 86, 107
NAPIER, Sir Charles, 93, 102/3
Natural History Museum, London,
    178
NICHOLSON, John, 96, 100
Nil Durpan, 134
Nile river, 8
Nilgiri hills, 90
Non-officials, 12/3, 33, 74, 79,
    193/203
NORTHBROOK, Lord, 194

O
OMMANNEY, Lieutenant, 131
Ootacamund, 90
Opium, 108, 160
Opium war, 104
Orissa, 103/5
ORLICH, Leopold von, 55
Oudh, 108/9, 115
OUDH, ex-king of, 107, 115
OUTRAM, Sir James, 121

P
Palanquins, 25, 60/2
Palki-garee, 60
PARKES, Mrs Fanny, 91
Peliti's Grand Hotel, Simla, 177, 185
Peninsular and Oriental Steam
    Navigation Company, 8/9, 147,
    151, 155
Pests, 44, 70, 87/8
PETER, Kishnagur khansamah, 63
'Peterhoff', Simla, 174/5
Planters, indigo, 12/3, 133/40, 193
    tea and coffee, 136
Plantations, life on, 136/40
Plassey, battle of, 106
Police, 167/70, 183, 193/4
Political officers, 14/5
Poona, 26/7, 86, 88/9
Pornography, 76, 173
Precedence, 32, 154
PRENDERGAST, General, 188
Prickly heat, 156
PRINSEP, Val, 141/2
Prostitutes, amateur and registered,
    173
Punjab, 15, 19, 96, 101/2, 176
Punkahs and punkah-wallahs, 65, 150,
    156

Q
'Qui-his', 22

R
Rangoon, 188/91
RANJIT SINGH, 96, 100
Red Sea, 8
Religions, Indian, government patro-
    nage of, 45
Residents, political, at native courts,
    20, 77, 165/6

Index

RIPON, Lord, 198/202
ROBERTS, Lieutenant Frederick, 49, 62
Rothney Castle, Simla, 178/9
RUSSELL, William Howard, 49, 58/9, 74, 115/6, 130
RUSSETT, Charles de, 180

S
Salt monopoly, 108
Sanitation, 46, 48/9, 51, 164
Sepoys, see Army
Servants, 67, 137, 151/3, 159/60
    In Madras, 38/40
    Treatment of, 20/1, 40
    Written characters, 39, 151
    For Cooks, see Kitchens
Sexual life, 13, 34, 59, 67, 173, 190/2
SHAH JAHAN, 78
Shepheard's Hotel, Cairo, 8
Shoemakers, Chinese, 31
Shops and shopping, 28, 30/1, 89, 138, 146, 150/1, 181
Sikh war, first, 96
    second, 98
Simla, 91/5, 110, 173/85
    Hotels, 177, 185
Sind, 102/3
SKINNER, Colonel James, 79/80
    Robert, 79/80
Slavery, 103
SMITH, Public-Spirited, 159
Snakes and reptiles, see Pests
Soda water, 9, 27, 31
Spence's Hotel, Calcutta, 49
Sphinx, the, 8
Sport, 70/1, 91, 139
    see also Horses and Hounds
'Station, The', 42, 60, 64, 66/76
STEEL, Mrs Flora Annie, 152, 156/9
Suez, 8
    Canal, 147

SUPAYALAT, queen, 188
Sutlej river, 77

T
TAGORE, Dwarkanath, 54/5
Telegraph, electric, 114, 147, 170, 176
Thacker and Spink's Gallery, Calcutta, 128
Theosophy, 178/80
Thermantidote, 64/5, 156
THIBAW, king of Burma, 187/9
Thugs, demonstrations by, 74
Ticca, 154
Times, The, 49, 130, 145, 198, 201
Tonga, 176
Travel:
    To India, 5/9, 147
    In India, by rail, 60, 147/8, 164, 176, 194
        by road, 25, 60, 62, 90, 95, 137, 154, 158/9, 176
        by water, 1, 53, 60, 62
Tum-tum, 154

V
VANS AGNEW, Peter, 98
Vellore, mutiny at, 107
Venereal infections, 173
Viceregal Lodge, Simla, 175
Viceroys, see Governors-general
Victoria Hotel, Bombay, 22
VICTORIA, Queen, 1/2, 101
    1858 proclamation, 131/2
    1877 Empress of India, 142/3
    1901 death and memorial, 204/5
    Visiting, etiquette of, 28/9

W
WILLIAM IV, king, 1
Wines and spirits, 67, 72, 75, 154, 176
Wives, British in India, 18, 44, 90, 101/2, 146/61, 184/5